Animation in Croatia
Zagreb School and Beyond

Midhat Ajanović

CRC Press
Taylor & Francis Group
Boca Raton London New York

CRC Press is an imprint of the
Taylor & Francis Group, an **informa** business

Designed cover image: Krešimir Zimonić

First edition published 2025
by CRC Press
2385 NW Executive Center Drive, Suite 320, Boca Raton FL 33431

and by CRC Press
4 Park Square, Milton Park, Abingdon, Oxon, OX14 4RN

CRC Press is an imprint of Taylor & Francis Group, LLC

ISBN: 9781032451473 (hbk)
ISBN: 9781032451480 (pbk)
ISBN: 9781003375623 (ebk)

DOI: 10.1201/9781003375623

Typeset in Times
by KnowledgeWorks Global Ltd.

Contents

Introduction

A VIEW OF THE ORIGIN, HISTORY AND BASIC TRAITS OF THE PHENOMENON OF THE CROATIAN ANIMATION

The intent of this book is to provide an overall framework for understanding Croatian animation. Croatia is a small country that belongs to the Central European cultural circle, which has been independent only since the beginning of the 1990s. A small man recognizable by his typical Central European humour and culture, who fights for his independence and freedom, is the central symbol of Croatian animated film and is also one of the arguments of my discussion.

The main subject of this study is "animated cartoon", which could be defined as **humorous drawing in motion.** Of course, I am aware that the term "animation" as a form extends beyond the realm of the "cartoon film". However, I only marginally dealt with other techniques and types of animation such as stop-motion or 3DCGI, since "animated cartoon" strongly dominated Croatian animation throughout the entire historical period discussed in this book with the exception of the last chapter.

Around the same time, at the beginning of the twentieth century, film animation appeared as a medium and as an artistic discipline in almost all Central European countries (former Czechoslovakia, Hungary, former Yugoslavia, more precisely Croatia, Poland etc.). Central European animated film developed into a striking chapter in film history in the period between the 1950s and 1970s, when a large number of animated film studios were established throughout the region, which during the Cold War firmly belonged to the socialist part of the bloc-divided world. One of these studios was Zagreb Film, in which the brightest pages of Croatia and the entire culture of the former state Yugoslavia, a federation of which Croatia was a part for 74 years, were written. At the beginning of the 1980s together with the death of the Yugoslav leader Tito, the fame of Zagreb Film slowly began to fade and darken.

What the world recognized as Zagreb school of animated films, actually a stylistic direction, was mainly based on a modern understanding of the medium, caricature drawing, stylized movement within the technical possibilities of cel-animation and global satirical metaphors that expressed resistance directed towards the arms race, possible nuclear war and other fears and anxieties about the future that marked an era commonly called the "Cold War".

My concern as an animation researcher is the animated image as a historical source. Animated films are often successful pictures of "micro physiognomy" of a certain society and time; precise and "realistic", so that they are faithful witnesses of the time and environments they were made in.

Such an approach draws upon the history of animation in a wide socio-cultural context as well as analysing animated pictures for the purpose of understanding deep history within society. Consequently, the key question in the text that follows is whether Croatian animation interacted with historical circumstances that influenced the development of culture in that country, including of course Zagreb school as its important part.

Consequently, the manuscript which you are hopefully going to read to its end provides a highly selective survey based on my own reading and research conducted over several decades. The central intent of this text is to present and examine in detail a very interesting cinematic and cultural phenomenon that has not received enough attention so far. In order to analytically interpret the values of the School, I will offer my own hypothesis regarding the aesthetic, ideological and cultural foundations on which this value is based. I will use the films themselves as an argument that confirms my hypothesis. In many ways, it is the backbone of this study.

In my view the Zagreb School is a successful combination of (1) general modernist tendencies that appeared in animation in the 1950s, (2) the Central European cultural and historical context, (3) aesthetics based on the close connection between Croatian caricature, comics and animated film and (4) practices and ideologies in the former Yugoslavia, known as Titoism.

Following that hypothesis, the structure of this study was created where each chapter can be seen as an argument that confirms such an understanding of what is called the Zagreb School of Animated Film and the Croatian animation as its wider context.

1 Some Introductory Thoughts on Modernist Animation

Let's start with some important circumstances that led to the revolutionary development in the field of animation. A new trend appeared in American animated cartoons between the 1940s and the 1950s, embodying a different sensibility both in visual stylization and in artistic and intellectual approach to animation.

In the book *Cartoon Modern*, Amid Amidi gives a whole list of the "wide range of modernist sources and inspirations, among them art magazines, cartoons, graphic design and illustrations in children's picture-books", under whose influence comprehensive changes took place in the treatment of visualization and of movement in American and European animated films. The late 1940s and especially the 1950s were a period when a powerful proliferation of the mediated image began, which suddenly started to decisively affect events and the experiencing of reality. Animation, which at that time still mostly appeared in animated cartoons, became an active part of this far-reaching social process, marked by a changed view about the role and importance of visual communication in the development of mass information, education and democratization.

Modernist animation was first introduced in animated war propaganda and was later intensively developed by young animators who worked in independent studios, especially successful among which was UPA (United Productions of America) seated in New York, founded by a group of young animators who had left Disney.

Primarily through abstract backgrounds that reflected contemporary tendencies in art, posters, design and illustration, and which is very important, through characters created by applying the modernist cartoon as drawn by *The New Yorker* cartoonists, especially Saul Steinberg, their films undermined the very foundations of the aesthetic model that Disney's studio had formulated for the eternity of animation.

Right from the time when people first began to mass-multiple pictures at the end of the eighteenth century, the authors of cartoons and proto-comics had honoured the basic laws of perspective. In modern cartoons, however, the representation of space depended on the artist's free interpretation of the character and its surroundings and was usually shown in two dimensions. Besides this flat representation of space, cartoonists became increasingly radical in abandoning the classical principles of art composition, adopting a pure and plain line and decorative cross-hatching or colouring in cases when drawings were printed in colour, and at the same time discarding the optical principles that define halftones.

DOI: 10.1201/9781003375623-1

ANIMATED WAR PROPAGANDA

World War II also played a great role in the leaning towards minimalist cartoons and the simplification of design and animation in the 1940s, so that one might say that modernist animation was born under the wing of the war against Nazism and Fascism.

Allied military strategists, American and Canadian in the first place, recognized the immense propaganda potentials of the animated image. It was thus very important for Donald Duck and other popular characters to serve in the war against Nazism, and the military authorities took possession of parts of Disney's studio for the needs of anti-aircraft defence already in December 1941. In films such as *Victory through Air Power* (1943), about the importance of strategic bombing, basically a documentary film with animation, and especially in the satire *Der Fuehrer's Face* (1943) with Donald Duck, showing him in the middle of a nightmare in which he is working in a Nazi munitions factory, Disney gave his manifest contribution to American war propaganda. It is noticeable that Disney moved away considerably from his aesthetic model in these films, and that *Der Fuehrer's Face*, for example, contains animated caricatures of real people – in this case Hitler, Mussolini and Hirohito – and visual gags in the so-called crazy style, which is completely untypical of Disney's mature phase. A closer analysis of the rendering of movement and timing shows that Disney came close to the kind of animation used by Tex Avery and his followers, which could not even be imagined in the animation giant's peacetime films. The modernist updating of the Disney model is also evident in the rapidly accelerated pace, where the scene on the assembly line is modelled on scenes borrowed from Chaplin's classic *Modern Times* (1936). As the pace of the film accelerates, Donald's behaviour, because of his hectic confusion and hysterical nerviness, becomes like that of Warner Bros' (WB) character Daffy, which must really have seemed like blasphemy to Disney.

Warner Bros's animated series *Private Snafu* can be taken as an example of a project in transition from the (more)traditional to modernist animation. Its star is a completely new animated character created to the order of the military to spread war propaganda in an amusing way. WB produced 26 black-and-white episodes between 1943 and 1945, which were part of *The Army–Navy Screen Magazine*, a film programme shown all over the world in Allied barracks and on warships (Figure 1.1).

How seriously the studio approached this task is clear from the fact that it employed its leading authors on the series. Chuck Jones directed 12 episodes, Friz Freleng 7, Frank Tashlin 5 and Bob Clampett 2. The legendary Mel Blanc was in charge of sound effects, Carl Stalling composed the music for the series and the script with the accompanying text in verse was written by the equally famous Phil Eastman and Theodor Geisel, better known as Dr. Seuss.

In their research into animated war propaganda, Shull and Wilt (1987:23) emphasized that American animated characters had served in earlier wars, too, illustrating this on the example of one of the first widely popular animated cartoon heroes created by John Randolph Bray, Colonel Heeza Liar, who spread patriotism during World War I, among others, in the episode *Col. Heeza Liar in the Trenches* (1915). Other well-known animated film characters of that time did the same, such as Mutt

FIGURE 1.1 *Private Snafu* (1943). prod. Warner Brothers Company.

and Jeff, Happy Hooligan or Sullivan-Messmer's cartoon version of Charlie Chaplin. One should also remember that the fascinating animated documentary *The Sinking of the Lusitania* by Winsor McCay, from 1918, was basically an anti-German propaganda film.

In the years after World War I, animated films dropped political subjects almost entirely, but they appeared again with the Great Depression and the rise of Fascism in Europe and Asia. In the late 1930s, Warner Bros. made several animated films as more or less open satire against the Axis Powers. After the Japanese attack on Pearl Harbour, practically all the Hollywood studios produced animated propaganda. Between 1 January 1939 and 30 September 1945, almost 500 animated shorts were produced, of which 46% were thematically linked with war events (Shull & Wilt, 1987).

Especially important was the production created outside the Hollywood system, in the small animation studio of the US Army Signal Corps. The studio was founded in the mid-1930s to make training animated films, diagrams, maps and similar production of an informative content, which some experts in animation classed in the documentary cartoon sub-genre. This was the embryo of the later First Motion Picture Unit in Culver City during World War II. The need to efficiently spread important messages and information among soldiers on the front lines was one of the most important factors behind the decision of the top military authorities to engage considerable material and human resources for the production of animated propaganda.

There are several reasons why animated propaganda became such an important step in the overall development of the animated picture. The successful propaganda and informative film series *Why We Fight*, which started in 1942 and whose main creator was the famous Hollywood director Frank Capra, delighted the army and encouraged them to continue using the moving picture in all its forms. A very important event was the great strike in Disney's studio in 1941, when many competent animators, dissatisfied with the low pays and creative restrictions, left their jobs and found new employment in the barracks, waging war against Nazism with animated propaganda and under the command of Frank Capra. The proficiency in technique and technology, and other skills that the fired animators had learned with Disney, were the foundation on which the essential innovations were built, first in propaganda films produced as part of the war effort, and later in the UPA Studio and other independent animation productions.

The fact that animated films played such an important role in the country at war gave a boost to young animators, novices in war propaganda, to sail uncharted aesthetic waters without hindrance (which was forbidden in the large studios). Since these films were not in the first place made for entertainment but for information, there was practically unlimited creative freedom under the roofs of the barracks in which they were produced, and however paradoxical this may sound, it was there that all the Disney clichés and rules about how to produce a cartoon film and what it must look like were rejected. The generals, whose only interest was for the message to be clearly expressed, did not interfere in the form it would be given. Thus, the war years were a period of creative enthusiasm and experimentation for animators.

Many authors with liberal ideas about art and also about politics, who believed in the possibility of stimulating social reform through art, gathered under the same roof in the barracks. Animators such as Zachary Schwartz, Stephen Bosustow, David Hilberman and Jules Engel sought for alternative paths in animation, in the first place by modernizing design in their films. One of these soldiers was John Hubley, a young artist equally active in drawing and design who worked for Disney for a short time and then found himself in the army. Several of Hubley's films may be considered the foundation on which modernist animation was built. Another important author was Robert Cannon, who cooperated with Hubley as an artist and realized *Brotherhood of Man* (1945), the first animated film that based its visual expression on Steinberg's minimalist style (Figure 1.2).

Young artists embraced animation, that eclectic and widely open art form, as an ideal medium for their fresh new ideas about visual expression. They introduced a completely new animated picture, marked by a drastically reduced and simplified drawing made with a geometric, angular line and, in comparison with Disney, a completely different style of animation. Instead of Disney's soft O-line, they used the straight and sharp Steinberg line, or the knotty line taken over from another influential cartoonist and illustrator, the Briton Ronald Searle. Besides designing the characters with the use of simple geometric shapes, these characters moved with jerky, jumpy movements created within the context of a general concept of a particular film, instead of always resorting to the same imitation procedure and animating characters by adapting natural movement.

Dave Hilberman once said that work on war propaganda gave him and his colleagues a "chance to discover something about themselves and animation which would never have been possible with Disney". In a lecture he gave at the University of California, John Hubley emphasized the "greatly new development of technique" and the "inherently human appeal of the new understanding of the medium of animation and its application to all kinds of animated production, which young artists had accepted during work on films commissioned by the army" (Barrier 1999:503).

FIGURE 1.2 John Hubley.

Finally, mention should also be made of the production conditions in the improvised army studios as another factor that contributed to the discovery of new paths in animation using graphic stylization and simplified animation. Films were made by much smaller teams than in normal Hollywood production. Furthermore, the deadlines were very short and the budgets more than modest.

FLATTENED SPACE AND THE CHARACTER OF THE SIMPLE LINE

At the end of the war, it finally became clear that a new style had been born in animated cartoons, (dubiously) named "limited animation", whose main features were modernist design in art form and, one might say, efforts to achieve maximum expression through minimum means in animation. Cinema studies often describes this trend as a modernist rebellion against Disney's animation model and usually links it with the activities of the UPA Studio, although Disney was "dethroned" as the result of many years of activities of various American and world studios, including, of course, the one in Zagreb.

The small animation workshop already turned attention to itself in its first work, the successful use of animated humour and graphics in the still rather conventionally designed and animated propaganda film *Hell-Bent for Election* (1944), which was part of Franklin Roosevelt's presidential re-election campaign. WB's leading animator Chuck Jones directed the film, and in his other work he also showed a leaning to more modern expression and form. The studio's second success was the film *Flat Hatting* (1945), made by John Hubley while still a soldier by working at night in the studio. The film was commissioned by the US Navy, which wanted to produce a series of propaganda films about the safety of flying. Hubley designed the film by using very detailed background drawings and a very simplified treatment of the foreground figures. It was constructed as a series of scenes made from unusual angles of observation and rapid changes of perspective, simulating the pilot's experiencing of space when flying above California and San Francisco. Using what is known as carry-over editing, where the transitions from scene to scene softly morph one into another, the aeroplane turns into an axe, book, mouse and other shapes, transferring the film's propaganda message through easily readable pictorial metaphors. What makes *Flat Hatting* an important film, however, is in the first place its visual stylization, one that modernist animation later embraced, and which can easily be read on three levels: design, characters and animation.

Naturally, this was not the first time that American animators resolutely rejected Disney's canons. The most outstanding example of this kind was certainly the work of filmmakers in the WB studio, in the first place Tex Avery. Their films pioneered a new and revolutionary narrative model and type of humour, since Avery and company introduced crazy humour in animation, which meant the use of the dynamic visual gag. But on the level of visualization, the central model of design remained basically Disneyesque, with the typical construction of the characters from circles of different sizes set in motion by the use of squash and stretch animation.

On the other hand, studios such as UPA introduced a radical change of visual aesthetics and animating procedures. Under the motto less is more, UPA offered a clear alternative to the dominant model in American (and world) animation. Instead of Disney's realistic and detailed treatment of the picture and respect for the laws of perspective, UPA films feature fundamental graphic simplicity in rendering backgrounds and design of characters, for which they were somewhat inspired by minimalist cartoons and illustrations, and partly by consumer cubism, a style that developed in modern drawings for advertising, which were rational, efficient and purpose-oriented and expressed in schematic and basic geometric forms. This design made modernist animators, when creating the space of the film, partly or completely reject depth of space in favour of two-dimensional and flat representation devoid of excessive detailing and figuration, and in some cases the forms were completely abstract. In addition to this two-dimensional geometric ornamentation, animators and artists used basic colours in strong contrast with the aim of creating graphic tension and dynamics.

Unlike Disney, whose models in art were nineteenth-century illustrators of pastoral picture books, young animators were inspired by contemporary art. Some animation scholars, Norman M. Klein (1993) for one, claim that modern painters decisively influenced UPA's cartoon films, among others Dali, De Chirico, Matisse, Cézanne, Picasso, Modigliani, Klee, Léger and Pollock, and so did new theories of design (Bauhaus, Kepes, etc.), which erased the difference between fine and commercial art. Amidi noted that some background artists came to UPA after gaining experience as the authors of posters, which played an important role in the overall development of the modern style. He also gives the example of Bob McIntosh, who defined his own poster style as a "minimum of technical rendering plus pure geometric forms" (2006).

Klein finds similarity between UPA films and the abstract animation – non-figural forms and geometric characters brought to life and set in motion by the film animation technique – that appeared in Europe in about 1920 with the originators of this movement, artists like Hans Richter, Viking Eggeling, Len Lye and especially Oskar Fischinger, who fled to the USA from the Fascists (Nazis) and worked for Disney for a time. It should also be noted that some of the leading UPA authors, for example Hubley, underlined the influence on their work of the Canadian animation and experimental filmmaker Norman McLaren.

On the other hand, there is an obvious difference between the approach of the artists mentioned above and the way in which the UPA artists designed the film picture: the first was a case of abstraction, the second of abstracting. Modernist animation uses recognizable shapes, however geometric and stylized they may be. Even when an abstract picture is applied in a background, it has a concrete function in the film's discourse, which de-abstracts it because the viewer recognizes some object in it and attributes to it certain characteristics that emerge from its position in the narrative structure. Abstract films may have inspired modernist animators, but only in a limited measure and only concerning the understanding of film space.

The fact that modernist animators, instead of placing their characters in a space with perspective and depth, used a flat, abstracted surface and two-dimensional space, or to put it more simply, a coloured plane, made some animation scholars, such as Amidi, call the entire movement design animation or stylized animation, overlooking the simple fact that every image in all the animated films that were ever made, whether signed by Disney or McLaren, was designed and stylized in some way. Thus, in analogy with the status of Disney animation as classical, the name modernist animation seems more suitable for the stylistic tendencies that developed in UPA and some other American animation studios between the 1940s and 1960s.

The basic characteristics of this style are even clearer if we analyse the design of the characters, which were dominantly made, as Klein says, in "the simple line drawing", and the animation itself. Suddenly these films no longer have charming little figures typical of Disney's films, whose movements are like those of a small child; nor is there any of the excessive violence in the manner of the WB or MGM school; there are no talking animas, instead, the characters are human figures shown in the manner of the modern minimalist cartoon. Earlier animated cartoons also had human figures, of course, for example the series *Mutt and Jeff* (1916–1927) or *Little Herman* (1914) made between 1910 and 1920, which were succeeded by Fleischer's animated film stars of the 1920s *Koko* and of the 1930s *Popeye* and *Betty Boop*. But these human characters were deeply overshadowed by the anthropomorphic animal figures in Disney's, and also WB's and MGM's globally popular films.

Modernist animation, therefore, marked a return to the film screen of the human figure in cartoon rendering. These figures were constructed using basic geometric shapes with only several simple lines depicting very clear facial expressions and feelings, which showed that the UPA animators were aware that how we see is based on our visual experience, not on the amount of information given. Just like on Steinberg's cartoons, for example, the UPA animators shaped the face or body using the least possible number of lines, but the figure is nevertheless not only recognizable but also expressive. From this manner of visualization, which Gombrich in his essay on Steinberg calls the utmost simplicity, this great art historian concludes that "our reaction with respect to visual representation is completely independent of the degree of realism that it contains" (1996).

Moving towards unexplored realms at lightning speed, in some works modernist animators even freed themselves of the contour line and showed their characters only by using colour, sometimes they were drawn only with a line without colouring, allowing the background to be seen through them, which emphasized filmic design, and so on.

"LIMITED" ANIMATION

The creators of the modernist current did not only use minimalist stylization of the picture, but they also adapted the animation to the modernist design, as well. The name limited animation resulted from the fact that UPA used many fewer drawings per unit of film time than was the rule with Disney. Disney-style animation had a soft and naturalistically constructed movement harmonized with a background rendered as a three-dimensional and perspective-based picture, while the characters in UPA films from the 1950s moved rhythmically, schematically and mechanically consistent with the stylized background space, sometimes shaped like a pure geometric or completely non-figural composition. Norman M. Klein calls the space of these films "suprematist non-space" basically characterized by the "absence of markers and by ambiguity" (1993). Modernist animators concentrated on design, timing and drawn pantomime and were not at all interested in imitating the laws of nature, perspective or anatomy, which resulted in a special kind of animated movement never seen on screen before. Animation now became rhythmically structured with emphasis on the key positions in movement; the main starting point of animation, which I elsewhere called the micro shot (2009), became longer and with much greater variations. Nevertheless, the mere fact that there were fewer drawings, with frequent cuts and complex compositing as well as the manifold use of the same drawings, tracking shots, and in some cases even animation without inbetweening, does not lead to the conclusion that this was reduced, and especially not limited animation. On the contrary, in this case animation showed itself as a field of unlimited possibilities. One of the outstanding scholars of modernist animation, Jules Engel, wrote in one of his essays that this was in fact an attempt to "create movement, create action style, come up with the gesticulation calligraphy that was appropriate to the graphic stylisation and sensibility of the stories", concluding that "there is no limited animation, only limited talent" (1946).

The bodies of the animated characters in Avery's films, for example, are in constant movement (rushing around) and keep changing shape, growing smaller or bigger in turn, their bodies take emphasized poses and gestures that express particular feelings, their eyes bulge, their necks stretch, their heads grow and so on. There is none of this in modernist animation, where the figures are pictured in a very simply way, sometimes with only a triangle for a head and rectangles for body and limbs. In accordance with the new, more rational approach to animation, studies were made of certain mechanical aspects of movement and the possibility of *designing movement* for cartoon characters instead of having them move in analogy with the movements of people and animals in nature. One of the leading UPA animators, Bill Melendez, described this revolutionary approach to the animation aesthetic as follows: "In Walt Disney's studio we were taught to animate as closely to real life as possible. Years later, at UPA, my colleagues and I tried an opposite approach. We wanted to caricature life like cartoonists do, not imitate it like a camera does" (Pintoff, 1988).

Editing, between film shots and equally within each of them, became another field in which Disney's precepts were rejected. With Disney the line of the horizon is horizontal and inaccessible to the characters, in UPA films there is no horizon, and the design is often constructed by vertical lines. Most modernist films are marked by urban indicators typical of large cities, dominated by human-made buildings, the vertical lines of skyscrapers, and this also introduced the frequent use of the vertical camera movement (tilting). In standard animated films the camera moved relatively rarely, and the same was true of changing frames in the picture; the frame would already be fixed in the second shot of the film, immediately after the initial establishing shot. Modernist animation, however, used the camera as an instrument of narration. Shots such as close-ups, various angles of shooting and perspective, aspect ratio or zooming now appeared with much more complexity and variation than in earlier films.

CARICATURED SOUND AND THE DANCE OF COLOURS

The choice of what strategy to use as a basis for the narrative and humorous discourse in modernist films was adapted to the stylization of animation and the visual nature of the design. For example, in films produced by WB it was usual for a cartoon character to literally disappear into the ground, its body jumped and bounced off the ground in rhythmic convulsions, various tempers were expressed by exaggeration, outbursts of violent rage, excess, impossible physical acrobatics, a generally furious pace and the total absence of logical, physical and perception rules. The characters in modernist cartoon films had expressionless faces and movements devoid of any emotion. Thus, the humour in UPA films was based on a balance between comical verbal ambiguity and a degree of cautious visual gag. This was conditioned by the design of the picture itself and the way of representing space, because incongruent visual humour cannot exist without a minimum degree of realism, i.e. without a three-dimensional treatment of space. Many gags, for example those built on impossible and illogical body postures or movements, could simply not be communicated in an abstract film space.

The same is true of the narrative structure in most modernist films. Unlike the tradition to which Tex Avery and his companions in WB belonged, where the film script was a succession of various gags, the stories in UPA films had a beginning and an end connected by a logical narrative thread, with respect for the principle of continuity and the cause-and-effect structure. Nonetheless, considerable innovations and changes were also made in the fields of storytelling and subject matter. The abstract surface was filled with "good political animation", as formulated by Klein. The concept of "political animation" in his definition should not be understood literally, as a satirical revolt against the American political system or way of life. It was more a case of soft satire very similar to what we find in *The New Yorker*, whose cartoonists liked to create situation-humour about the ordinary man's existential confusion and weakness in a society undergoing dynamic modernization. Many animated cartoons from the 1950s also came as a reaction against the dramatic changes caused by technological progress that seemed frightening, threatening to turn people into mere machine supplements and cities into vast concrete jungles. To emphasize the increasingly complex circumstances of contemporary man, the UPA film characters usually had some obvious physical handicap which prevented them for fitting into the environment they lived in – just like Snafu was too short, which made it difficult for him to perform the daily tasks of soldiers. On the other hand, these characters managed to outdo physically superior opponents thanks, in the first place, to their brains, which worked overtime, and second, thanks to the actual physical handicap which enabled them to see what others could not see or to do what was impossible for others who were "normal".

It must be added that the cartoon film medium itself was placed in the position of having to adapt to the new circumstances, just like any misfit member of society. In the first post-war years, Hollywood went through its greatest crisis by then, a result among other things of abolishing the so-called film bill, the evening-long cinema programme composed of cartoons, documentaries and feature films under which had upheld the production of animated films which were on the margins of the film industry in any case. In addition, in 1954 the medium of television started its victorious campaign and the suddenly wealthier middle class began to move to the suburbs, which not only decimated but radically changed the movie public. However, in the end it was television that saved the production and further development of animated cartoons, becoming their most important producer and distributor. Thus, this whole decade seems like a transitory period for animation, from the film format to the TV screen. This is clear if we examine UPA production, which was in the 1950s dominated by cartoons made for the adult cinema audience, and by the end of the decade turned almost completely to cartoons made for the children's TV programme or TV commercials.

In one of the first great artistic and commercial successes of modernist animation, the cartoon *Gerald McBoing-Boing* (1951), which both Klein and Amidi consider "the quintessential UPA product", director Bob Cannon had both child and the adult audiences in mind. In his treatment of the relationship between picture and sound, Cannon completely rejected Disney's Mickey-Mousing principle of creating substitutes for diegetic sound through perfect synchronization. Instead, asynchronous sound was used, sometimes completely incongruent with the film's picture. This is in fact the very idea of *Gerald McBoing-Boing*. The story was written by Dr. Seuss (Ted Geisel), prominent child writer and illustrator, scriptwriter of the Snafu series, and it describes the life of the boy Gerald who has a serious speech disability. Every time he wants to say something, a terrible unarticulated sound described as "boing" comes out of his throat. But after great troubles at home and at school, Gerald goes to

Hollywood where he gets a job making sound effects. The activated sound, modernist visual concept and Cannon's skill as an animator brought sensational success to the small studio with only 14 permanent employees: the first Oscar for UPA, reviews of the film in, among others, the weekly *Time* magazine, and its use as the basis for the animated television programme *The Gerald McBoing-Boing Show*.

Another show-off example of modernist animation is certainly Hubley's *Rooty Toot Toot* (1952) made exclusively for the adult viewers, in which it is important to underline the contribution of the artist Paul Julian, besides that of the director John Hubley (Figure 1.3). This was an innovative and brave work in each of its elements, inspired by the folk song Frankie and Johnny, with the sung refrain "rooty toot toot", and the earlier successful Broadway musical. Many people consider this film the peak of UPA production. A cross between a musical and a courtroom-film, it tells of a love triangle and jealousy-motivated murder and is primarily outstanding in rhythmic elegance in creating movement and the expressive use of colour. The film leaves the impression of an unbroken dance of colours, where the surfaces painted in watercolours move to the time of the accompanying jazz music and pour like water from a restless lake, crossing the boundaries that outline the forms and shapes of characters and objects. The result of this approach to colour, as a fidgety smudge that plays

FIGURE 1.3 *Rooty Toot Toot* (1951) by John Hubley.

with temporary and instable contours, is an effect of translucence and fluidity which makes the drawn figures literally pulse with life. Hubley did more than relax the outlines, in several places he did away with them completely at the same time changing the colour scheme in accordance with changes in the atmosphere of the film and the mood of his characters, which underlined the drama and emotional charge of the entire experience. For the same reason Hubley used points of view that were very unusual in animation at that time, and stylized movement inspired by modern dance.

At the same time distinct colour shades portray the characters psychologically. Thus, for example, Frankie is coloured red, and this colour dominates all the scenes in which she appears, which indicates her temperamental nature. Frankie is passionately obsessed by love, which is shown as her weakness because she reacts before she has time to think. On the other hand, her competitor Nelly is shown in shades of blue, which reveals her cold and calculating nature that is, of course, better adapted to the world as it is.

Bill Hurtz, who was also head artist of *Gerald McBoing-Boing*, finished and signed *The Unicorn in The Garden* (1953), whose real author was John Hubley. This cartoon was based on James Thurber's somewhat misogynist illustrated story. Because of his leftist views, the notorious House Un-American Activities Committee (HUAC) blacklisted Hubley, so forcing him to leave UPA and all the projects he had started, including that film. In accordance with Thurber's original, the film was extremely minimalistically stylized, made with a line whose spontaneity and simplicity reminds of a child's drawing. The animation is equally relaxed, the characters' movements rather stilted and unpolished, for example, when a man wants to telephone, his hand simply grows until it takes hold of the receiver, and so on.

If the boy Gerald was a misfit because of his physical handicap, the girl Frankie because of her fiery temperament, here the hero is a middle-aged resigned man whose life is out of balance with the modern times. He is terrorized at his job but even more so at home because his marriage has turned into everyday complaints made by his emancipated, domineering and egotistic wife, two heads taller than himself. The comic effect in the film (and earlier, in the story) is created with the help of the irrational, which suddenly interferes in the couple's everyday life and disturbs their set ways. The appearance of a unicorn in the garden, which only the couple can see, causes a chain reaction that leads to the husband's liberation from the great burden and terrorizing of his wife. The psychiatrist, who openly sides with the member of his own sex and generation, sends the wife for treatment to a psychiatric hospital, and the husband remains alone and free.

After this certainly most adult UPA film, their subject matter radically moved towards films for children. The next noted UPA film was Bob Cannon's *Madeline* (1952), made after Ludwig Bemelmans's picture book. The reason for this must be sought in changed production conditions and the current requirement for animation to adapt to television. What is more, UPA was the first studio that turned to this new, gigantic channel of distribution. The minimalist style of modernist animation has shown itself as a foundation for building the television animation aesthetic right to the present. The course of development of the animated series *Mr. Magoo*, UPA's greatest commercial success, is an example that clearly illustrates the turning point in the history of animation (Figure 1.4).

FIGURE 1.4 Mr. Magoo (1949). prod. UPA.

In the early 1960s film animation definitely came under the influence of radically changed production and distribution circumstances, a new taste and changed viewer habits. This led to the birth of a new type of animated picture. Animators who had changed from film to television production were forced to bow before the television budget, which was much smaller than that for films, and the resolution of the pixelated screen of that time, which made subtle variations and visual details impossible. The result was animation which in the beginning could really be called reduced (limited) in the literal sense. The demand of the moment was to produce as many minutes of animation as possible in as short a time as possible, which minimized the number of drawings and film operations. The pictorial content was reduced to a clearly contoured foreground and a simply stylized background, while the animation usually consisted of otherwise immobile figures blinking and opening their mouths, with the maximum use of supplementary lines such as speed lines taken over from comics to provide a graphic representation of movement. The first popular animated TV series like *Crusader Rabbit* (Alexander Anderson, after 1949, production 500 episodes) or *The Bullwinkle Show* looked like illustrated radio. William Hanna and Joseph Barbera brought this approach to (commercial) perfection. This experienced duo, who used to make the animated series *Tom and Jerry* for MGM, consciously brought this extremely limited animation style, as Paul Wells says, into harmony with the "established narrative codes of radio and television storytelling" (2002), which should by no means be confused with the UPA modern art-animation style.

THE IMPACT OF MINIMALIST MODERNISM

To sum up this historical survey of the development of modernist animation, one could say that the influence of UPA and other studios of a similar approach from the 1950s left a deep mark on the entire world of animation, and the aesthetic then created has in fact remained present until today in the form of the modern 2D computer-generated animation. Thanks to UPA production, academic and elite-art cultural circles became aware of animation and began to take serious notice of that medium, which led to the exhibition *UPA: Form in the Animated Cartoon*, held in 1955 in the Museum of Modern Art, in which animation was established as an art form. But the most important consequence of this revolution in animation aesthetic in the 1950s was the appearance of the great variety of stylistic currents and formal strategies in the next phase of development, and this can be compared with what happened in all other art expressions. Animated cartoons and animation in general were never again uniformed and constrained inside rigid models, rules and principles; instead, the field of animation opened up to styles, expressions and techniques of undreamed-of variety and possibilities, a phenomenon which we are witnessing in our time.

The UPA did not influence only small producers, it influenced even Disney's studio and other Disney-like productions in the world. The UPA tore down all Disney's rules and dogmas.

The first and most important rule was the following: "The line had to be drawn exactly and accurately. In no circumstances should the line vibrate, or the colour pulsate on the screen". The UPA animators did exactly the opposite: lines and colours on their drawings were shivering and shaking lively. What used to be considered a mistake now presented an unlimited space of creative freedom.

The second rule was the following: "Round head, round eyes and nose, round body. Animator should not worry about angles: no matter which way a character moved; it could be drawn with circular strokes. Arms and legs moved like rubber hoses. No such things as elbows, knees, or wrists concerned the animator. Tubelike and rubbery limbs could be drawn fast and moved in any direction or elongated if necessary" (Thomas, 1991 28).

The UPA's reply was the following: "Circle is just one of geometrical shapes". Their figures were drawn in the spirit of current tendencies in graphics or painting. Or, as Swedish film historian Lars Lönnroth (1979) defined the UPA style in his book *East European Animated Film*:

> The shortest route between two points is a straight line, provocatively replied the UPA. Why would it be forbidden to draw squary or angular figures, thus producing an original shape. Why always insist on the realistic background when the story can be told on a neutral background or milieu drawn with several quick, simple movements? The UPA was looking for stylized, but representative energy in movement.

Next rule on the list proscribed that animals in cartoons have to be anthropomorphic animals, drawn to appear nice and cute. Principal characters in the UPA cartoons were stylized human figures, which in the case of Mister Magoo, the UPA's greatest commercial success, resulted in an obvious caricature of the comic W. C. Fields, a character who was anything but nice.

The most important rule of the UPA was the following: "There are no rules".

Although many UPA animators, largely because of Disney's fervently enthusiastic cooperation with HUAC, were accused of participation in an alleged communist plot and blacklisted, the UPA style strongly influenced Disney's studio, as well. Disney made several short films in the modernist style, and one of them, *Toot, Whistle, Plunk and Boom* (1953), won an Oscar. The impact of modernist animation can also be seen in feature-length projects such as *101 Dalmatians* (1961), *The Jungle Book* (1967) and *Aristocats* (1970).

In 1952, John Hubley made five animated inserts for the live-action film *The Four Poster* (Irving Reis), which was shown worldwide, including in the former Yugoslavia. World animators immediately accepted the minimalist animation and modern design of the characters, with abstract, geometric backgrounds; first in the British films from the 1950s produced by John Halas. Canadian animation also owes much of its success to the innovation and freedom born in UPA, as does the Central European animated film, especially the Croatian animation tradition in the part called the Zagreb School of Animated Films, or Zagreb Film, which Amidi considers undoubtedly the "most important producer of modernist animation in Europe" (2006).

2 Little Man at the Turn of the Worlds

BETWEEN TWO MASTERPIECES

In 1962, in Santa Monica, a European animated film won an Oscar for the first time. The film was *Ersatz* by Dušan Vukotić, one of the leading masters of the so-called Zagreb School of animated film.

In 1979, the Oscar went to animated film noir *Special Delivery* made by Canadians John Weldon and Eunice Macaulay, much to the disappointment of many fans of film animation, who wished for the Oscar to go to the film *Satiemania*, a masterpiece by Zdenko Gašparović, which did not even get a nomination. From today's perspective, it is more than obvious that *Satiemania* belongs to the pantheon of supreme artworks made in the medium of animation as one of the most beautiful animated films ever made. *Special Delivery*, on the other hand, despite its unquestionable qualities, paled under the influence of time.

The two masterpieces, *Ersatz* and *Satiemania*, more or less marked the beginning and the end of the period that could be called the golden age of the Zagreb School of animated film. Between the 1960s and 1980s, Zagreb film studio produced dozens of extremely significant animated films, which, seen as a whole, constituted an important epoch in the development of film animation as an artistic form. Most film historians and many great animators considered that Zagreb film took classic cel-animation to one of its highest peaks (Figures 2.1 and 2.2).

FIGURE 2.1 *Ersatz* (1962) by Dušan Vukotić.

DOI: 10.1201/9781003375623-2

FIGURE 2.2 *Satiemania* (1978) by Zdenko Gašparović.

POLITICAL AND SOCIAL SURROUNDINGS

Over its 74 years long existence, Yugoslavia had a taste of rightist dictatorship by the Serbian royal dynasty from 1918 to 1941, leftist dictatorship by Tito from 1945 to 1980 and finally fascism and extreme nationalism from 1941 to 1945, and in the 1990s. In addition, the 1980s were a decade of instability and fighting between the federal states' bureaucracies started by Serbia's attempt to reclaim total hegemony it had lost under Tito's rule.

One thing Yugoslavia has never tested was democracy.

Today, it is more than clear that the only period of economic and cultural prosperity of South Slavic peoples was the time of Tito's soft dictatorship, or liberal socialism that developed after 1948, when this skilful communist politician and indisputable hero of the antifascist war refused to be one of Stalin's servants. During the years of crisis and pressure from Moscow, Yugoslavia managed to develop an original system, communism with elements of democracy, unofficially called "something in between". In political terms this meant a more influential role of working councils in factories and, more importantly, due to Soviet blockade, the economy turned to Western Europe and the USA.

Yugoslavia's cooperation with the West had far-reaching consequences on the culture. Reformed communism and a high degree of political decentralization enabled a quick and definite breakup with the theory and practice of social realism. This resulted, among other things, with a relatively high degree of freedom and independence of film companies, which could make deals with foreign companies unhindered by central state institutions, as was the case in other socialist countries. Yugoslav producers made successful contacts with foreign distributors and importers, so that Yugoslav film production participated in most important world film festivals. Each federal state developed its own film production, so that in some periods film production in Yugoslavia reached between 30 and 40 feature films and more than a hundred short films. Production was also expanded by the TV networks built in all republics' capitals.

Two international festivals played an important role in the presentation of Yugoslav cinematography to the world. First was the Belgrade FEST, the annual review of the international feature film production, and the international animated film biennale in Zagreb, which, soon after it was founded, became one of the most important festivals of that kind in the world.

In short, film authors from Yugoslavia had much better chances to present themselves at the international market and a far greater freedom than their colleagues from Eastern Europe.

The authors of animated films took full advantage of this situation.

PRODUCTION CIRCUMSTANCES

Croatia may have been the most developed Yugoslav federal state, but Croatian feature and documentary films had much less success on the international scene than Serbian, or even Bosnian and Herzegovinian, for that matter. Probably one of the reasons was the fact that in Croatia, animation developed up to the point that it completely eclipsed other film forms. Nevertheless, the phenomenon of the Zagreb school, although exclusively belonging to Croatian legacy, cannot be linked entirely and only to Croatia. Primarily because the development of the School was carried out by the artists from the whole Yugoslavia but also because of the Yugoslav cultural context and generally accepted ideological values, and specific production circumstances. All these factors significantly influenced the School's formation. Contrary to their East European colleagues, Yugoslav animators were not regularly employed but instead had the status of free artists and signed contracts with studios for each new film. In Zagreb film, only colourists, in-betweeners, copiers and other assistant staff had permanent jobs. This created a technical service able to offer production services for the whole studio production. On the other hand, directors, head animators, cartoonists, art directors and other authors changed roles from film to film, for purely practical reasons.

If a person was an in-betweener in, for example, Sophia studio for animated film, or in Moscow Soyuzmultfilm, he could expect with fairly certainty to be retired as in-betweener. In Zagreb film, on the contrary, a young man who started off as in-betweener had real chances to rise on the hierarchy of professions linked with animated film. Many known animators, especially those who came in during the Studio's second phase, began their careers at the lowest level of the professional ladder and slowly worked their way up to become character designers, animators and even directors.

To earn for their living, many freelance animators were forced to run from one project to another, between theirs and the films of their colleagues. Direct consequences of such practice were close relations between the authors – they worked together, their roles constantly changed, once they were screenwriters, on the other occasion directors, or even simple animators or art directors in their colleague's film. Authors exchanged ideas and experiences, learning the tricks of the trade, and influencing each other at the same time.

Alongside animation, many animators worked on comic strips, caricatures, illustrations, posters and similar things. These studio outings kept them in touch with other media, which expanded their insight into actual tendencies in other art forms. In consequence, Zagreb School's films often followed actual trends in graphic and visual art of the day.

PREDECESSORS: EUROPEAN AVANT-GARDE AND THE PIONEERING MODERNIST

Disney was the most important personality in the history of animation, not just because of his huge contribution to all possible components of film animation, from production to technological and commercial aspect, but primarily because whole modern animation developed in opposition to Disney. Giant Californian studio created rules that creative animators of the world would break and surpass.

Disney attempted to make animation uniform, to turn art into industry, and actually managed to do it. Strong individuals, on the other hand, refused to accept animation as product of the assembly line, and in that they were successful too.

This is the history of animation in shortest terms possible.

During the first decades of the twentieth century, several aesthetic movements developed in film animation in Europe, all very different to what would become Disney's animation model. Wladislaw Starewitch and Alexandre Alexeiff were two authors born in Russia, who mostly worked in France; the first one established stop-motion by animating strange insect-like puppets or reanimating dead insects thanks to *frame-by-frame* technique, while the second one used the unique pin-screen technique, which was in a way a mechanical forerunner of computer animation. Avant-garde authors like Eggeling, Ruttman or Fischinger used animation as their basic technical tool in attempting to realize the idea of "pure" film, liberated of all, as they called them, redundant elements, primarily narration.

Great authors, besides their explicitly individualistic understanding of the medium, realized their ideas mostly with newly conceived, experimental techniques: Lotte Reiniger made her films as animated silhouettes, using the technique similar to Chinese shadow theatre; George Pal developed a unique form of object animation based on replacement of puppet models, while Hans Richter, Len Lye and Norman McLaren launched direct-on-film animation, or in other words, animated films made without the use of camera. Obviously, all these authors differed from Disney, as far as both the content and the form were concerned. However, European film experimenters never showed much interest in commercial production, so that their films never caused much of a headache to Disney studio heads.

Still, as I discussed in the previous chapter, Disney's greatest challenge came from the USA. Warner Bros. animated film department stood out as a clear alternative to Disney. Original, bold cartoons produced in WB were characterized by wild tempo, surrealist humour spiced with politically incorrect jokes and the use of slang. Creators like Tex Avery, Friz Freleng or Chuck Jones made cartoon equivalents to a tradition within American humour whose representatives were Groucho Marx or the magazine *Mad*. Quite understandably, Avery and the gang never missed a chance to mock Disney's anthropomorphic, sugary world. Still, all the films made in the WB followed more or less the aesthetical rules and recipes prescribed by the animation Mastodon.

However, it would be no exaggeration if we said that the UPA studio made the most important shift in the development of film animation; the UPA marked the beginning of continual production of creative animation. Artistic animation no longer depended on the person and the activity of some freely working, independent genius. A company was founded whose basic goal was to create art and experiment. Animators started to create movement and shape instead of imitating nature. Before the UPA, creative animation was an exception – after all the efforts made by the UPA's animators, it became a rule. In short, after the UPA united technical possibilities developed in Disney with European experimental tradition, it was time to make another step forward towards combining all the above with Central European cultural heritage, Slavic sense of absurd humour and satire and the inclination towards little peoples' destinies, like that of the brave soldier Schweik on one side, or the likes of Gregor Samsa on the other.

The encounter of two traditions happened halfway – in Zagreb.

PIONEER'S MOVING SILHOUETTES

The first cartoons in Croatia were made by Sergej Tagatz, a Pole born in Russia that became the Soviet Union in 1917. Until 1920, he lived in Yalta and worked in Ermoljev's film studio, where he had his first encounter with film animation. Among other things, Tagatz made Studio's trademark in the form of a short cartoon. Like many of his countrymen, he emigrated to Yugoslavia in 1922. After having arrived in Zagreb, he did all kinds of odd jobs before eventually returning to his old trade. He produced several commercials the same year, while in 1923, he made opening credits for Bosnia Film and animated trailers for films stared by Jackie Coogan.

The School of National Health had its own photo-film laboratory and made film animations. Its founder was Milan Marjanović, a writer and prominent personality of Croatian public life in between the two world wars. Marjanović was the only educated film worker of the School and the first head of its film department. At his initiative, the School started producing short teaching films with animated inserts, with the goal of spreading important information about hygiene and ways of preventing epidemics.

In 1929, Aleksandar Gerasimov, another emigrant from the Soviet Union, became head of the photo-film laboratory and remained so until 1961. With the cooperation of cameraman Stanislav Noworyte and cartoonist Peter Papp (and later on Vilko Šeferov), the School of National Health produced films: *Wizzards* (*Čarobnjaci*, 1928), *The Outbreak of Dysentery in the village of Prljavor* (*Kako je počela griža u selu Prljavor*, 1929), *Pussy's nose, Ivo's Tooth* (*Macin nos, Ivin* zub, 1929), which combined live action with silhouette animation – a technique similar to that of the Chinese Theatre of Shadows. In 1929, the School realized an especially important achievement – 300 metres long film *Martin in the Sky* (*Martin u nebo*) (Figure 2.3).

The School of National Health was evidently very much influenced by Walter Ruttmann and Lotte Reiniger, since animation in the films was mostly combination of static drawings and moving silhouettes. Unfortunately, a certain portion of their work was lost and only owing to secondary sources such as photographs and newspaper clips do we conclude that their films were content-wise very naïve, while their shapes were quite unpolished. Animation was probably not much better than the drawings so that it all boiled down to an amateur attempt that could not catch the attention of wider public, resulting in the studio's failure to fulfil its goals.

The third pioneering contribution to Croatian animation came from Berlin with brothers Zvonko, Ivo and Vlado Mondschein. As soon as they arrived in Zagreb, the brothers started their own company Maar ton – film commercials. Owing to a

FIGURE 2.3 *Martin in the Sky* (1929), an educational film produced by the School of National Health.

significant amount of capital invested in their firm, the brothers succeeded in creating a big, professional studio, which produced around a hundred commercials per year, from 10 to 100 metres long. Sergij Tagatz was the company's first employee; from Berlin they brought a skilled animator, Ilsa Polley, and hired many renowned Zagreb visual artists, like Gerty Gorjan or Pavle Gavranić. High production quality of Maar resulted in huge commercial success. They were receiving orders from all over, including the foreign countries. The number and quality of Maar's products soon listed the company among the best European producers of animated commercials. Despite that, the production was terminated in 1936 for reasons unknown to the author of this study. From the foundation of the Independent State of Croatia (NDH) in 1941 until the stabilization of the communist government in the second Yugoslavia, more or less all of Maar's production was destroyed. Reasons for this loss were not evident from the sources the author of the study had researched.

Apart from the three already mentioned, there were also some other attempts to revitalize Croatian production of animated film. Hardworking film enthusiast Oktavijan Miletić also experimented with animation; photographer Viktor Rybak made a wholesome animated film 8 metres long; Professor Kamilo Tompa used animated puppets, while Kosta Hlavaty, artist and member of Tito's liberation movement, made eight animated propaganda films during the war, working on the territory under partisan's control.

Within State Propaganda centre founded by the Ustasha government following Nazi Germany's example, also existed the studio for animated film. Its productions, however, have not been accessible to me during writing of this study.

"PRESCHOOL": EDUCATIONAL FILMS AND PROPAGANDA

Immediately after World War II, several enthusiasts continued developing animated film in Zagreb. On political directive, state film production houses were founded in all federal states' centres. In Zagreb, this was Dubrava Film, soon renamed Jadran Film. The company promptly constituted several production departments. One of them was the department of educational films, where several films were made in the technique of animation. Their cartoonist and animator was Leontije Bjelski, formerly known as comic strip author. However, the most interesting individual who worked with Jadran Film was Bogoslav Patenjak. In 1949, he returned to his homeland after many years in Argentina. In Buenos Aires he worked as animator in the Cristiani studio for animated film and gathered lots of experience. As a skilful animator he was given a chance to make films that mostly applied Disney's aesthetic. Apart from making teaching films, Petanjek made one gag produced by Jadran film, *Blackman Miško* (*Crnac Miško*, 1949), and was studio's main animator until 1957.

However, true initiative for Croatian animated film production was born in the editorial board of the satirical magazine *Kerempuh*. When in 1948 Tito refused to obey directives from Moscow, he came into fierce conflict with Stalin. The consequences reflected as crisis in the whole area, enormous pressure and blockage of Yugoslavia on the part of the Soviet Union. Yugoslavia finally stepped out of the so-called socialist block, countries under Moscow's command, and got closer to the West. One of the outcomes of the Yugoslav politics and its international standing included a breakup with the ideology of the so-called socialist realism in art and the development of a much more relaxed cultural model in respect of the dominant ideological dogmas, unlike in other countries of Eastern Europe.

As the only existing satirical magazine in Croatia, *Kerempuh* rounded up many known caricaturists and cartoonists. On the wave of sudden anti-Soviet atmosphere, their caricatures and comic strips in which they mocked Stalin became very popular. The sales of the magazine reached the unimaginable number of 170,000 copies. Instead of a small, state-funded firm, *Kerempuh* magazine became a wealthy company. Strict Yugoslav economic regulations required all unexpected incomes to be paid back to the government. Young editor Fadil Hadžić took a risk and did not obey the directive. He decided to use the money for an unusual adventure with his collaborators – the making of an animated film.

Thus started the production of *The Big Meeting* in 1950, an extremely important film for the future development of Croatian animation. Namely, the project gathered the people who later on formed the core of the Zagreb school. Despite their inexperience, during one year of working on film, the group managed to master technical know-how and practical details of one so complicated job, as was the making of an animated film. *The Big Meeting* was a success, both in theatres and political committees (Figure 2.4).

Fadil Hadžić could have finally relaxed and continued with his day job. But then, a 25-year-old writer from Bosnia who came to Zagreb to study founded Duga film, a film company that announced itself as specialized in animated and puppet-films.

FIGURE 2.4 *The Big Meeting* (1951) by Norbart & Walter Neugebauer.

This was the beginning of what had in few short years become a phenomenon renowned all over the world. Before starting Duga film, Hadžić described his and his co-workers' ambitions as the following: "We shall try to depart from the usual schemes of foreign cartoons as much as possible and find new visual elements from our cultural legacy" (Munitić/Sudović, 1978).

Duga film assembled almost all important artists (Kostelac, Dovniković, Marks, Kristl, Jutriša and Dušan Vukotić, at that time a young Montenegrin who came to Zagreb to study architecture), whose creative peak signalled the first of three most important phases of the evolution of the Zagreb school. During its short existence, from 1951 to 1952, Duga film produced five films meeting high professional standards. Animators completely mastered the assembly line production, in other words, working in an effective team where the roles were strictly divided between the head animator, cartoonist, in-betweener, director, art director, colourist, copyist, cameraman and other specialist jobs.

First film produced in the studio was *Happy Event* (*Veseli doživljaj*, 1951) by Walter Neugebauer, which was yet another perfect imitation of Disney's short films.

However, already the second film, Dušan Vukotić's *How Kićo Was Born* (*Kako se rodio* Kićo, 1951), came out with certain differences in respect of the Disney tradition. Instead of the usual anthropomorphic animal characters, Vukotić created a human figure, a short man named Kićo, the antihero whose adventures took place in the ordinary routine. The drawing in film was very stylized and simplified, and he tried to apply the so-called limited animation, or in other words, animation was freer and more creative. These became the main traits of the Zagreb School in the years that followed (Figure 2.5).

While the animators of Duga film were preparing their first colour film, *Little Red Riding Hood* (*Crvenkapica*, 1954) arrived an unexpected administrative directive: due to the general shortage caused by the Soviet blockage, and as a measure of cost cutting, Duga film was closed. Despite this heavy blow, the seed of Zagreb animation

FIGURE 2.5 *How Kićo Was Born* (1951) by Dušan Vukotić.

planted in *Kerempuh*, and transferred to Duga film, carried on growing and evolving, to finally reach unimaginable peaks. A group of Duga Film animators went on to work for Zora film, company that specialized in teaching films, and where *Little Red Riding Hood* was finished, bringing the first international award to Zagreb animators from Berlin in 1954. The film was directed by Nikola Kostelac and Aleksandar Marks, whose accomplishment consisted in going one step further in search of an original style and means of expression. The same year, a studio for animation was formed as part of the advertising agency Interpublic, where several very successful commercials were made. New, irrational administrative directive liquidated even Interpublic. Still, young people who decided to devote their lives to animation did not let bureaucracy stand in their way. They moved to Nikola Kostelac's apartment, who was the oldest member of the group, and there made new 17 animated commercials.

In 1965, Zagreb film was founded, whose management, after a short period of fluctuation between documentary and feature film, made a reasonable decision to specialize in the production of animated films. Finally, young artists had a place they could turn to.

"ELEMENTARY SCHOOL": YOUNG AND MODERN

Owing to the fact that they had mastered the craft, had fresh ideas and were absolutely aware of their ambitions and ways to realize them in the chosen medium, young Zagreb animators won international acclaim shortly after the new studio was founded. Their first production was Vukotić's *Playful Robot* (*Nestašni robot*, 1956). The same day he finished this film, Vukotić started working on the next, *Cowboy Jimmy*. This time the animation was even more "reduced", almost "paralyzed", while characters, rhythm and movement were synchronized with individual film ideas, instead of some dogmatic rules. His characters were two-dimensional geometrical symbols that, united with the background, resonated the most important aspirations of modern art. Furthermore, Vukotić was much influenced by Paul Klee. Dialogues were excluded, sound and music integrated with animation and the drawing, not being "above" or "outside" of film. It was obvious that Vukotić perceived animation as something absolutely dynamic. In one film he created rules; in the next one broke them. *Cowboy Jimmy* brought the author and the Studio first international award from the Berlin Film Festival. More important than the prize itself was the fact that one of the members of the jury was Norman McLaren. Vukotić's true successes were yet to come. *Concerto for Sub-machine Gun* (*Koncert za mašinsku pušku*, 1958), *Piccolo* (1959) and *Ersatz* (*Surogat*, 1961) collected awards at almost all important film festivals on the planet, while the author was celebrated as the new genius of animation. At the end of the 1950s and the beginning of 1960, Vukotić and McLaren stood as the most important names of artistic animation in the world. While *Concerto for Sub-machine Gun* was a humorous irony inspired by Hollywood, offering original animation and drawing solutions, *Ersatz* was a satirical allegory full of carefully studied visual gags on the subject of human existence in the abyss of consumer society. All that we saw in the film was an illusion and artificial; the only purpose of our existence was to consume and be consumed. Even the film's main character, although seemingly in control of the situation, was actually a plain inflatable doll,

FIGURE 2.6 *Playful Robot* (1956) by Dušan Vukotić.

which deflated when having stepped on a nail – the only three-dimensional detail in the film – in the film's excellent finale (Figure 2.6).

However, from today's perspective, *Piccolo* is Vukotić's most intriguing work. Evidently influenced by McLaren's *Neighbours* (1952), the film was an obvious metaphor on the subject of Serbs and Croats, two of Yugoslav biggest nations. Two neighbours lived in one house (Yugoslavia?) and their relations were quite good. They visited and helped each other (in an ingenious sight gag one neighbour even cut rain drops so they would not fall on his neighbour), until one of them bought a piccolo, small mouth organ, and started playing. The other neighbour was envious and bought a bigger instrument and started playing louder. The first neighbour went for an even bigger instrument – and so on and so forth. Finally, a war broke out between the two families (tribes), and the house was destroyed. It is hard to speculate what Vukotić's intention was, but it would simply be impossible not to see piccolo as a symbol of nationalism (Figure 2.7).

In the book *Masters of Animation*, John Halas (1987) described his colleague from Zagreb:

> Vukotić's formula is a combination of expressive graphics and enthusiastic drawing calligraphy, which he skilfully uses in the medium of animation, with a great feeling for time equalled only by Hollywood slick-films. He is an intelligent director perfectly capable of controlling the material and manipulating the means at his reach. He also knows how to structure the film and where to put the main emphasis to achieve the desired atmosphere.

FIGURE 2.7 *Piccolo* (1959) by Dušan Vukotić.

The second prominent author of the Zagreb school was Nikola Kostelac, whose films also won numerous awards. His major film was *Opening Night* (*Premijera*, 1957), an excellently structured and skilfully directed story about snobbism. The film also owed much to the work of cartoonist Aleksandar Marks and animator Vladimir Jutriša. The first was a very capable and educated cartoonist and graphic artist with a fine sense for geometrical stylization, the second was an animator with an unusual awareness of timing, and together they were a harmonious team of performance artists who helped many authors realize their ideas.

This particularly referred to Vatroslav Mimica, the Zagreb school's great exception. Namely, he did not draw or animate, but instead he was a born filmmaker with a modern perception of the medium. He considered animation an aspect of cinematography. The special quality of animation was that it was defined by something called "total editing". This meant that editing did not consist only in cutting scenes; it meant editing every single frame. In a cartoon, director made 24 cuts in a second! His films, like *Alone* (*Samac*), *Happy End* (1958) or *At the Photographer's* (*Kod fotografa*, 1959), mostly dealt with alienation of individuals in a modern society. The individual was lost, trapped in urban quarters, frustrated and terrified by the hyper mechanized surroundings. These were generally the subjects of many contemporary European films (Figure 2.8).

During this initial period, another artist made a meteoric career: Vladimir Kristl, who was probably the most gifted artist in the history of Zagreb school. If Mimica was a born filmmaker, Kristl was a born artist, interested in writing, film, theatre,

FIGURE 2.8 *At the Photographer's* (1959) by Vatroslav Mimica.

painting, directing, acting and almost any other artistic form. Film *La Peau de chagrin* made in 1960 was based on Balzac's famous story about a man obsessed with gambling to the extent that he was ready to sell his youth for money; this was not a typical cartoon subject. In view of the graphics, direction and animation, the film was many years ahead of its time. Kristl shaped it in Art Deco manner, using newspaper clips, advertisements, containers and other unusual objects, which created a collage background. His animation was much richer than Mimica's, characters were carefully studied, and animation had authentic rhythm and dynamics. *La Peau de chagrin* was one of the first animated films without humour or gags, which instead directly addressed viewer's emotions (Figure 2.9).

The following year he made *Don Quixote* (*Don Kihot*, 1961), his life work. Young viewer, accustomed to electronically edited music videos or computer animation, today would probably be very confused about what the point of Mimica's *Alone* was. He would have great difficulty to understand why the film was praised all over the world. Special features in *Alone*, among others, were intersected images, multiplied scenes seen from different angles or Mimica's treatment of space as two-dimensional surface that "acted" three-dimensional. Today, none of these things sounds special; much more complicated procedures can be found in any TV commercial.

Contrary to that, 64-year-old film *Don Quixote* still appears impressive! In this masterpiece, Kristl managed to accomplish his old avant-garde desire to create film as visual music. The film was entirely abstract, with no figurative elements.

FIGURE 2.9 *La Peau de chagrin* (1960) by Vladimir Kristl.

Nevertheless, squary heroes expressed drama and poetry through rhythm and animation, telling a "story" that any of us could "read" as he pleased.

Ralph Stephenson (1967), for example, gave the following interpretation:

> *Don Quixote* (1961) has locust shaped structure of cans, tubes and pipes. Sancho Pansa is a combination of a square sea urchin and a meat refrigerator with glasses. Against them line up dots, shapes, creatures, trailers, wheels, moving in flocks, buzzing, halting. The background is filled with forward lines, shapes, and projectiles. What do these strange shapes represent? There is no doubt about that. These are radars, cannons, tanks, aircrafts, patrols, and armies. It is a vision of chaos, at the same time eccentric and terrifying.

The 1958 Cannes Film Festival marked the international ascent of the Zagreb studio. Screenings of Vukotić's, Kostelac's and Mimica's films took place as part of the programme Journes du Cinema, and they were received with equal enthusiasm by the viewers and the critics. On that occasion, critics Georges Sadoul and Andre Martin first wrote about a "school" of animation founded in Zagreb. The school was characterized by an authentic vision of reality and the original use of the medium. Cannes success was followed by worldwide successes on festivals: Venice, Melbourne, San Francisco, Moscow, Montreal, Buenos Aires and London. Finally, in 1962, *Ersatz* won an Oscar.

Zagreb School became known all over the world.

"HIGH SCHOOL": FRESH IDEAS AND INNOVATIONS

Next phase in the development of the Zagreb School began with a short crisis. After creating another masterpiece, *The Game* (*Igra*, 1962), a combination of animated children's drawings and live-action footage, which also won an Oscar nomination, 37-year-old Dušan Vukotić decided to turn to feature film. As the only Yugoslav author who had won an Oscar and a politically very active person, he never had problems with funding for his feature films. Vatroslav Mimica followed Vukotić's example, Kostelac turned to commercials, while Kristl left for Germany.

The gap left after the departure of four great authors soon began to fill former assistants and helpers, who got a chance to make their films. Introducing fresh ideas and innovations into the auteur procedures, new authors made a step forward in expanding authors' freedom and further individualize the process of filmmaking. In time, Zagreb film completely abandoned assembly line production, transferring the responsibility to the author, who was coordinating all important elements of his film: drawing, rhythm, animation, direction and often screenplay and editing.

The first to take advantage of the opportunity offered was the pair Marks and Jutriša, which introduced elements of horror in their animations. Their main work, *The Fly* (*Muha*, 1966), had anecdotal structure and related sensations of discomfort, anxiety and impotence. The pair managed to conjure up nightmarish atmosphere with the help of drawings, colour, sound, editing and minimal use of animation. The film featured unusually long frozen shots of a human character blinking. However, even this barely visible movement allowed the viewer to see the character's inside and to recognize his fear as his own (Figure 2.10).

Borivoj Dovniković, a popular caricaturist and experienced animator, working in the School from its beginnings, was finally given a chance to make his own

FIGURE 2.10 *The Fly* by Marks and Jutriša.

FIGURE 2.11 *Curiosity* (1966) by Borivoj Dovniković Bordo.

films after having cooperated on others for so many years. After several short gag films, such as *No Title* (*Bez Naslova*, 1964) and some less appreciated works such as *Costumed rendez-vous* (*Kostimirani rendez-vous,* 1965), in 1966, he made *Curiosity* (*Znatiželja*), a very important work, which established him as one of the central figures in the history of the Zagreb School (Figure 2.11).

On a bench in a park, sat a sleepy little man, with a bag at his side. Every person who passed him wanted to peek into the bag, including the viewers. This was the first time "living white" was used in a Zagreb School film. This was another original invention of the School, white background functioning as an active participant of film action. We see something only if it was serving some aspect of the story. The moment its function was fulfilled, the character or detail would drown in white haze. The feature of functional whiteness, at the same time the surface and space, spat out particular details only when they were inseparable parts of the story, fire brigades, military units on practice, even a ship with passengers peeked into the bag, only to get lost again in the white (un)reality.

The same procedure Dovniković used in his next works, *The Second Class Passenger* (*Putnik drugog razreda*, 1972), *Learning to Walk* (*Škola hodanja*, 1978) and *One Day of Life* (*Jedan dan života*, 1982) of which I will tell more in the next chapter. Dovniković's heroes stood as symbols of the Zagreb School of Animation. They were antiheroes, little people whose only wish was to be left alone in their simple everyday routine. However, for some unexplainable reason or event, their peaceful lives were always messed up by the cruel surroundings.

John Hallas mentioned even Dovniković as one of the three most important authors of the Zagreb School (two others mentioned were Vukotić and Dragić), explaining his choice with the following:

> Dovniković is a caricaturist of great natural talent: an observer of human weaknesses and comical situations caused by greed, stupidity and a wish to dominate. He is a fearless critic of traditions and practices that take away our freedom, but he is never malicious or revolutionary in political sense of the word (...) His characters seem honest, even naïve, although they frequently hide the inside of an aggressive beast when confronted with corrupted society. Or when they become victims of their own inconsideration.
>
> **1987**

FIGURE 2.12 *Far Away I Saw Mist and Mud* (1964) by Zlatko Bourek.

Several other authors of Zagreb film appeared in this period.

Zlatko Bourek, a top graphic artist, began in 1964 with *Far Away I Saw Mist and Mud* (*Vidio sam daljine maglene i kalne*), artistically impressive poetry adaptation of the great Croatian writer Miroslav Krleža. His next film was *Dancing Song* (*Bećarac*, 1966) a collage-animated film inspired by music motifs of Slavonic folklore music. *Captain Arbanas Marko* (*Kapetan Arbanas Marko*, 1967) was based on a folk epic, while *The Cat* (*Mačka*, 1972) could be seen as an artistic piece based on a beautiful ballad by Zvonimir Golob, inspired by Aesop's fable, in which Bourek flirted with pop-art under the influence of George Dunning's long feature pop-art animated film *Yellow Submarine* (1967) (Figure 2.12).

Another extremely important name in the history of Zagreb School was Zlatko Grgić, undoubtedly one of the best gagmen who ever worked in the studio. His films *Little and Big* (*Veliki i mali*, 1966), series *Maxi Cat* produced from 1971 to 1976, and his major work *Dream Doll* (made in cooperation with Bob Godfrey) from 1979, besides the features characteristic of the Zagreb School, also had much in common with films made in the Warner Bros. studio for animated film. It was no wonder that Grgić ended his career on the North American continent. In addition, he was the main author of the internationally acclaimed series *Professor Balthazar* (dating from 1967), while his auteur film *The Musical Pig* (*Muzikalno prase*, 1965) can still be interpreted as an actual metaphor for human prejudices. Little piglet sang beautifully. Roaming around it encountered people fighting, at war, with various problems. Owing to the piglet's beautiful song, people put their differences behind and decided to celebrate – by eating the piglet (Figures 2.13 and 14).

FIGURE 2.13 *Dream Doll* (1979) by Zlatko Grgić & Bob Godfrey.

Here is how Bendazzi characterized Grgić's contribution to the school:

> Grgić relates freeing laughter, but his humor differs from that of the golden times of comedy. Although his style follows that of Chaplin and Avery, he finds comical elements in the worse human feelings, hostility and tension. Like other Slavic humorists, he is cracking jokes about the least pleasant life's experiences avoiding the happy ending.

1994

The Fifth (*Peti,* 1964) was a small musical metaphor about loneliness related through the anecdote about a stubborn musician who wanted to become the fifth

FIGURE 2.14 *The Musical Pig* (from 1966) by Zlatko Grgic.

member of a quartet. Here, Grgić cooperated with Pavao Štalter, another original and prominent animator of the School. Štalter reached his creative peak with *Mask of Red Death* (*Maska crvene smrti*, 1969), produced in the very successful technique of collage. Štalter took over the production from Zdenko Gašparović, author of the screenplay, who, after having started drawing for the film, immigrated to Canada. Made in the old technique used already before cel-animation was invented (each drawing was cut out of paper and glued to the background), the film remained until today the best interpretation of Edgar Allan Poe in the medium of animation.

In 1964, young Boris Kolar made *Warf-Warf* (*Vau, vau*), a boldly and originally stylized peace, characterized by nonchalant line, meaningless when static, but when animated it assumed unexpected shapes and meanings (Figure 2.15).

Another good gagman was Ante Zaninović. Two of his funniest films date from the same period; *The Wall* (*Zid*, 1965) and *On Holes and Corks* (*O rupama i čepovima*, 1967).

Despite many great authors working in the Zagreb School during the 1960s, one author stood out – Nedeljko Dragić. He was probably the only animator whose contribution could be compared to that of Dušan Vukotić. Dragić, formerly known as caricaturist, began his career as assistant animator in 1965. His debut came with *Elegy* (*Elegija*), an average black-humour gag film. His next work already, *Tamer of Wild Horses* (*Krotitelj divljih konja*, 1966), won a Grand Prix at the most important festival of animated film in the French city of Annecy in 1967. The film was technically consistent and was a credible visualization of Vatroslav Mimica's scenario. It was no surprise that his funny anecdote about a highly technological society and the growing sense of alienation won sympathies of the jurors. The award meant a

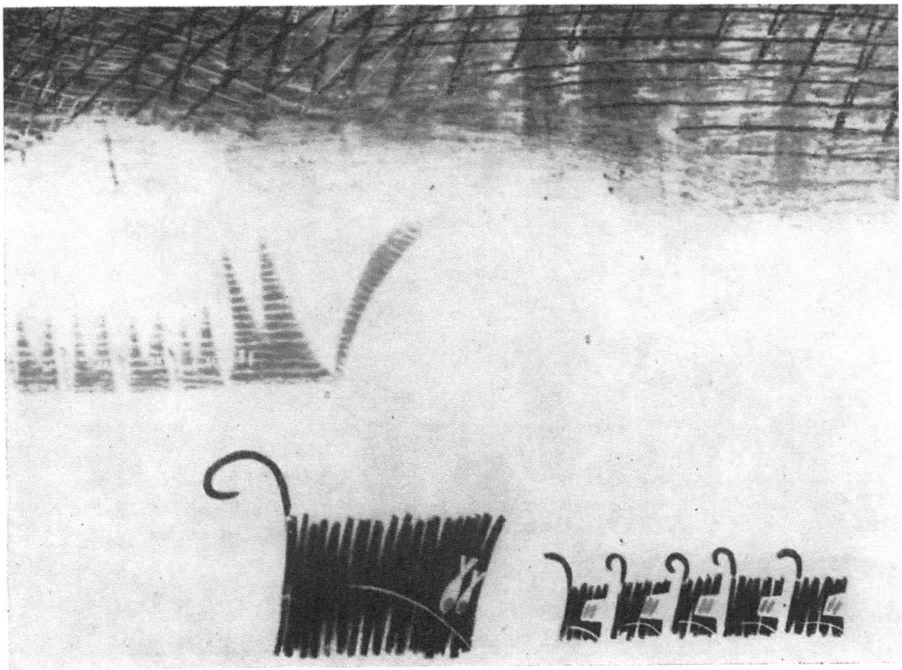

FIGURE 2.15 *Warf-Warf* (1964) by Boris Kolar.

great opportunity for Dragić, and he capitalized on it. His next two films *Diogenes Perhaps* (*Možda Diogen*, 1967) and particularly *Passing Days* (*Idu dani*, 1968) were characteristically individual, of temperament style of animation, carrying a pessimist vision of reality spiced up with bitter humour. Actually, Dragić managed to incorporate all the elements characteristic of the Zagreb School of Animation. His animation was fast, full of energy, tempo was fierce, drawings created with live, free line, and characters reduced to the essential. Filmic space is materialized through movement. This implied that even set design was movable and changeable. Literally everything moved in Dragić's films, and literally nothing was stable. The consequence of this procedure was a lack of "classical" editing; whole film was made in one "shot". A scene was born and died in the moment when another appeared. Interwoven scenes would come and go without any chronological order, precisely as we remember past days, as mixed and fused images with no beginning, and no ending (Figure 2.16).

In *Passing Days*, probably the most important film that came out of Zagreb studio in that period, once again we meet a small, ordinary man whose only ambition is to live his simple lifestyle. Obviously, he fails in doing so because his whole surroundings conspired against him. Everything and everyone joined in against the man. *Passing Days* may not only be the most typical film of the Zagreb School of Animation but also a representative example of what in the world was known as the "Yugoslav Style of Animation".

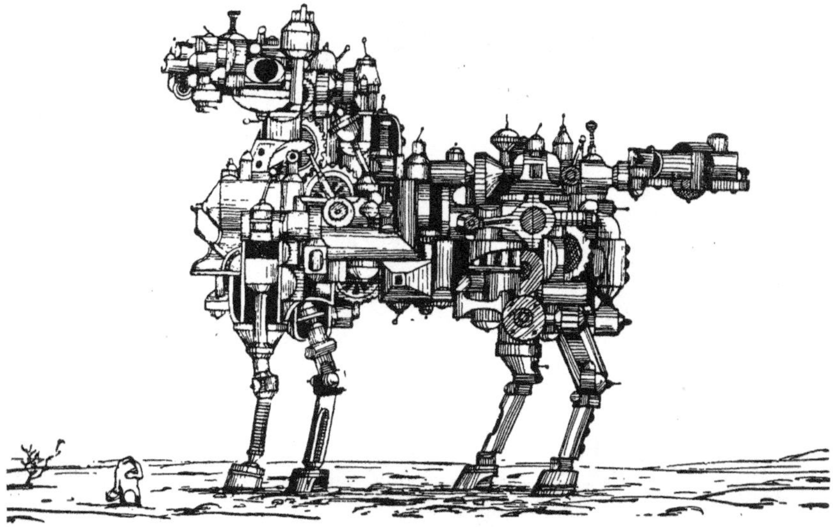

FIGURE 2.16 *Tamer of Wild Horses* (1966) by Nedeljko Dragic.

At the time of *Passing Days* and other previously mentioned films, Zagreb film reached its peak. The awards were coming from all parts of the world, many leading critics praised Zagreb artists, while at the same time, production was well organized, and most creators were in their best years.

At the beginning of 1968, The Museum of Modern Art in New York organized a grand retrospective of the Zagreb School's films. Cartoon masterpieces made in the small Zagreb Studio had definitely conquered the world.

"UNFINISHED COLLEGE": THE SCHOOL's SWAN SONG

The third and last phase of the golden era of the Zagreb school was marked by creators who reached their creative peaks in the 1970s. Unfortunately, the studio did not renew its creative capacities, and at the beginning of the 1980s, it became quite obvious that the phenomenon of the Zagreb School of Animation wore down.

Owing to film *Tup Tup* (1972), which won an Oscar nomination, Dragić got the opportunity to get to know the New World. He collected impressions from his travels across America in a fascinating "animated documentary" Diary (Dnevnik, 1974) which I discuss more thoroughly in the coming chapter. *Diary* was an important event in the world of animation, won countless awards and was celebrated by many respected animators as one of the highest accomplishments in the contemporary world animation.

After *Diary* it was hard to imagine that two-dimensional cartoons could go any further. Namely, at the beginning of the 1970s, it was obvious that new technique, three-dimensional model animation aided by computer graphics, was gaining on the old methods. Nevertheless, four years after *Diary*, a new creation came from Zagreb, made in the old cel-technique, which surpassed not only Dragić's film, but all its contemporaries regardless of the technique they were made in.

Zdenko Gašparović's *Satiemania* was one of the best films ever made in Zagreb film, and also the School's swan song. Before *Satiemania*, Gašparović's name was known only in narrow professional circles. He participated in some important creations; he was one of Grgić's few collaborators working on Professor Balthazar. He also worked in some of the world's greatest studios of commercial animation where he acquired impressive experience. His love of avant-garde composer Eric Satie's music, which he listened to for years while he worked, turned out to be an exceptional source of inspiration. Visualizing the beloved music imprinted in his memories, Gašparović created an impressive work. According to Giannalberto Bendazzi *Satiemania* was "the best film ever to come out of the studio on the Sava river" (1994) and remained an unrivalled visual composition bursting with life, charged with eroticism and love, full of nostalgia and a certain intimate element that eluded explanation, but which every viewer felt as soon as he saw this masterpiece: *Satiemania* awoke memories of short moments of love and beauty worth living for. Technically, it was a work that subtly used the possibilities of double exposition, giving the author free hands to present all his luxuriant artistic talent. Soft transitions between the images and scenes presented a visual experience of irresistible charm, strength and beauty. The shot of female face reflected in restless waters is still one of the most beautiful and most exciting things seen in animation (Figure 2.17).

In his book *One Hundred Years of Cinema Animation*, Bendazzi also wrote:

> In 1978 he finished *Satiemania*, in which Eric Satie's music connects scenes of the woman he loves, woman getting bored, Grand Canyon, and Montparnasse, bars, butchers and malls, breasts, sliced stakes and ships in the rain. It is a grotesque and sensual film, a long journey into the subconscious where Otto Dix and George Grosz mix with underground comics, Reginald Marsh, Covarrubiasom and Ralph Steamon.
>
> **1994**

This work of unparalleled beauty marked the highest peak of Zagreb film, after which came sudden downfall, both on organizational and creative level. True, even after *Satiemania* several important films were made by two representatives of the younger generation. Joško Marušić in *The Fish Eye* (1980) created a modern horror in the animated medium, while in the *Skyscraper* (1981), he recreated the atmosphere of his excellent urban caricatures and produced a funny voyeuristic film with dozens of gags appearing at the same time. Prominent member of the unforgettable comic group New Square (Novi kvadrat), Krešimir Zimonić, in his film *Album* (1983) introduced visual tendencies of contemporary comic books in the Zagreb School's house style, a topic I will return to later. The old masters had not given up either. Pavao Štalter made *House 42* (*Kuća broj 42*, 1984), in a bold, risky and complicated technique of oil on celluloid, while Nedeljko Dragić recalled the best days with *Pictures from Memory* (*Slike iz sjećanja*, 1987), his last film before he emigrated to Germany.

Still, this was only a shadow of former successes. Several individual titles could not substitute for the past continual production of top films. Nobody experimented with new techniques, young animators mostly repeated already seen and achieved

FIGURE 2.17 *Satiemania* (1978) by Zdenko Gašparović.

instead of making new breakthroughs in content and form. On the other hand, in some other countries, animation was gaining in speed. New techniques and a new culture introduced with electronic media started to dominate and Zagreb film slowly began to lose the title of internationally important centre of animation.

Zagreb film remained a good school, but the University of Animation was built in another place on the planet – the Canadian National Film Board.

IDEA OF "THE THIRD ROAD" AS IDEOLOGICAL FOUNDATION

Art deals with man and the big secret of life. Social circumstances in given time and space, and a particular situation a person finds itself in, define each individual in a particular society and the art that develops in that society. Reality of human existence from the perspective of Zagreb authors was strongly marked by the value system formed in the political atmosphere they worked and lived in.

Democracy and dictatorship are not the only two systems existing in the world, just as there are more colours than just black and white. Between these two distinct poles lies a whole multicoloured world, a spectrum of countless colours and nuances. One of the ornaments in this vast mosaic of political history was Titoism, a strange combination of dictatorship and democracy, which will probably be forgotten as soon as the last generation born in that system eventually passes away. Tito maintained his power skilfully balancing between federal and republic institutions on the home turf, and East and West abroad. Yugoslavia introduced the idea of the so-called third road in foreign politics. Geographically, and ideologically, Yugoslavia stood on the border between two confronted blocks but belonged to neither. In Belgrade, in 1961, the Non-Aligned Movement was founded, in which Tito was the central political figure. Even if they disliked communist ideology, most Yugoslav people respected the political stability of the country, and a relatively good economic development. The idea of "the third road" was extremely popular; people really saw their country as an alternative to imperialist West and bureaucratic East. Many, including artists, believed that Yugoslavia presented the best combination of the two worlds. Although Yugoslavia had its share of political engaged films, especially at the time of the so-called black wave, Yugoslav live-action authors never confronted the system as fiercely as did Kadar, Menzel, Passer or Forman in Czechoslovakia, Wajda and Zanussi in Poland, Jancso, Makk, Fabrio or Szabo in Hungary.

Yugoslav regime was rarely criticized for lack of democracy; it was more fiercely attacked by the nationalist right wing, which sheds much light on the catastrophe that happened after Tito's death. Like most of the people, Yugoslav filmmakers rarely confronted the system; they were mostly its ardent propagators. This was also true of the "third road" idea that was unusually popular even among the creators of Yugoslav's best films – members of the Zagreb School of Animated film. Except for Vladimir Kristl, Zagreb authors were mostly opportunistic towards the regime. Besides active participation in politics, Vukotić also made several regime films; Mimica and later Dragić were members of the republic Central Committee of the Communist Union. Other leading animators were also loyal citizens of the Federal Yugoslavia.

Still, satire was an important element of Zagreb films, but the satirical razor was directed towards actual global problems, racism, colonialism, pollution, hunger, poverty, fear of the A-bomb, war etc. Criticism was present, but it did not include social criticism. Yugoslav system was not only spared of criticism, it was, indirectly but indisputably, celebrated. The idea of a small, spiteful country existing on the borderline between two gigantic and hostile worlds was interwoven in many films made in the Zagreb studio to which I will concentrate in a separate chapter.

A small freedom oasis, surrounded by pressures, terror and danger, was an all-present motif in animated anecdotes of the leading school's masters. A small man abused by his surroundings, who, despite the troubles, kept fighting for his way of life, his independence and his neutrality was a common denominator of all the authors of the Zagreb school, regardless of their artistic profile and their filmic and visual expression. The interest of Zagreb animators to keep repeating the phrase "one against all" or even better, "everything and everyone against one" described one of the contemporary connoisseurs of the Zagreb School, the critic Ranko Munitić (1982):

> ...the tendency to place in the middle a small, plain person, a representative of the average, not at all special participants of this existence. Of course, this anti-hero, pathetic-free symbol of life's banality, will assume different character depending on the author's individuality. (...) His fight is mostly directed towards keeping his personality and autonomy intact from various kinds of social pressure: the antihero of the Zagreb School is always the untameable exception negating the general social rule (...) Even when moderated with comical elements, the conflict between global and individual is always present as a clear ideological trend of these multi-coloured anecdotes. The typical little fellow of the Zagreb school defends his integrity and intimate freedoms with persistence and stubbornness.

Probably the most representative example of this trend was *Learning to Walk* by Borivoj Dovniković. At the beginning we see a small, happy man walking across the screen, hopping, bouncing, whistling and smiling. However, soon he meets other figures, much bigger and stronger, which are marching, limping, dragging their feet, twitching their elbow or waving their head back and front while walking. Each of them tries to teach the small man "the right way" of walking. Trying to follow their advice, he starts limping, marching, twitching and waving... all at the same time. But he is no longer happy. His attempt to please everyone turned out ridiculous. In a virtuously animated finale, we see the small man physically and mentally handicapped. Exhausted by other people's advice, he finally returns to his bouncy walk (Figure 2.18).

FIGURE 2.18 *Learning to Walk* (1978) by Borivoj Dovnikovic Bordo.

Again, he is hopping, bouncing, whistling and smiling, now a master of his own destiny.

A similar metaphor about the small man defying the big world can be found in a whole range of films of the Zagreb School. In Dovniković's second film, *Passenger of Second Class* (1972), the small man's universe was his compartment. In *Curiosity* (1966), it was a park bench. Even in these miniature places hostile surroundings will not let them be. The small man, this time a tramp, was a hero of Dragić's *Diogenes Perhaps*, and *Passing Days* (1968), where he was a simple taxpayer sitting in his living room. In Vukotić's *Ars Gratia Artist* (1970), he was an artist, in Štalter/Grgić's film *The Fifth* (1964), the small man was a musician rejected by the quartet. In Dovniković's *N.N.* (1979) and Dragić's *The Day I Stopped Smoking* (*Dan kad sam prestao pušiti*, 1982), we saw nothing but the small man, everything else was white, at the same time everything and nothing, the place out of which lurked invisible dangers. In Zaninović's film *On Holes and Corks* (1967), the small man was living in a strange fortress when somebody or something started drilling his living space. In Marks/Jutriša's *Sisyphus* (*Sizif*, 1967), the small man was attacked by chairs, drawers and other bits of furniture in his apartment. And so on, and so forth. Dozens more films featured this basic metaphor based on the small, bold and optimistic man and his self-confident slalom between hostility, malice and injustice in his surroundings (Figure 2.19).

The small man, often wearing his hat, was one of rare Croatian national traits that could be seen in animated films, and it became a symbol of the Zagreb School and more generally, for the idea of neutrality, independence and a big NO to the block politics. A small defiant fellow coming from the border between the worlds in conflict won many sympathies at international festivals. It was no surprise since his philosophy was interpreted as resistance to the arms race, prospect of nuclear war,

FIGURE 2.19 *The Fifth* (1964) by Štalter & Grgić.

and other fears and anxieties that have marked the time we usually refer to as the "Cold War era".

The Zagreb School films were not always received with equal enthusiasm in the world of animation. Joe Adamson in his book *Tex Avery: King of Cartoon* mocked Stephenson's delight with European, and particularly Zagreb animation, claiming that the authors of Zagreb School would imitate Avery "if only they had sufficient funding" (1975). William Moritz, editor of the animation chapters in some of the *Oxford History of World Cinema*, mentioned the whole phenomenon as a marginal group of caricaturists "gathered around Dušan Vukotić" (1996).

However, they were only exceptions. The leading world authorities in the domain of animation, such as Bendazzi, Wells, Cotte or Horn, writing in their capital books (whose covers frequently included shots from some Zagreb School film), treated the Zagreb School precisely as this phenomenon deserved it – as an extremely important chapter in the history of animation, especially its modern turn-off.

THE CRISIS AND THE END OF SCHOOL DURING THE 1980s

Soon after Tito's death in 1980, the idea of the "third road" turned out to be completely "unrealistic reality", a kind of "La Grande Illusion". After Gorbachev, perestroika, the fall of the Berlin Wall, and the end of the Cold War, the idea of the "third road" and a country in between lost its initial meaning. Yugoslavia lost its international position and, moreover, dissolved in a bloody war.

Political chaos that extended over the country at the beginning of the 1980s caused economic crisis, whose first victim was culture. Zagreb film was one of the institutions whose funding was radically cut. Small studio place in the Old Town of Zagreb found itself in the worst crisis ever. The number of productions was constantly decreasing until it fell to only several films a year, whose quality was far below the Zagreb School's reputation. Times like year 1962, when, besides all the commercial work, the studio produced 23 animated films, seemed out of reach in the 1980s. Many great names left Zagreb film; they kept changing the management, while one humble attempt to rejuvenate the studio and production succeeded only partially. International awards stopped coming to Zagreb.

Yugoslav political crisis, however, was only one of the causes for the downfall of the Zagreb School of Animated film. Even without the catastrophe, it is highly probable that Zagreb film would not have been able to hold the position in world animation competing with the National Film Board of Canada, Polish or British studios in full swing. The main reason for Zagreb film's stagnation was the absence of any other technique apart from classic cel-animation. In the studio's history, only several films were made in the collage technique, even less in stop-motion and everything else was done as classical cartoon film.

From its beginnings, the studio recruited newspaper cartoonists for animators, which always remained caricaturists, cartoonists or illustrators, even after becoming animation directors. Leading authors of the Zagreb School showed no interest in puppet-film, claymation or other forms of model animation. The possibilities of Zagreb style, based on two-dimensional drawing and anecdote, began to wear out already in the 1970s, when most of Zagreb film production seemed like déjà vu.

At the same time, their strongest competitors, Canadian National Film Board and CBC, invested greatly in the development of new techniques. Countless animators from all around the world, including one of the leading Zagreb animators Zlatko Grgić, come to Canada, where they had excellent working conditions, and created with the home artists the "Canadian phenomenon" in animation, making films that filled some of the most brilliant pages of the history of cinema.

Other countries also produced successful animated films: the Soviet Union, Great Britain, Poland, Czechoslovakia or Japan. Each of them started researching different materials as early as the mid-1960s; they were making significant steps into the third dimension; experimenting with camera movement, and the use of computers etc. World animation was gradually abandoning two-dimensional surface of the film image and diving into the depth of film space. With several exceptions, *Satiemania*, for example, two-dimensional Zagreb "cartoons" were rapidly losing their breath in the race with their competition.

New techniques, primarily computers, quickly changed the face of animation. During the 1960s began the research whose goal was to adapt computers to visual media. The 1970s marked an extremely fast development of computers in the USA, Japan and Western Europe. One of the first renowned authors who made a computer-animated film was John Hallas, and the film was *Dilemma* (1981). Only eight years later, John Lasseter won an Oscar for his computer animation *Tin Toy* (1989), produced in his studio Pixar, specialized for computer animation.

The 1990s have been a time of serious crisis in the Zagreb studio, along with other world studios, including Canadian. Technical progress made animation in the 1990s all-present in our ordinary lives: electronic commercials, music videos, computer-animated introductory credits, the so-called visual effects etc. At the same time animation got more and more impersonal. During a period of time when technique dominates traditionally understood animation is having hard time. The dominance of the technical aspect stimulated the authors of the traditional understanding to react in the form of strong personal profiled films, in which computer was just a tool subordinated to the author (*Father and Daughter*, 2001, by Dudok de Wit, *Fugue for Cello, Trumpet and Landscape*, 2014, by Jerzy Kucia, *The Physics of Sorrow*, 2019, by Theodore Ushev…). This brought back hope that animation, as the art of individuals and primarily handmade, would manage to overcome all technological challenges.

Zagreb film continued to exist and produce animated films, today as a cultural institution of Croatia, which has been an independent state since 1991. New generation of animators have basically terminated the period of stagnation, and some of them have already made noticed films. As we will see in the last chapter, the old place helped generate new quality that once again attract attention of the world of animation. But it is another story.

The term Zagreb School of Animation has been a part of history for a long time. Just like the country this phenomenon sprang from.

3 Central European Humour in Regional Animation

GOOD SOLDIER SCHWEIK IN CIVIL SUIT

He is about 40 and has an ordinary job. He does not make much money, but he has enough to pay for the rent, treat himself with an occasional pair of sausages and a bear before finally ending in bed. That is all he wants from life, but everything that is happening around him – wars, assassinations, political conspiracies, nationalism, revolutions, communism, capitalism, constant upheavals and alarms – simply will not let him be.

He cannot comprehend the turbulences surrounding him and despises change, unrest and confusions of any kind. He can be defined in a single word – anti-revolutionary. He is a fighter for ordinary life, hero of everyday, advocate of the average and normal. What makes him happy is repetition, monotony and things that never change.

He wants to be nothing more than an average citizen and a simple taxpayer. Traditions, customs, habits and conventions represent the world he feels at home with. He has no interest in politics; his ambition in life is – to live. He is the character we usually call the "little man".

Nevertheless, although against his will, he still became a hero.

When exterior circumstances endanger his ordinariness, he is forced to fight. But he is not a true fighter, and his fight is different from what we normally understand as "fighting". Under occupation, during wars or revolutions, his only shelter and shield is a special kind of humour, full of pessimism, absurd and surrealism. Pessimism is his way of refusing to submit to political lies, military idiotism and ideological fogs. Absurd space of his humour is a sanctuary in which he hides from reality.

Despite his "unheroic heroism", this character became the national hero. While many nations take pride in their warriors, conquerors, winners, saviours, and knights, one little, plain man named Schweik became the greatest Czech hero. And not just Czech. Such a hero, more precisely, pessimist antihero, is one of the central figures of the whole Central European literature, oral literature, visual art, theatre, film and cinema animation.

Tradition of pessimist humour, which stems primarily from the territory that was for a long time known as the Austrian empire, and later on Austro-Hungarian, is a reflection of a hundred years longing of small nations for freedom, equality, right to publicly use their language and be autonomous in culture. Even after the fall of

DOI: 10.1201/9781003375623-3

FIGURE 3.1 Good soldier Schweik (1954) by Jiri Trnka.

Austro-Hungarian Empire after World War I, Central European pessimist humour or humoristic pessimism remained vital and often functioned as an irreplaceable spice to many forms of artistic expression and important works made in this field.

In the area we call Central Europe, the term itself has much more cultural than geographical meaning, between 1950 and 1980, worked a significant number of animated film studios. Many successful films, regardless of their origins, be it Prague, Budapest or Zagreb, relied precisely on the tradition of humour whose main character was a plain man whose main feature was pessimism.

Little Schweikian character with an ironical smile, a character whose humour is his means of survival, is the leitmotif of Central European animated film, the phenomenon to which film history has not yet paid sufficient attention (Figures 3.1 and 3.2).

CENTRAL EUROPEAN AUTO IRONY AND ABSURD

It is often the case that the notions of Eastern and Central Europe are perceived as one and the same thing, although these are two different things that have common features but are by no means the same. The first notion implies primarily a political term, dating from the end of 1940s and mostly referring to the countries included in the former Warsaw pact, while Central Europe is defined by its spiritual and cultural content. Geographically, the area cannot be outlined with exact borders; it is rather defined with common mental features and cultural legacy of its population. On the map, Central Europe figures as a vibrant blob, as from some animated film, continually moving across history. Still, it can be approximately outlined, the "blob" spreads from Krakow to Sarajevo.

FIGURE 3.2 The Hand (1965) by Jiri Trnka.

Central Europe presents a complicated ethnical mix, as the consequence of great movements of the peoples, wars and conquests, and the longevity of the Hapsburg Empire. The Hapsburgs, which ruled Austria and parts of Bohemia, formed a union with Hungary and Croatia at the turn of 1526, which was considered the beginning of the empire that would fall apart only after World War I, in 1918. Imperial family Hapsburg ruled over a great number of nations: Germans, Hungarians, Ukrainians, Czechs, Croats, Slovenes, Bosnians, Serbs, Italians, Romanians, Gypsies, including Jewish communities situated in most of larger towns of the empire.

For centuries, these small nations dreamed of freedom, independence and a right to create their culture in their own language. One of the characteristics of their battle for freedom was that it was fought with peaceful methods: negotiating table was a much more frequent choice than rebellious barricades. With political strategies, compromises and occasional protesting, small nations gradually acquired their rights. However, every portion of freedom demanded a lot of time and patience. For example, after many years of persistent Hungarian manoeuvring, the empire was formally divided (in 1866, when the empire was officially renamed Austro-Hungarian), although Franz Josef remained sovereign on both territories. This encouraged the Czechs to demand their sovereignty, while Croats, on the other hand, developed the idea of Yugoslavia as a way of freeing from the Austro-Hungarian hegemony. Neither the Czechs, nor the Croats succeeded at first, but they won some other privileges. For example, Zagreb got the independent university in 1874, and Prague in 1882.

The constant fighting for independence and equality in respect of the Hapsburgs and their strict regime was the basic characteristic of the almost 400 years long empire, and as such has defined political and cultural history of the nations constituting the Empire.

This conglomerate consisting of many mixed nations, which applied the politics of small steps with more or less success, developed authentic regional traditions, way of life and surviving. A superior state that could not be defeated by other means than negotiation, which regularly extended over whole generations, produced a strong sense of impotence in the subjects of the Empire. Unable to control their own lives, people could choose between despair and laughter at their own expense. Of course, they chose humour. Of course, the result of this humour was not necessarily laughter.

With a risk to oversimplify, satire can be defined as humour whose object is the government – i.e. those with social power or advocates of the ruling dogmas. Humour, however, is possible only if its creator, humourist, is prepared to laugh at his own expense (too). Of course, humour can be an artistic activity, healing therapy, entertainment and many other things. Still, the basic assumption that has to be satisfied in order for something to be called humour is that the subject of the joke has to be ready to become its object. Otherwise, the result is mocking, prejudice, provocation or insult; anything but humour, one of the most sublime qualities and abilities of human being. Humour and satire are directly related to the social position of their creator. A poor man can easily make a good joke at the expense of the rich; however, it is not so the other way around. Sense of humour and satire is most frequently found among the poor, humiliated and oppressed victims of all kinds of injustices and repressions.

In Central European humourist tradition, object and subject of humour are often one and the same, while the line between humour and satire is practically inexistent. Since he cannot change his life by rebelling against the government, the man mocks his own situation. Humour has the power to transform impotence to superiority, while at the same time the humourist is perfectly aware of the situation he is in: he is not living in the society of his choice, he serves in the army of the state he does not care about, he pays the taxes to someone he considers his oppressor, he is forced to read and learn in foreign language, while his mother tongue and cultural heritage are, if not forbidden, than at least unwanted. Already by birth, owing to his name and nationality, the man finds himself on the other side of law; he is supposed to hide, or at least keep quiet about his proper culture, customs and language. For a member of a particular national or linguistic group, living itself becomes, in a way, a subversive, underground activity.

"Let's be Czechs, but keep it a secret", said one of the characters from the novel *The Good Soldier Schweik* (Hašek, 1998: 142).

However, this metaphorical underground is usually the most fertile ground for humour.

Central European humour always simultaneously refers to the rulers, its proper origins and the reason for humour. Humourist from Central Europe never puts himself above or outside of his work but is instead its active part. He gravely mocks the big and the powerful but with the same irony displays his own oppression and impotence to change his situation.

Since he does not respect the government and power, Central European humourist has no illusions about himself. This type of humour produced one typical figure of the little people's man who is constantly joking. Despite the troubles that never cease, this disillusioned kidder often makes sarcastic jokes at his expense; his laughter hides his real face from his not very humoristic surrounding. Every Central European national community has in its cultural legacy one such humoristic character, but as mentioned, by far the most famous of them all is already mentioned *Good Soldier Schweik*, creation of the Czech writer Jaroslav Hašek.

In the last hours of the Hapsburgs, the Austro-Hungarian Empire evolved into a modern state with ever growing bureaucracy, which appeared almighty, making people, especially in the big cities, feel even more impotent, fearful and desperate. Humour became the imprint of (un)reality ruled by the absurd. In real life, nothing was possible, so to counter that, humour created the world in which everything was possible. Jews, which were a minority in a double sense (in the Empire as a whole, and in every town and quarter they inhabited), gave a significant contribution to the development of the element of absurd and surrealism in Central European spiritual heritage. The classic of the literature of absurd was undoubtedly Franz Kafka, writer of Jewish origin from Prague.

As the historian Hermann summarized in the following citation, the relationship between small, impotent man and mighty bureaucratic or military system is common denominator of the tradition personified by both Kafka and Hašek (1975):

> Jews belonging to the German cultural circle of Prague were minority in a double sense and this perhaps more than anything explains the extraordinary sensitivity, which they displayed. In Franz Kafka they were the first to express, in surrealistic form, the anguish of modern man. But it was not long before – in the early twenties – the same theme of the small man facing a soulless power was treated in Czech and in a quite different style (and with greater contemporary impact) by Jaroslav Hašek, in *The Good Soldier Schweik.*

After World War I, Austro-Hungarian Empire vanished from the political and geographical map of the world. Poland became independent in 1919, in the Czechoslovak Republic, legendary opposition leader in emigration Tomas Masaryk became first democratically elected president, while Yugoslavia was founded in 1918. All this accompanied by other events signalled the definite ending of the four century-long empire. However, as the future would show, this did not mean that nations in the region were any closer to happier and more prosperous existence. Humour heavily characterized by absurd, auto irony and pessimism continued to dominate Central European life. Central European man still had many reasons to change the world he was living in.

With humour at least, if there was no other way.

SCHWEIK – A PHONY LUNATIC

Good Soldier Schweik is probably the most famous unfinished novel in the history. The book's author, Hašek, died in 1923, before having finished the manuscript. He managed to write three chapters of the book entitled *In the background*, *Road to the Battlefield* and *Glorious decline*. His obvious intention, however, was to write the fourth chapter in which he would describe the hero's return from the war.

Despite the novel's mosaic structure constructed of interconnected anecdotes with Schweik as their main protagonist, and the fact that the writer did not get to write "the end", *Good Soldier Schweik* can be read as a whole and coherent story. Literary worth of the book is still questionable, and there is significant controversy among the critics as to the real literary worth of Hašek's prose. While some think that the work deserves status of the classic of world literature as one of the best humoristic novels ever, others claim that it is nothing but pure propaganda.

In the book *Essays on Czech Literature*, Rene Wellek (1963) wrote the following:

> Jaroslav Hašek (1883–1923) has given a grotesque picture of the Austrian Empire in dissolution in his *Good Soldier Schweik*. The book is not much of a work of art, as it is full of low humour and cheap propaganda; but the type of the foolish, smiling, cowardly Czech Sancho Panza who goes unscathed through the military machine of the Empire is difficult to forget, however unheroic and uninspiring he may be.

What was definitely not questionable was the nature of humour and characterization of the hero, but both had many qualities typical of the cultural milieu the book was created in.

Hitchcock famously said that excitement is produced when ordinary man finds himself in an unusual situation. A possible paraphrase of this definition could be that a characteristic type of humour is created from normal, everyday behaviour in an utterly abnormal situation.

There is hardly any situation more abnormal than war. The war we are faced with is World War I, which caught Schweik in its net, a nice Czech man, plain little bear lover from Prague, decisive to stay independent despite the horrors of war. Nobody knows, and the reader cannot say for certain, who Schweik really was. The writer put him among epic figures, whose greatness surpassed many of famous historical personalities (Napoleon, Alexander…). At first sight, however, Schweik is not the type that would inspire such human qualities as bravery and heroism. He is not even a soldier – he was forcefully mobilized to go to a war he could not care less about. Moreover, he did not even satisfy minimal physical demands for a soldier: he suffered from rheumatism. In addition to this, he was once already freed from serving in the army after having been certified by an army medical board as an imbecile. Finally, he was spending his warring days as batman to Austrian officers.

Schweik's civil job is also not very impressive. He lived by selling dogs "ugly, mongrel monstrosities whose pedigrees he forged", spending his free time visiting beer pubs in his beloved Prague. When the Emperor calls him into war, he seems more like a saboteur and simulator, than a hero. Yet, that is precisely his main heroic deed.

The book starts with great news brought to Schweik by the cleaning lady, Mrs. Miller who told him that "they had killed our Ferdinand, back there in Sarajevo". Instead of being alerted by the assassination, Schweik comments on the late Archduke's weight ("a fat archduke's a better mark than a thin one"). In this scene, the author already introduces typical "Schweikian" irony: talking about something totally out of context or simply said: talking gibberish in most critical moments.

In the next chapter – anecdote, we see Schweik in a pub in his quarter, discussing the event with other guests, of which one was a police snitch. Due to silly bar talk, Schweik is arrested and charged with high treason, which triggered a series of misunderstandings between him and hyper bureaucratic Austro-Hungarian state. Schweik is not at all excited or scared because of his arrest. Moreover, he almost looks pleased.

"What is the use of police if not to punish us who are talking too much?", he comments on his own situation. He confuses his prosecutors by admitting to whatever they accuse him of. Even that he assassinated Ferdinand by his own hand and thus caused the outbreak of war between the Empire and Serbia, and consequently the outbreak of World War I.

"I am a certifiable imbecile. I admit to everything!", was his motto during the whole novel.

After the investigation, the police send Schweik to a mental hospital where he enjoys himself even more.

> I honestly do not understand why lunatics get mad when closed in the nuthouse. One can crawl naked on the floor, howl like a jackal, scream and bite. If man would do such a thing in the street, others would be amazed. This is clear as day! Even socialists cannot dream of such a freedom.
>
> **Page 32**

As the war is expanding, the state, needing "fresh cannon fodder", addresses all nations of the Empire and drafted all men, including the incompetent Schweik. Despite the bloody war and the fact that he is wearing Austro-Hungarian uniform, Schweik is having tons of fun. His sanctuary is joking, best cure for human stupidity and madness, and all it carries with it. Pretending to be a fool, Schweik is pulling the leg of the whole Empire, and especially its military section.

He performs every order to the letter and literally transfers the messages from officer to officer ("Colonel sends you his regards and says you are an ass"); he is proud and erect even when saying the utmost stupidities, for example, when he pulls the handle on the train to check whether the brake is functioning properly, or when he is singing patriotic songs in most inappropriate places, or when he starts talking gibberish while the outcome of war is being decided.

"There was this doctor in the pub Špirk…" starts Schweik his usual gibberish every time the Imperial army finds itself in a critical situation, driving his superiors nuts. His infantile behaviour and nonsense talk, his "philosophy" and "deep" conclusions turn the battlefield in the theatre of nonsense, the theatre of absurd. Lines between geniality and stupidity in Schweik's case simply do not exist.

He passes through the inferno of war wearing the jester's mask that helps him escape from reality. We laugh at his ability to keep his usual civil behaviour even amidst the most inhuman situation such as war. Laughter breaks any link between his actual situation and his acts: a rheumatic is forced to fight for his oppressor, and his behaviour is still perfectly casual.

Actually, the more ordinary his behaviour, the more pointless is his situation. The result is humour.

Still, we should not forget that Schweik has no other choice. As was the case with many people of that region, history gave him only two choices: to accept the situation, however hopeless, totally serious, or to mock everyone and everything, and particularly himself, or in other words, to survive.

Of course, there are many examples in the book where Hašek reminds the reader whom his hero is representing.

> Listen, Schweik, are you really such a fool?
>
> Yessir, replied Schweik proudly. – Yes, I am! Ever since I was little I had no luck with myself.
>
> **Page 148**

An interesting curiosity connected with the book were the vignettes made by Josef Lada used as illustrations for the first issue of the novel. The illustrations integrated with the content of the book so strongly that it is simply unimaginable to publish Schweik in any time and any language with any other illustrations. Lada visualized Schweik for eternity: clumsy and staunch beer lover dressed in a uniform one size too large, whose face always wears a good-natured smile. Lada's perfect visual interpretation of Schweik and other characters showed immediately after the publishing, how much the novel was pliable material for other media apart from literature.

PESSIMISM AND IRONY AS FORM OF HUMOROUS RESIGNATION

Schweik is making fools out of his military bosses although he is aware that he could easily end up in jail or even dead. However, he has nothing to lose – living in his situation, being a soldier of the army he despises is not worth lamenting over. If he cannot live his life as he would like to, the only thing left to do is to turn despair into fun, no matter the cost. Still, this nonchalant nihilism is simply a façade. His foolishnesses are, according to Herman, much more frightening than Kafkian absurd labyrinth of reality:

> The conflict between bureaucratic machinery and the conscience was treated differently by Jaroslav Hašek, whose way of life was pub-crawling. His Schweik has no need of conscience because he cannot decide anything anyway, and cannot afford the luxury of truthfulness and decency if he wants to survive. The foul-mouthed joviality of Schweik, who says "Yessir" to his officers and kicks them in the pants every time they turn away, contrasts sharply with the suspense of Mr K's ghostly trial. But there is less hope in Hašek's nihilism than in Kafka's soul-searching, and the ready acceptance of Schweik as a national prototype was a terrifying experience.
>
> **1975**

The inch of hope and joy that can still be found in Schweik is actually a result of great expectations of the future that Hašek must have felt when he was writing his book, when his country and people were set from centuries-long occupation. The time that came, however, clouded the optimistic visions, while with the arrival of "little moustache" and "big moustache", Hitler and Stalin, they completely vanished. The region was the first and most difficult victim of Nazi Germany, while as the outcome of World War II, the whole Central Europe found itself in the grasp of another imperialist government, situated in Moscow. New Empire, the so-called communist block, made of the Soviet Union and its vassals, turned out to be as brutal as the Hapsburgs were. On the smallest sign of rebellion and openly expressed wish for freedom and independence, "comrade" Stalin sent punishing expeditions in the form of tanks of perhaps the mightiest army of the world, as was the case in Budapest in 1956 and Prague in 1968.

Characteristically Central European humour, product of not very joyful pessimist telling jokes, continued existing in the modern times. Man forced to live his life under the dark sky, used humour to reveal the invisible chains that prevented him from walking freely. The message of this humour is black: our world is anything but a beautiful place and life are a lost bet. We are only actors in supporting roles and have little chance of influencing our faith. The whole civilization is actually one sophisticated jungle trotted by helpless human beings. That is the reason why a person wants so little out of life, still even that is often unattainable. All that a person does is more or less pointless, and there is almost no joy in life. Even work, which often turns out to be a futile activity, does not make one happy.

In his analysis of East European (basically Central European) film comedy, Charles Eidsvik (1991) singled out the example of character from Kieslowski's *Short film about love* and formed a conclusion applicable to a much wider area than was just that film:

> The characters are beyond protest; there is nothing that can be changed nothing to complain about. The world of Kieslowski's characters has been crushed by history. And so Tomek, Magda, and landlady do not resent work even though they do not work for reasons of ambition. They work because work can help people to reach, however clumsily, toward each other. Work is an excuse for contact between ludicrous and funny but suffering human beings.

Still, despite everything, little Central European man is not fatalist. Pessimism, materialized in his humour, became his rebellion. Existence seen from the viewpoint of a looser, life as a complete nonsense and confusion, person's impossibility to understand the reality in which idyllic picture from the media and political rhetoric constantly collide with the everyday hell and are a fertile source of humour. Whole phony picture created by the police and one-party state was unmasked with the help of bitter humour and irony, as defined by Eidsvik (1991):

> Irony regularly questions identity. Whether verbal or visual, particularity of irony is that it questions the existence itself, presenting it as apparition and illusion, just like our knowledge of ourselves and others.

"THE GREATEST ENEMY" OF SOCIALIST DOCTRINE

"Orwellian" system that called itself socialism developed gigantic propaganda machinery whose task was to persuade the population that they were living in the best society there is. Newspapers, magazines, film and television controlled by the regime, featured photographies of smiling workers by their machines, radiant smiles also graced the faces of farmers on tractors, metal workers in steel factories, even miners were "happy" in reportages showing them coming out of dark mines. The biggest lie consisted in the claim that working class had won the battle against exploiters and that workers were ruling the country. Figure of worker dressed in a typical suit became a falsified icon, while work itself became a cult. In some of the so-called socialist countries, the official greeting was "long live work". Work was actually celebrated by the bureaucratic nomenclature, the class of the worse slackers in the history, those who unscrupulously robbed the poor who officially "ruled" the society.

The party was at the helm of the society which was allegedly moving towards a brighter future – communism – where all were going to be equally valued. Everyone was supposed to give according to their abilities and take according to their needs. To prevent the people to go astray, the party had to rule with iron discipline and the utmost seriousness. This seriousness, however, demanded the citizens to smile. Their faces had to radiate optimism and faith that they were on the way to the best social system possible and the final phase of history – communism. Milan Kundera (1987), Kafka's and Hašek's spiritual son, described it in his landmark work *Joke* (*Žert*) with the following words:

> The strangest thing concerning this seriousness was that it did not have a dark face, instead it looked like a smile; yes, these years were proclaimed the happiest of them all, and those who were not happy immediately became suspicious as someone who did not rejoice in the victory of the working class or (which was no smaller sin) for the individualist drowning in the inner sadness.

Ludvik, the hero of *Joke*, encountered troubles after having written a humorous postcard to Marketa, girl he met in work camp, with the following lines: "Optimism is opium for the masses! Sense reeks of idiotism. Long live Trocki! Ludvik". After this, he had to undergo a hearing before the party committee and was accused of having betrayed the revolution and "historical optimism of the working class". Finally, due to his pessimism, Ludvik was forbidden to go to college and was sentenced to "reforming", in other words, slavery in a mine, and life in a work camp.

What was called pessimism – in other words, scepticism and openly expressed disbelief in official happiness – was labelled as the greatest threat to the so-called socialist doctrine and many subjects of socialist countries went through the same ordeal as Kundera's literary hero. Artists were particularly stricken by this, because of "pessimism" they lost the possibility to present themselves to the public, they were imprisoned or forced to continue their careers in emigration.

Central European humourist tradition with its bitter points and bleak representation of reality continued to flourish across the region, defying difficult political climate and the attempts of political heads to harness creativity. A good illustration of the circumstances in which artists created was effectively summarized in the famous political caricature by Fritz Behrendt showing a political official sitting in his armchair telling a writer, already dressed in striped prisoner's suit: "We give you ten years to rewrite your book in optimistic-realistic spirit".

Small demands of little people for an ordinary life eventually tore down the huge statue raised to the honour of those who symbolized dogmatism, state terror and other perversions resulting from totalitarian interpretation of freedom. Sceptical artists who refused to believe political and ideological lies and reflected in their works their disbelief and hopelessness were the first saboteurs of the steel construction of the so-called realistic socialism. Among them, creators of animated humour played one of the most prominent roles.

CENTRAL EUROPEAN ANIMATED HUMOUR – IT IS FUN TO DIE

Another characteristic of Central European humour was its totally nonchalant relationship to death. Central European art in general, and humour in particular, relates to death as to a close relative. This approach greatly differs from western humoristic tradition. Western European humourists are trying to forget the grim fact that death is the only certain thing in life. While western civilizations often encourage the naïve belief that death is something far away (and happening to others), Central European spiritual heritage considers death, physical and mental, as an everyday event. Happy end is rarely seen in Central European art works. There is no good ending; there is only naked truth: the only epilogue of life is death. From birth, man is sentenced to die, and that is the only firm knowledge we have. No other. Time never stands still; even when something resembling a happy end occurs in one moment, it is inevitably followed by death.

The notion of death is rarely understood in its religious sense, as the beginning of new, spiritual life, be it in heaven or hell. Death is nothing more than a huge black spot signifying a more or less welcomed end to life sufferings. It is not something we should be afraid of; on the contrary, dying can even be fun! If there is some life after death, it would be welcomed. Even hell could not be as horrifying as everyday life.

Dark nuances of death always painted Central European humour, including the drawn satire; means of expression with great tradition in the region. Drawings featuring suicide as the only real answer of the little, ordinary man to the world evil could regularly be found in Central European newspapers and magazines, exhibition catalogues and posters. Such drawings elicited laughter, but the one that gave you cramps in the stomach, because their motives mostly included things like guillotine, gallows, prisons, firing squads, coffins, handcuffs, cemeteries.

Posters, design, caricature and graphic with humoristic content were successfully produced in the region since the nineteenth century. However, the golden age of creation came after World War II, mainly in the 1960s and the 1970s. Central European graphic art stood out with its expressiveness, originality and the ability to transfer messages in original manner. Although they followed national trends such as surrealism and pop-art, regional graphics always managed to keep their own original visions, passion for experimenting and their authentic subtle black humour.

It seems that a rule can be created according to which production of caricature or graphical aphorism is in direct opposition of democratic development in the particular surrounding. There are numerous other examples supporting the claim that dictatorship is fertile ground for drawn satire, art that seems to grow best as forbidden fruit.

In the countries of the so-called socialist block, large numbers of humoristic magazines were published with the state support and blessing. The most famous of them were Szpilki in Poland, Eulenspiegel in East Germany, Dikobraz in Czechoslovakia, Ludas Matyi in Hungary, Jež (Serbia) and Kerempuh (Croatia) in Yugoslavia etc. The purpose of these magazines was to serve as some sort of safety valve for the people and to be a surrogate for real critical debate in the society. Humour was not allowed to question the doctrine, but it was desirable to criticize (or even better, mock) rivalling political and ideological block, which sometimes turned humour and satire to plain propaganda.

Most of humoristic artists found it frustrating to work within strict, state-defined limitations imposed on humour. Working with satire assumed great risks, so that those who drew cartoon and caricatures were always facing possible trouble with authorities. For that reason, best caricaturists, instead of balancing on thin line between allowed and forbidden, resorted to abstraction. Their polysemic line included much more than simple interpretation of the actual situation. In the shadow of everyday life filled with agitation, propaganda and humour in the service of ideology and regime, intelligent visual aphorism started to develop, whose grim and absurd ideas hit the great political lie right between the eyes. Absurd and abstract camouflaged the real intention of the drawings: unmasking of social mechanisms in the political system whose official ideology proclaimed bright eternity but in reality created short suffering in the darkness.

Pessimistic artists mocked false optimism. Their hero became a confused little man who pretended not to understand the lack of logical connection between the daily horror he was exposed to and the overall success and happiness that party-controlled media and socialist realist art were full of.

Schweik was no longer a soldier, dressed in a civil suit he started asking tricky questions which had nothing to do with revolutions and bright perspectives, but with the poor state of his pocket, plate and soul. The answers he got were illogical, absurd and disjointed. He stood in the midst of ideological mist and parodied the situation, himself and the proclaimed notion of man as the society's "greatest treasure", while in reality this "treasure" was no more than a punching bag for insatiable and fast-growing bureaucratic machinery.

Abstract caricatures painted "socialist realism" as the theatre of absurd where nothing was possible and everything was impossible. All that a man could see was a frame for the grand illusion invented to deceive the people. Little ordinary man thus became a rebel against political and economic powerholders, by showing on his own example all the pessimism, hopelessness and nonsense created in the "best and historically final social system". Generalized in caricature, this man, whose only ideal was plainness and normality, became the prototype of counterrevolutionary in the society of "permanent revolution".

He had a noose tied around his neck, and an ironical grin on his face.

Pessimistic view of life transmitted in the form of Central European black humour turned out to be extremely effective for enabling individual voices to be heard, to make it known that they protest and disagree with the terror of bureaucracy and domination of stupidity. Occupied, ideologically and territorially, if they could not free themselves, they could at least refuse to accept the situation. Official system was seen as total chaos, while reality with allegedly all the answers concerning human existence was depicted as a nightmare.

Despite the ruling ideology which "made people happy", in drawings death was featured as the only and final place of human freedom: the face of a convict about to be guillotined is horrified and in tears, but when his head is cut off, the expression on the face changes into a smile. On one Bartak's drawing, made with his typical broken line, there are numerous signposts pointing nowhere and the little man, although at first glance it appears nonsensical, shakes hands with them. On another drawing by the same author, we see the newspapers which exclusively publish ideological fairy tales, in other words nothing, make their reader invisible, in other words, nothing. Hungarian cartoonist Jelensky drew a man standing behind a corner, waiting for a potential victim to rob. Behind him stood his hungry family waiting for the catch. On another drawing we discover homeless people even on another planet, which is exaggeration characteristic of cartoon, signalling the chronical lack of flats, one of the typical problems socialist fortune makers were never able to solve. Satirical drawings showed fully developed brain, the obvious symbol of knowledge, as a big handicap for his owner: It was better to know less, life was simpler. Books, another symbol of learning and science, on Kosobukin's drawing are made of glass; "the truth" coming out of them is something extremely fragile.

And so on and so forth. There are piles of drawings representing the world as something rotten, inhabited by tortured and haunted people; drawings that transparently illustrated the only success of the deviation called real-socialism – the making of overall darkness, depression; people so desperate that death was their close friend.

Everyone and everything resemble itself more when presented in a caricature. Life in the society that turned Marxism upside down and pulled it out of the historical context was no exception to that rule. Consequently, caricaturist drawings were unusually realistic portrayals of horrors the so-called socialism was producing. Strong pessimist feelings emitted by these works pictured something very real, something that was hidden deep in the people trapped in the ideological castle in the clouds. It was not unusual that in the "classless society" it was the lowest class that intuitively understood the message in caricatures far better than bureaucratic nomenclature. In absurd, paradoxal, black world, the oppressed recognized themselves.

ANIMATION – ART OF ACCELERATED METAMORPHOSIS

Already in the course of the first decades of the twentieth century, film animation appeared in almost all Central European countries. Still, the golden age of this medium in this region lasted from the 1950s to the end of 1970s. After World War II, a significant number of animated film studios were founded in the region. Animated film was not considered "dangerous" for the system and the regime, so that censorship was much more frequent in other medias, like literature, theatre or feature film. Indeed, innovative and fresh art of animation was state funded, especially when at international film festivals animators from socialist countries stood out as superior to their western colleagues, thus "proving" the advantages of living and creating in socialism.

However, animated films came out as utterly subversive. In best works of animated film, reality was painted in colours and tones quite the opposite of those socialist bureaucrats wanted.

In the focus of interest of Central European animated film artists was maximally generalized individual, little man surrounded by absurd, trapped in the world where even most ordinary was often turned into something totally mystifying and incomprehensible. Everything the man sees or experiences represents an incomprehensible metamorphosis with no beginning and no end.

There was no Central European equivalent of Popeye or Superman. Much like in regional literature and drawn humour, in animation too there were heroes who were not heroes. Leading characters in Central European animation were often characterized by the "Schweikian" anomaly: little man, who felt like a looser, bearing no illusions towards the presence or the future, was forced to live unfree in the ideological casemate. Therefore, he was not afraid of death but instead saw it as a way to trick the torture and absurd of his ordinary life by escaping from it.

Film director builds an artistic reality by connecting longer or shorter temporally separated details of life. In practice, it is more than a curiosity when film time is of identical length as the reality represented. Contrary to director of feature film or documentary who are basing their storytelling on chosen, isolated shots and sequences, namely film sentences, animator deals with the molecules of film expression: 24th fragment of a second. Life in a film can be presented with the help of few consecutive shots of our face in the mirror. One day we see a child's face, the next, the face is mature and finally, it is old covered with white beard. The following day we do not wake up. Animator can represent the same thing in a single shot, in which our aging will be a continual process, unbroken movement lasting only several minutes. The whole life is represented as an accelerated metamorphosis; man grows, ages, his surrounding constantly changes. The medium of animation condenses time and allows for the invisible to be seen. It is capable to reduce the notion of life to a visual aphorism. Owing to the animation method, which can be defined as accelerated metamorphosis, in several short seconds we see a series of changes of our face, which normally spread throughout our whole life. In the same way it is possible that our face, in one continuous movement, transforms from old to young or becomes a female face, some animal's muzzle, an object or anything else. There is nothing impossible, unnatural or illogical for animation metamorphosis. In an animated film, literally anything can be made alive or represented as such.

In his book *Understanding Animation*, Paul Wells (1998) emphasized the importance of metamorphosis in animation saying that

> Metamorphosis also legitimises the process of connecting apparently unrelated images, forging original relationships between lines, objects etc., and disrupting established notions of classical story-telling. Metamorphosis can resist logical developments and determine unpredictable linearities (both temporal and spatial) that constitute different kinds of narrative construction. It can also achieve transformations in figures and objects, which essentially narrate those figures, and objects, detailing, by implication, their intrinsic capacities.

As the art of metamorphosis, film animation is almost an ideal medium for transferring absurd, surreal and black-humoured ideas, in other words, all that was for centuries integral to Central European cultural heritage. The whole opus of the father of absurd in literature, Franz Kafka, especially the famous story *Metamorphosis* with its endlessly recited introductory sentence ("Als Gregor Samsa eines Morgens aus unruhigen Träumen erwachte, fand Er sich in seinem Bett zu einem ungeheueren Ungeziefer verwandelt"/"As Gregor Samsa awoke one morning from uneasy dreams he found himself transformed in his bed into a gigantic insect".) quite logically, was always greatly cherished inspiration to the world's animators. The pair Marks and Jutriša from Zagreb dedicated most of their creative energy to making animations dealing with human existence as a nightmare (one of their films was called precisely that, *Nightmare,* from 1977) filled with Kafkian feelings of anxiety and discomfort. Something similar can be found in the work by the Pole Piotr Dumala, film *Franz Kafka* (1992), while the idea about a certain Gregor Samsa waking up transformed into a cockroach also attracted the ingenious American-Canadian author Caroline Leaf, who made the film *Metamorphosis of Mr. Samsa* in 1977, that is to say at the very beginning of her career (Figure 3.3).

As early as 1931, Berthold Bartosh, Slovak artist of left orientation who also worked in Germany and France, made his anthological animated film *Idea.* The film featured a man who came up with an idea in the shape of a beautiful naked girl. A group of people whose looks reveal that they are members of the ruling social classes are trying to dress

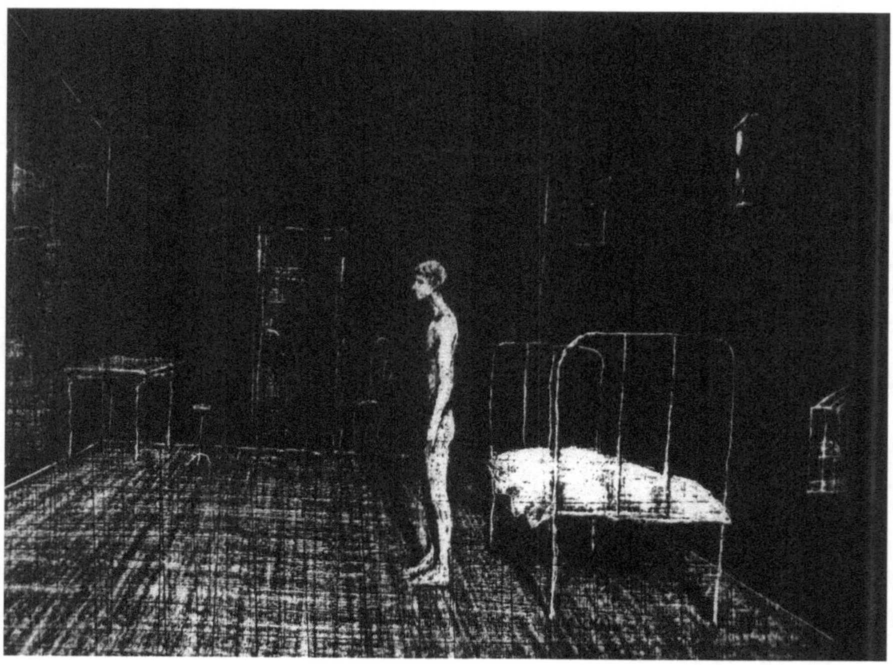

FIGURE 3.3 Freedom of the Leg (1989) by Piotr Dumala.

the girl and hide her naked body, the symbol of her purity. They are trying to turn the idea against the workers and its creator. When the idea refuses to succumb, its creator is shot, while the idea leaves this world. Bartosh's pessimism and scepticism (even concerning the utmost the human being can offer: an idea) greatly differed from contemporary American animated films founded on gags and jolly rides of anthropomorphic animals. His visual language, relying on contemporary trends in graphics, was completely different from the style overtaken from comic strip, which was the main characteristic of American animation from its very beginning. Until today, American (and western films in general) and Central European animated films continued to evolve, traveling different paths, as far as the expressive form and the content transferred were concerned.

Wells shed some light on the phenomenon by comparing animated illustrations by Terry Gilliam made for *Monthy Python's Flying Circus* with the film *Bartakiada* (1985) by Czech animator Oldrich Haberle, which consisted of animated and functionally connected abstract caricatures drawn by Miroslav Bartak. He found many similarities between the western animator and his Central European colleague but also pointed out one crucial difference:

> When two ideas that do not seem to naturally relate, meet, and indeed, fundamentally conflict, this can create a comic event. The joke comes out of a resistance to logical continuity (…) Incongruity follows incongruity but, unlike Gilliam's work, this is played out slowly, and consequently, Haberly creates a different atmosphere and tone. The speed and zany insanity of Gilliam's animation possesses the spirit of comic anarchy and violation whilst Haberle's jokes are essentially recognition of the absurdity of humankind's attempts to bring logical order to the world. Eastern European humour like this may be viewed as black irony – the surreality is a philosophic and political statement as well as the vehicle for humour. The incongruity is used for different comic purposes – Gilliam's to shock, Haberle's to reveal. One is the comedy of revolution, the other, the comedy of resignation.
>
> **1998**

It is not difficult to agree with Wells that precisely in this resignation or humoristic pessimism lies the essential difference between "socialist" and western European animated films. Political and ideological fog in which Central European animators worked significantly defined the content and form of their films, which were often clouded with abstraction, illogicalities and dilemmas.

Or, as Wells (1998) stressed it in another place in the same book:

> Working in oppressive, often authoritarian regimes, animators needed their work to represent their point of view but remain ambiguous enough not to incur the wrath and intervention of the authorities.

Little man enclosed in incomprehensible and unclear surrounding was the hero of many Central European films. Pessimist humour or humoristic pessimism was a feature of most important Central European animated films, whose authors were Poles Jerzy Kucia, Daniel Szczechura, Jan Lenica, Walerian Borowczyk, Miroslaw Kijowicz, Zdzislaw Kudla or Witold Giersz, Hungarians Attila Dargay, Marcell

FIGURE 3.4 Dimensions of Dialogue (1982) by Jan Švankmajer.

Jankovics and Joseph Nepp (together they created successful animated series Gusztav, featuring another typically "Schweikian" character) or Croats Zlatko Bourek, Zlatko Grgić, Vladimir Jutriša, Aleksandar Marks and others. Same characteristics can be found in puppet-film, animation genre to which Czech and Slovak animators definitely made the greatest contribution (Figures 3.4 and 3.5).

FIGURE 3.5 Rhynoceros (1965) by Jan Lenica.

ZAGREB SCHOOL: FREEDOM LIMITED BY AUTO-CENSORSHIP

Yugoslavia was a great exception among the socialist countries. It could be said that it was the most democratic country of the East block, or the least democratic country of the West. The country was independent in relation to the blocks, ruling communist ideology was significantly reformed and the society was liberal enough: life there had much more in common with the western way of living than the east. Yugoslavia parted early with the ideology of social realism in art so that censorship was much less strict than in other countries of the so-called socialist system. Instead of censorship, Yugoslavia developed a sort of auto-censorship; in practice, this meant that the authors more or less knew how large their manoeuvring space was. More importantly, they mostly accepted those limitations. This was also true of the leading animating studio in the country, Zagreb film. One of the leaders of the Zagreb school of animation, Borivoj Dovniković, explained it in the following way:

> We had no problem with censorship in Zagreb Film or with the Government. However, you must know that we had "a policeman in our brains", as we've described it, and that we knew what subject matter should be avoided, which included anything against politicians, the Communist Party and the Federal State of Yugoslavia.
>
> **Furniss (1998)**

Another important difference between Zagreb and other animation centres of central Europe was an obvious American influence on the aesthetics that formed in the Studio. Graphical language typical of caricature and strip defined the visual style of American animated film, whether it was gigantic Disney studio or Disney's rivals such as Warner Brothers, the UPA or others.

Owing to an important tradition of comic strips in Croatia, it happened that caricaturists and cartoonists founded a production of animated film in Zagreb. The founders were mostly artists whose main role models were Americans. Puppet-film did not develop in Zagreb, just as it did not develop on the other side of the Atlantic, while collage animations were quite rare.

Nevertheless, Yugoslav social system was still based on Marxist theory. Besides, former Yugoslav federal state Croatia was a Central European country with long history as an integral part of the Hapsburg Empire. Content of the films made in Zagreb thus much more resembled that of the films produced in the neighbouring Central European countries, and much less followed the clichés which developed in American animated comedies with anthropomorphic characters in main roles. Humoristic pessimism was the common denominator of all Central European animated film, including the works of the "Americanized" Zagreb studio.

One of Zagreb's animated films that could function as the prototype of Central European pessimistic humour is *Passing Days* by Nedeljko Dragić's, made in "rebellious" 1968. Little man whose life this film depicts is everything but rebellious. As is always the case with Dragić, here too we observe caricature drawn with utter simplicity, on which only several details stand out. In this case, this detail is slippers, clearly expressing the hero's only ambition in life: to live and ordinary, normal family life. However, he is prevented from doing so. Little man's life is full of misery and

FIGURE 3.6 Diogenes Perhaps (1967) by Nedeljko Dragic.

suffering, he is molested by the police, politicians, and has problems with money, even his love and sex life elicit only disgust (Figures 3.6–3.8).

It was mentioned earlier that Dragić successfully used an animation solution which earlier proved effective in Borivoj Dovniković's films: white desert where everything simultaneously exists and does not exist, a space abstract in the same

FIGURE 3.7 Passing Days (1969) by Nedeljko Dragic.

FIGURE 3.8 Passing Days (1969) by Nedeljko Dragic.

way as time. White background is first flat and formless; however, in the next instant changes into a deep, hollow, cave-like space. A chair appeared when the man wished to sit down, as soon as he stood up, the chair vanished; window, door, soldiers, wife, angel and everything else began its existence only when it came in active contact with the man. Contrary to Dovniković who perceived this whiteness as abstract and absurd reality surrounding his characters, in Dragić's film this "all-nothing space" was something very subjective. In this case, it was a philosophical view. Our absolutely most important contact with our surrounding is made with our sight. We see only what exists in material world, nothing else. The only thing we can know with the certainty is what we are seeing, and only in the moment we are watching it. That is the only reality we can state as a fact, everything else can only be assumed. We only assume that the big whiteness hides the people, objects and nature we know. "Life is more than what we are seeing", wrote McCloud in his book (1995) many years after the premiere of *Passing Days.*

Dragić's heroes were regularly total losers. His heroes inhabited one rotten, corrupted, utterly cruel world in which people were unimportant and apathetic puppets. With time, they accepted their position in the world and stopped resisting, which was practically their greatest defeat. This pessimistic view of the world, scepticism and cynicism concerning human ability to influence his/her own life and relationships with others, was a constant feature of Dragić's films.

In the opening scene we see the little man sitting next to his wife Matilda. She pulls a drawer out of white "all-nothing space", takes from it her hidden lover and eats him. Little man blows on the bulb which turns black. His chair suddenly transforms into a pool and he almost drowns in it. Policemen come to the door that appear all by themselves on the white surface and beat him with the sticks. Soon after, another door opens, and two secret agents enter and give him a good slapping. A closet opens with a skeleton in it, a lover Matilda had forgotten about. Little man tries to read but is disturbed by a motorcycle buzzing through the room. A doorbell rings. He opens previously invisible door and a swimmer enters, swimming in his floor. Little man wants to swim to, so he jumps in the "water", but physical laws still apply to him and he only manages to break his nose. Swimming in the floor is forbidden so policemen swarm in again and give him another beating.

At this moment a figure resembling an angel appears flying over him, offering him a red apple. He refuses the gift.

As soon as the angel disappears, another agent bursts into the room and tears the little man's book. Reading is forbidden. His wife Matilda enters shaking her hips, takes the agent under his arm and leaves with him. Out of the off-space we hear sounds typical of sexual activity. Suddenly, the agent runs through the shot, trying to escape lascivious Matilda. Desperate little man is watching all this, pulls a cord out of white "all-nothing" and tries to hang himself. Unexpectedly, a public appears before him clapping at his attempt of suicide. When he changes his mind, the public start whistling and try to lynch him. The cord breaks and the little man falls to the ground when a salesman appears offering him better quality ties. Little man calls Matilda, but she is busy riding her new lover. He continues to call her but he is heard by the policemen who come back and silence him with another set of beatings.

The angel flies in again offering him an apple. Again, he refuses.

The little man tries to calm down with the help of music, but a politician interrupts him with his boring speech. He attempts to escape to the politician's babble, but policemen catch him and force him to listen. A whole series of seemingly pointless and unrelated events follows, directed against the little man, as if the whole world had set out to get him: TV-face from the commercial for toothpaste "Puff" molests him violently brushing his teeth, a rock and roll musician comes out of the lamp on the ceiling bursting his eardrums with electric guitar, a war pours down out of the television screen in his living room, bombs are exploding, tanks firing, rockets whizzing...

He falls unconscious.

The war disappears all by itself, and it starts raining in the little man's room. He wakes up and sees the little angel hovering over him offering him the apple. He refuses. Just then Matilda appears with her new lover and his numerous children. She pulls another drawer out of the whiteness and takes another lover. The little man opens another drawer and crawls inside hoping that next time she would pull him out. However, this produces the most absurd moment in the film. A king enters the room, opens his mouth and we see a speech balloon saying: "A kingdom for a horse!". The king opens the drawer, takes his "horse", our little man, and leaves riding on his back. Immediately afterwards, the little man finds himself in a whole new set of troubles coming out of the white background: two groups of demonstrators appear, green and pink (in a short insert we see one green demonstrator joining the pink ones), which are pulling the little man to both sides, until they tear him apart.

He falls unconscious again.

Little angel wakes him up. He refuses the apple. He wants to listen to the radio, but the policemen burst in and snatch the radio from his hands and start searching their favourite radio station. They find one playing Yugoslav folk music. Although they are dressed in western uniforms, their true identity is revealed thanks to the music. After the policemen, an artist comes into the room, sells the little man a painting, rips him of all of his money and kicks him in the rear. Little man hangs the painting on the wall. The painting is not hanging straight, and that is forbidden. Because of this "misdemeanour" his house is bombarded by an army. A tank enters his demolished room and a soldier comes out waving his finger, warning the little man: "No, no!" Little man is trying to escape, but the angel stops him.

He takes the apple.

However, even this apparently surreal "Schweikian" sanctuary for the little man turns out to be only false hope. The apple is a grenade in disguise, which explodes when the little man bites it. His teeth break and fall on the floor. A cleaner appears and wipes away the teeth while spitting on the little man for polluting the surrounding. Totally desperate, little man starts calling Matilda again. She finally comes and they make love. Their intercourse takes no more than a few seconds and for that time we see only Matilda's hair, which looks like some hairy dog wagging its tail. Matilda is soon done with him and leaves.

He falls unconscious again.

When he wakes up, he sees a pliant skyscraper falling into his room, and when the night falls, the sky and the stars come pouring down his window. He escapes, runs like hell, but a marathon runner runs past him showing us how the little man is actually slow and exhausted, and how his running is taking him nowhere. There is no "Schweikian" sanctuary for the little man: his reality is twisted to the utmost limits of absurd. He opens the door, and a graveyard appears. He opens another door and sees the graveyard again, behind another door he sees another graveyard, and every new door leads him to the graveyard.

All that he is left with is the graveyard.

In one, when compared to the previous dynamics of the film, unusually long scene without any movement, the little man stares at us, the viewers. What Swedish film scholar Örjan Roth-Lindberg calls a "direct ironical correspondence between the picture and the public" (1995) takes place and we perfectly understand Dragić's hero. Soundtrack of this "frozen" scene is the sound of train leaving. There is no hope. The little man has been hopelessly trying to pick up the pieces of his life.

The last train departed; all days have passed.

He did not get to live.

At the end, a dark wave of rage overcomes the little man. Leaving this world, he is a totally broken-down person.

In the whole history of the medium, it is hard to find an animated film with such pessimistic view of reality as was the case with Nedjeljko Dragić's masterpiece *Passing Days*.

INSTEAD OF A CONCLUSION: HUMOUR IS MORE LASTING THAN POLITICAL CIRCUMSTANCES

We live in a culture where seriousness is overrated to the extreme. A sad person is assumed to be able to discern the true essence of things, to see people and values as they "really are". In this way, grief becomes an emotional marker of a deep personality.

This is perhaps why humour is often not taken seriously.

What is meant by humour tends to elude any precise definition. The field of humour is incredibly vast; it varies between different individuals, cultures, eras and is usually specific to a certain society and its dominant world view at a certain time. There are many different opinions about the extraordinary complexity of the phenomena that the term "humour" denotes. The eternal question why man actually laughs still remains unanswered.

My ambition here was not to give a firm answer to this question. Just like love, humour remains an unsolvable mystery. We do not know why we love someone, just as we do not know what the source of humour is. And that is a good thing. Life without secrets would be infinitely boring.

Still, if not humour itself, we can identify what humour carries in itself. Humour, just like art (and art and humour are often united), presents a vision of the world, one view of life.

Nations which were forced to spend most of their history between one big and one huge nation, Germany and Russia, have developed a special humoristic tradition in accordance with their mental heritage. Central European peoples conglomerate had lived through too much of history and too little freedom, which has reflected in its humour. The essential feature of that humour was pessimism. In this type of humour, the humourist was joking at his own expense, cracking jokes about his insupportable situation. The humour was painted with all nuances of black; it mocked human existence treating it as anything but sublime, and featuring death as a desirable escape from the tragedy called life. This was particularly true of the people of the "wrong" nation whose mother tongue, culture and nationality were the reason they were treated as the lowest class. Main hero of this tradition was the ordinary man, born loser who was running away from the cruel reality to absurd, paradoxical and impossible, a hero who was dying with a smile on his face. Apart from literature, theatre and visual humour, pessimistic humour and humoristic pessimism marked to a great degree Central European animated film. This unique phenomenon experienced its golden era between the 1950s and 1980s, in other words, in the time when ideological dictatorship called socialism molested Central European souls most fiercely.

The strength of humour of one culture usually lasts much longer than political circumstances that caused its birth and influenced its form. Situation in central Europe changed significantly after 1990. The hope remains that future will bring much less reasons for pessimism than was the case before. Humour, including pessimist humour too, is never preserved in a mausoleum; it moves and spreads over geographical, mental or temporal borders. It is highly probable that little "Schweikian" man will continue his victorious stroll not just within the borders of this region, but all around the "global village", carrying the ability to laugh at the impossible in his luggage. Today, little man lives in the "Empire" called planet Earth, which in our times, owing to electronic media, functions as a unique and compact whole.

4 The View from the Glass Dome

A CLOSER LOOK AT SOME CRUCIAL FILMS OF "ZAGREB SCHOOL"

Linking the term "animation" exclusively to the film medium, as it has been done for decades, is one of the wrong premises one can find in a large part of animation studies. In his extensive study on the history of visual special effects in *The Vatican to Vegas*, Norman M. Klain, however, pays special attention to pre-film animations, especially those that were performed on stage as a work of illusionistic theatre where inanimate objects were brought to life and the illusion of movement and metamorphosis was created by means of various mechanical-optical devices. Among the animation processes created by the fusion of the magic of the pre-industrial age and the technological outgrowths of the Industrial Revolution, the result of which is the panorama (from the Greek pan: everything and horama: view), which Klein sees as "part of the encyclopaedic impulses of the nineteenth century" (2004) mentioning as an example the long-lived panoramic theatre "The Colosseum", opened in 1826 in London, which, with occasional modifications, worked until 1875. The Panorama was a large circular stage room with painted walls and light from the ceiling. In the middle of the room, there was an audience that watched the scenes on the screen whose range was 360 degrees and where staged representations of famous battles, such as those at Waterloo or Gettysburg, were most often given. A visual simulation of reality was created with the help of a mobile light that emphasized individual details, relief structures of the image, various optical tricks and pyrotechnic effects were also used to create an atmosphere and mood of reality by simulating movement and depth perspectives so that the visitor could feel at the same time as an observer and participant of the presented event. According to Klein, the most important feature of the panoramic vision was that it provided the possibility of "the all-embracing view".

After more modern technologies supplanted the panoramic theatre, the term panoramic view moved from the realm of the concrete over time to the realm of the conceptual and remained a label for a way of looking at things in which the image was created after the view encompassed a full circle. The panorama is also established as the word for a circular movement of the film camera without a cut, which is a technique that has been particularly actualized in the last decade after the emergence and popularization of contemporary digital moving images, where the panoramic "camera" movement is one of the usual means of expression.

This analysis presents an attempt to illustrate, on the example of films of the Zagreb School, a panoramic way of seeing the world with an "all-embracing view" that first arose in the ideological domain and gradually took shape as an aesthetic principle. Namely, the sequence of socio-historical circumstances that arose in Yugoslavian

DOI: 10.1201/9781003375623-4

society after World War II conditioned the appearance of an illusory "comprehensive view" in the Zagreb cartoon authors who, in many of their works, created a panoramic vision created from a position that seemed to be central, "in between" or simply as an ideological glass dome in the middle of a block-divided world.

Great international successes and the objective value of what was created in the Zagreb studio between the late 1950s and early 1980s were mainly based on the superbly mastered technology of so-called cel-animation, stylized movement, modern understanding of the medium but also, which is the thesis of this text, effective global metaphors realized with caricature means, a simplified and schematized depiction of the world divided by the Cold War, but also its ideological satire made from the position of the ideological-political discourse we call Titoism, which reigned in the "glass dome". The hunger for power in socialist societies and the obsession with money in capitalist ones, as well as the constant danger of an all-destructive conflict with each other, was the central thematic area of Yugoslav cartoon humour in all forms, especially animators who circled the "panoramic" with an "all-embracing" image of the world of his time. Their global metaphors, which by satirizing phenomena that marked the "Cold War" such as the arms race, but also the inequality of the small and the poor, the neglect of ecology and the alienation of modern man in the growing concrete jungles, faithfully expressed the fears and anxieties of their contemporaries about the future.

Of course, like every model, this one has exhausted its capacity over time. Already in the 1970s, the classic "seven minutes" cel-animation began to stagnate in relation to other, new techniques in which enthusiastic and innovative animators created their original works, penetrating more and more into the "depth" of the screen and hinting at what we know today as 3-D digital animation. Animated films based on two-dimensional cartoon stylization and satirical humour resembled a told story and slowly disappeared. As I stated earlier, the time when Vukotić and company blazed and burned at world festivals and then international film authorities like Grierson, Sadoul or Martin established the "school" as a film-historical phenomenon was gone.

WALTER NEUGEBAUER – FROM COMICS TO FILM

We have seen that the core of the Zagreb School was, of course, newspaper cartoonists, comic artists and illustrators who also remained draftsmen as directors and as a rule showed no interest in puppet-film, plasticine animation, objects, the direct method or almost any other animation technique outside of cel-animation or, as it is popularly called, cartoon film. Of course, it would be completely wrong to describe the whole phenomenon as something monolithic and limited only to two-dimensional, caricature satires – but what is recognized as a "school" is contained in a unique stylistic approach through anecdotal film narration, graphic expression typical for newspaper cartoons, illustrations and comics, by treating the scenography as a flattened two-dimensional space, as well as in common conceptual characteristics that are primarily manifested in seeing the world as a panorama observed with a critical comprehensive view.

A particularly significant personality of Zagreb compared to animation centres in the countries of so-called socialism was the influence of comics that came across the

Atlantic, but also from the significant domestic comics tradition. The graphic language characteristic of comics largely defined the visual style of American cartoons, whether it was the gigantic Disney studio or Disney's competitors in "Terrytoons", "Warner Brothers", "MGM", "UPA" and others. While in the rest of the "socialist" world comics were suspected for a long time as something "capitalist" and therefore banished from the public, in Yugoslavia American and Western European comics were published en masse, and especially in Croatia domestic production was developed, which in the works of some authors (Maurović...) sometimes represented the top of what was generally being created in the medium.

One of the champions of Croatian and Yugoslav comics, Walter Neugebauer, established himself as the author around whom the team of the first cartoon film created in the editorial office of the humorous weekly Kerempuh was formed in 1949. This 29-year-old cartoonist and comic artist gained his authority among his colleagues and the editors of Kerempuh by the unattainable artistic quality of his comic works. Neugebauer, who would easily qualify for the place among Disney's "Nine old men", started his career as a 14-year-old and immediately, in his first published work, *The Adventures of Nasredin Hodža* (*Avanture Nasrudin Hodže*), published in "Oko" in 1936, he reached an enviable professional level. In the next three years, he cooperated with a large number of newspapers in Zagreb and Belgrade to start his own magazine Veseli vandrokaš with his older brother Norbert, who was the screenwriter of his comics. Later, during the war years and the duration of the Independent State of Croatia between 1941 and 1945, Walter Neugebauer not only completely mastered the Disney school of cartoon drawing, but also in many ways surpassed the quality of the comics of the time signed by "Walt Disney" (Figure 4.1).

FIGURE 4.1 Walter Neugebauer.

FIGURE 4.2 Everyone to the Election (1945) by Walter Neugebauer.

After the takeover of power by the communists, comics were suspected for a time as an "imperialist" medium, so the brothers got involved in the project of producing the first cartoons and got involved in the work of the "Film Company – Directorate for Croatia", where they realized the test film *Little Worm* (*Crvić*, 1945) and the propaganda films *Oral Newspaper* (*Zidne novine*, 1945) and *Everyone to the elections!* (*Svi na izbore,* 1945) (Figure 4.2).

However, real professional cartoon film production was born in Kerempuh, which Horn calls "the stepping-stone of many of Yugoslavia's top animators" (1976) for many reasons. The weekly gained enormous circulation and influence by publishing anti-Soviet caricatures and comics in which Stalin was ridiculed that, very popular as it was, created a market and a need for caricatures and gave a chance to many cartoonists to publish their works and get paid for it. Consequently, as the only satirical magazine in post-war Croatia, Kerempuh brings together many cartoonists and comic book authors who try to support themselves by drawing anti-Stalinist satires and parodies in cartoon form. As a typical example of the humour nurtured in Kerempuh, we can cite the parody of Ripley's classic newspaper column *Believe It Or Not* created by the then-young cartoonist Borivoj Dovniković Bordo, who in the coming decades would become one of the leading profiles of the Zagreb school. For example, in one of Bordo's versions of *Believe it or not* we have "information" that "a man without a spine lives in Sofia, Bulgaria. By profession, he is the president of the Bulgarian government". Another vignette shows a large concentration camp signed with the text: "The greatest forces of peace are concentrated in the Soviet Union". As is well known,

FIGURE 4.3 The Big Meeting (1951) by Norbart & Walter Neugebauer.

the huge circulation of Kerempuh also brought unexpected income, so the young editor of Kerempuh, Fadil Hadžić, took a risk and decided to use the money by investing one part in the establishment of a satirical theatre and the other in an unexplored adventure – producing an animated film.

After a year of learning animation techniques and working on film, the 20-minute *The Big Meeting* (1951) was completed, the production of which is extremely significant for the later development of Croatian animation. Namely, the people who will later form the core of the Zagreb School gather around the project. Despite their total inexperience when it comes to animation, during more than a year of working on this film, the group managed to master all the technical finesse and practical details within such a complicated job as the making of a classic animated film, for which credit undoubtedly belongs to Neugebauer before everyone else (Figure 4.3).

SOCIALIST REALISM IN DISNEY GUISE

Walter Neugeber's role in the credits is described as "lead artist and art direction" while his brother Norbert's contribution is formulated as "content direction and gags". However, the idea for the film came from Mirko Trišler, and it is interesting that the film had original music by Eduard Gloz, which was performed by the State Symphony Orchestra under the author's direction, while Fadil Hadžić was designated as the team director, and the Kerempuh editorial office was appointed as the producer.

On the performance level, the film functions as a hybrid composed of Disney figuration, but not with exclusively anthropomorphic characters, but, apart from the ducks, which have a symbolic and allegorical function, the main characters are humanoid figures, while in the second part, frogs appear as subjects of the film's narrative. Borrowing heavily from some of Disney's films, such as *Saludos Amigos* (1942), Neugebauer conceived and shaped the film within a newspaper editorial office, which is evident from the chosen topic and content, gags, central political message and the means by which it was shaped. The film opens with a text written (according to the testimony of Borivoj Dovniković) by Fadil Hadžić, where we are offered the interpretation and historical background of the term "journalistic duck" and then in the same long text prepares us for what we will see with the words: "This film of ours leads straight to the nest of a similar duck, to Bucharest, where the head of Inform-propaganda, Pavel Yudin, according to wise managerial directives from Moscow, inflates this naked bird to the miserable satisfaction of some and the laughter of others". The text is followed by a fade to a spacious square with a building reminiscent of the Kremlin, while the sound of a typewriter and the quacking of ducks can be heard in the background. The camera takes us into the building so that we see the sign above the door "For solid peace and people's democracy" – ducks fly out of the letters on the sign while in the off-screen a colporteur is heard shouting: "Buy 'Pravda'!" In the corridors of something giving the impression of being the newsroom, numerous ducks walk around, and in the scene after that, we see the editor Judin in his office, occasionally drinking from a bottle of vodka and writing his text. Every time he finishes writing a page, the paper transforms into a duck. When the phone rings, a duck comes out of it and lays an egg, on which Judin himself sits so that a new duck will hatch. Such a large number of ducks in the film's script certainly pleased Walter Neugebauer, a fanatical fan and follower of Disney, who drew them after his role model so that most of the ducks in the film, especially the one in the last scene, look like Donald Duck's relatives.

In the first change of view, we see Judin from behind while a deliveryman enters his office bringing several bundles of newspapers and magazines of the former communist constellation such as Rude Pravo or Unita. Of course, ducks fly out of the packages that fall out of the delivery man's hands and land on Judin's feet. Judin takes an article from the broken package and reads it into the radio microphone.

In the next scene, we are back in Judin's office and now for the first time we see a map of the Balkans on his wall, but Yugoslavia is not visible on it because that part of the map is covered with wallpaper that says "monster country". A small fellow, journalist Patkin, appears in the office, to whom Judin shows the place on the map where Lake Skadar is located and orders him to go to a rally in honour of the "great Enver Hoxha" who did not allow the "Albanian part of Lake Skadar to dry up". The purpose of this joke is clearly to show all the stupidity of the Information Bureau's propaganda. The streets of Bucharest that we see in the next scene are full of rats that run away from Patkin, who is on his way to the garage and pulls out of it a plane in the shape of a duck whose beak immediately transforms into a propeller. The journalist gets on the plane and takes off to his task accompanied by the sounds of a revolutionary alarm clock. While the plane-duck is among the clouds on the ground, we see two trains, one empty coming from the USSR and the other full of various materials and raw materials that are barely being dragged towards Moscow, which is obviously the application of one of the typical propaganda cartoons, which aims to suggest that the Soviet Union brutally exploits its satellite states.

The journalist lands on the shores of Skadar, where a large meeting of frogs and mosquitoes is taking place. The main frog croaks his speech directed against Yugoslavia while among the listeners who parade in front of the lectern carrying banners with inscriptions such as "Long live the wise leadership", "Long live Evner" (assume it is misspelled on purpose) or "We want a swamp". Then the squads of frogs and mosquitoes enter in false bandages and plasters bearing the inscription "Victims of Yugoslav Terror". Just at that moment, an unexpected storm thundered and blew. Frogs hide in a swamp, and a journalist who wants to return to Bucharest is blown away by a storm over Yugoslavia. Through the binoculars, he now sees white roads, a new factory with a large slogan "Factories run by workers", a modern building with the words "Farmer's Work Cooperative", a settlement made up of large white buildings, then a hydroelectric plant.

It is already dusk when the crazed journalist manages to reach Bucharest and his newsroom by crashing the mechanical duck on landing. The authors obviously did not trust that the audience would understand the language of the picture, so they had the need to retell everything we had previously seen by showing us in close-up the journalist's notes that Judin is reading, leaving us more than enough time for them.

In the final scene, we see how the enraged Judin throws the journalist into prison and then sits down and writes a new text himself. Judin tries to inflate the duck that he has now created to gigantic proportions, but this time he overdoes it. The air pressure from the duck overpowers him and he himself is first inflated and then explodes. The explosion destroys the entire building, and of course, Judin dies. On his grave is a duck and the inscription "For solid peace and people's democracy".

The Big Miting definitely remains an original example of socialist realism in specific conditions and mediums. The film achieved its purpose on two levels: the first group of professional animators was trained, which laid the foundations for the development of animation in Zagreb, and the film was extremely popular and watched, which means that it fulfilled the task of spreading the propaganda message embedded in it. At the same time, the film conceptually introduces a kind of critical panoramic perception of the Eastern Bloc, even though the "camera" will soon turn to the other side. The fact that *The Big Meeting* was realized by combining Disney aesthetics and socialist realism will also have a certain symbolic value since the film came precisely at a time when Disney was harshly criticized in the Soviet Union whose state studio finally broke with Disney's influence in the production of their animated films. On the other hand, one of the constants of animation in Zagreb will be an open preference for American style, of course not only Disney but later also UPA, WB and other studios on the other side of the Atlantic.

REBELLION AGAINST THE DISNEY MODEL IN DUGA FILM

On the wings of the success of that "first artistic cartoon" in Croatia/Yugoslavia, the director and editor-in-chief of Kerempuh Fadil Hadžić founded Duga Film in Zagreb with the decision and financing of the Government of the Republic of Croatia. Hadžić moves with the entire team of *The Big Meeting* to a new company and becomes its director. At the beginning of 1951, a public tender was announced for animators, copyists and colourists. More than 200 candidates applied, of which about 80 were selected. The new staff were trained by members of The Big Meeting team – cartoonists/animators Walter Neugebauer, Vladimir Delač and Borivoj Dovniković and the head of the copyist and colourist department Ladislav Šantak. "Duga film" brought together some of the most important artists (Kostelac, Vukotić, Dovniković, Grgić, Kolar, Marks, Kristl, Jutriša, Bourek…) who will lay the foundations of the Zagreb School and upgrade it to the first of the three most important stages in its evolution. During the short life of the "Duga film" studio, between 1951 and 1952, five, still black and white, films of a high professional standard were produced. The animators have completely mastered the so-called production on the conveyor belt, which means working in an efficient team where the roles are strictly assigned to the main animator, cartoonist, in-betweener, director, set designer, colourist, copyist, cinematographer and other specialist occupations.

The idea was to form two groups, one under the direct supervision of the art director of the house, Walter Neugebauer, who was supposed to continue working within the Disney conventions already mastered in The Big Meeting, and the other whose task was to find a "national style" – the management of that group was entrusted Dušan Vukotić.

As mentioned before, the same team that realized *The Big Meeting* was behind the first film produced by the new company – *The Happy Event* (1951). It is worth noting that within Neugebauer's group, their first independent film works were also realized by two famous names of Croatian humorous drawing, Vladimir Delač, a prominent representative of the so-called style of clear line in comics, was signed as the main cartoonist and animator in *Review in the Yard* (1951, directed by Andro Lušičić). Delač would draw a large number of comic pages later in his life, but unfortunately, he would not return to animation. Unlike him, Borivoj Dovniković – Bordo, after his first author's work, *Gool!* (1952, director Norbert Neugebauer) in which he was the main cartoonist and animator, achieved one of the longest and most successful careers in animation, not only in Zagreb.

However, for the future of animation in Croatia and the formation of the "school", the emergence of Vukotić was of greater importance, who from his first film, and "Duga's" second, *How Kićo Was Born* (1951, signed Josip Sudar as director), created hints of something that will become a feature of Zagreb cartoons: the comic character is no longer a crazy anthropomorphized rabbit or a duck whose eyes constantly pop out of their sockets, but a small drawn man, an antihero whose adventures take place in everyday life – Kićo. That Chaplin-inspired cartoon character was supposed to be the main character of the first domestic animated series, so a year later Vukotić completed the second film about Kićo (*The Enchanted Castle at Dudinci*, 1952), this time as a completely independent author, signed on the credits as cartoonist, animator and director. The idea of a small, caricatured man who plays the role of a punching bag that is pounded by all those around him. They are involved in a darkly humorous conspiracy against him, which will later develop into the leitmotif of a large number of "made in Zagreb" films.

Yugoslavia's approach to the West, but also the existence of a pre-war tradition (Maar Brothers) results in the birth of a new market for animated advertising films. Thus, the group from Duga Film were the first in the country to start making commissioned films for foreign countries (among others, for the renowned German car manufacturer BMW). The group around Dušan Vukotić and Nikola Kostelac, including several colleagues and collaborators from Duga Film Aleksandar Marks, Vladimir Jutriša and Vjekoslav Kostanjšek produce 30-second colour advertising cartoons in which the new aesthetic model created under the obvious influence of the UPA studio is fully applied. Ron Holloway (1972) states that the Zagreb animators encountered UPA films thanks to a newly opened English-language print shop, which included magazines that published images from Cannon's film *Gerald McBoing-Boing* (1950) and through the film *The Four Poster* (Irving Reis, 1952) shown in Zagreb, which contained animated parts realized by the leading author of the UPA studio, John Hubley. In any case, working for the most part in Nikola Kostelac's apartment, which is one of the reasons why Holloway believes that with Zagreb animators it was more about "a family, a group of people who like to work with each other" than a "school", the basics of limited animation were outlined as a method that achieves maximum expressiveness in movement with a minimum of necessary drawings. Of course, the introduction of limited animation was partly a consequence of economic scarcity, and the lack of celluloid drawing foils and special paints for them. In one of his later author's texts "Yugoslav School of Cartoons", Vukotić himself analyses the limited method, defining it as "creatively placed animation", which made it possible to radically reduce the number of drawings needed for one cartoon from, initially, 12,000–15,000 to 4000–5000 "without the film losing any of its visual richness" (Munitić & Sudović (3), 1978).

The most important result of the efforts of the young animators was that the management of Zagreb Filma, a company founded by the Croatian Film Workers Association in 1953, engaged the Vukotić-Kostelac group three years later on the project of establishing a Cartoon Film Studio, where, after a break of several years, continued work on animated films film in Croatia.

VUKOTIĆ: "VERFREMDUNGSEFFEKT" AND "JUMP-CUT" IN THE CARTOON

In one of the first international publications dedicated to the "Zagreb School", Ron Holloway's already quoted book *Z is for Zagreb* from 1972, Dušan Vukotić was labelled as "The most important name in Yugoslav animation", a reputation that Vukotić would keep until the end of life. The author whose name is most often associated with the fact that he was the first European animated filmmaker to receive the most popular film award "Oscar" which, however much it is not appreciated among experts and among animators themselves, considering that many great works of this type of cinema (let's mention only Youri Norstein's *Tale of Tales* from 1979 or number of Jerzy Kucia's masterpieces) have never been awarded an "Oscar", so prize at specialized festivals such as Annecy, Ottawa or Zagreb are objectively much more valuable. However, it sometimes happens that the American Film Academy, by

FIGURE 4.4 Ersatz (1961) by Dušan Vukotić.

awarding its statuette, symbolically marks an entire era in animation. That was the case at the Oscars in 1962 when, instead of the usual film produced by Disney, WB, UPA or MGM, a non-American animated film triumphed for the first time in history. The film was *Ersatz* (1961), one of the films from the impressive series of brilliant works that Vukotić created during the most fruitful decade of his career, roughly from the mid-1950s to the mid-1960s (Figure 4.4).

Vukotić came to Zagreb at the time of the fiercest conflict between Yugoslavia and the bloc of socialist countries and began publishing his own caricatures and short humorous comics that expressed strong anti-imperialist satirical messages aimed both at the West and perhaps even more at the East. The preference for global metaphors expressed through caricature probably originates from that short but important period in his career, which leads Holloway to assess Vukotić as the strongest when he finds himself in the field of satire and caricature ("He is the best in the cool domains of satire and caricature") which, after all, also applies to most other Zagreb authors. Many of his caricatures were, in addition, ironic comments on the unstoppable infestation of low-level culture, banality and consumer society. Thus, his comic series *Špiljko and Goljo* from 1953 about two cavemen dealing with problems analogous to those in modern consumer society seems like a precursor to Fred and Barney from the famous American animated television series *The Flinstones* (starting in 1957). The will to power in socialist societies, as well as (especially) the consummatory fixation with money in capitalist ones, will remain Vukotić's main preoccupation when he soon finds himself at the animator's desk.

Somewhere around 1950, when Yugoslavia became more noticeably closer and opened to the West, the ideological matrix in the country was partially corrected and the idea of a country open to the world began to be created, which left a huge impact on Vukotić's creative worldview and philosophy. Thus, in cinemas of larger Yugoslav cities, one could see both American and Eastern Bloc films, including animated ones, primarily films by the champion of Czechoslovak animation Jiri Trnka, such as *The Gift* (*Dárek*, 1946) or *Springman and the SS* (*Pérák a SS*, 1947). The influence of Trnka's cartoons, shown in Zagreb, is obvious and acknowledged by Vukotić himself on several occasions.

Trnka's influence is particularly felt in Vukotić's film *Playful Robot* (1956), the first realized in 1956 in Zagreb film, where, although he is still timidly cautious in animation, he announced his step towards originality both in terms of expression and on the thematic level, creating character of a good robot, which is one of the first such cases in popular culture in general, thus anticipating the later great success of Osamu Tezuka with the series *Astro Boy* (1963), whose opening episode is reminiscent of Vukotić's work in terms of its morphological and animation characteristics. A direct replica of Trnka comes in the next film *Cowboy Jimmy*, which Holloway rightly compares to Trnka's puppet-film *The Song of Prairie* (*Arie Prerie*, 1949) that was the first of a trilogy of cartoons in which Vukotić parodies American film genres and the increasing Americanization of the entire world. Already in that film, all the central features of Vukotić's style are clearly integrated; limited animation, rhythmically structured movement and characters constructed as geometric symbols that move on a background most often realized as an application of some of the current trends of modern art.

Vukotić uses a schematic drawing, and his cartoon expression is exact and clean: he is aware that the art of cartoon does not deal with nuances and ambiguities – you cannot caricature the unknown, in caricature snow is always white, a piece of coal is always black. As an innate caricaturist, Vukotić is particularly fond of parody and therefore he always deals with motifs that are easy to identify and conventions that are directly recognized as such, so his favourite target will remain the commercialization of human society and the trivial in man's daily life. Vukotić does not use dialogues, while noises and music are simply engraved into the animation and drawing, becoming an organic part of it, so that the characters communicate with each other exclusively through cartoon pantomime. Animated metamorphosis is almost a marginal procedure in his films. Instead of metamorphosis, Vukotić relies more on a static gag, combining often extremely effectively incompatible pictorial elements that create a kind of Brechtian principle of estrangement with their strong contradiction, even in the caricature's own world. Namely, when we have already established logical coordinates in the drawn world, he wakes us up by placing imaginative and original incongruent details and optical games in the cinematic image.

In 1958, Vukotić made as many as three films, *Abra Kadabra*, in which he experiments with the proportion of the frame, the film could be shown in cinemascope as well as in normal screen format, *The Avenger*, an adaptation of a Chekhov story, and *Concert for a Sub-Machine gun*, another parody of Hollywood genres, now gangster film and his first masterpiece in which he will fully develop his potential as an original film-cartoonist.

In his next two works, Vukotić will bring to perfection his harmonization of caricaturally stylized film images with rhythmic animation, where the influences of modern artists such as Klee, Kandinsky or Chagall are visible both on the surface, the visual envelope of those films and in the space of their inner driving energy. With those two films, we are talking about the works *Piccolo* (1959) and *Ersatz* (1961), he will attract a lot of attention from the international festival audience and experts and will definitely go down in film history and probably stay there as long as people study this discipline.

Unlike his parody films, where a critical comprehensive view was directed towards the western hemisphere of the planet, in *Piccolo* Vukotić builds a universal satire directed against the arms race that criticizes both sides in the so-called Cold War, of which there were plenty in the tradition of Zagreb animation (see for example *On the Meadow/Na livadi*, 1957, by Nikola Kostelac). In that animated allegory, Vukotić created many successful caricature ideas containing the "Verfremdungseffekt" as the already mentioned one in which the neighbour uses scissors to cut the rain jets. One of the neighbours starts playing a small harmonica, a piccolo and the other becomes envious, causing a chain reaction that eventually leads to the demolition of the shared house. A brutal war between yesterday's peaceful and sociable neighbours in which their relatives (compatriots) participate as an orchestra and choir trying to outshine the others is masterfully edited. The entire audio-visual montage composition depicting war with musical instruments as weapons suggests Vukotić's familiarity with some of Eisenstein's ideas about "vertical" montage, synchronizing conflicting directions, dynamics and rhythm, and harmonizing image and sound, colour and movement.

Ersatz was a satire about the vulgarization of the emotions of a dehumanized man and about the general existential conditions in the modern consumer society and the lack of substance caused by brutal materialism that was approaching Yugoslavia because of its opening to the West. Everything we see around us is apparent and artificial and the only meaning of our existence is reduced to consumption. A human possesses only one essential characteristic – replaceability. The experimental procedure that dominates the film is the reduction of movement in the way of creating a type of animation jump cut when a figure in an imagined space is simply moved from one place to another without any intermediate stages of movement. The figure simply appears in a new position in the frame without moving at all from point A to point B, which, without exaggeration, was a revolutionary shift in the understanding of animation aesthetics at the time of the film's creation.

In addition to several truly brilliant sight gags, such as the one when the main character changes his panties by hiding his head in the sand in front of the audience while his bottom is completely exposed, Vukotić demonstrates his mastery of the cumulative gag based on the creation of unexpected twists. Namely, in our everyday life there are always expectations and forecasts, starting with the simplest ones that we will see this and that around the corner or that the traffic light will turn red after the green one. But if someone with a bat is waiting around the corner or if the signal is broken and we wait an unreasonable amount of time, we are already on the trail of a cartoonish situation. Vukotić quickly gets us used to the fact that the figures and objects we see in *Ersatz* are inflated balloon-dolls that sooner or later burst into small pieces, but the key gag of the film comes at the very end of the film in the form of an unexpected twist; the main character, the almighty "inflator", himself gets killed when he steps on a nail and is deflated.

After completing *The Game* (*Igra*, 1962), Vukotić focused on work on feature films and pedagogy. Each of his occasional returns to animation as another combination of cartoon and live-action film *Stain on Conscience* (*Mrlja na savjesti*, 1968), animated *Opera cordis* (1968) or *Ars gratia artis* (1970) or special effects in the feature film *Maestro and Margareta* (Saša Petrović, 1972) confirmed that the decision to give up frame-by-frame cinema was far too early and that he probably did not use all his potential as an animator. Vukotić died at the beginning of the 1990s in his home in Zagreb while the country and world to which he truly belonged were collapsing and disintegrating like the final scenes in *Piccolo.*

CONCERTO FOR SUB-MACHINE GUN – A CARICATURE OF FICTIONAL AMERICA

As it was said before, "creatively set animation", polished caricature language and ideological panoramic view appeared in a perfect shape in *Concerto for Sub-machine Gun*, which makes that film a perfect example for understanding Vukotić's animation style. The fact that he almost literally materialized into a film what he wrote in the script also speaks of Vukotić as a thorough author who does not tolerate improvisation. Consistent adherence to the presented script when making the film was not a characteristic of many other Zagreb authors, such as Kristl or Dragić, whose "scripts" consisted of a few random sentences to which they later felt almost no obligation. It is also worth mentioning that two prominent profiles in the later development of the School, Boris Kolar as a character designer and Zlatko Grgić as an animator, collaborated on the film and significantly contributed to its visual quality and stylization of movement (Figure 4.5).

The film opens with a standard sight gag where we see a machine gun in a violin case. This is followed by a stylized representation of a large city, based on the appearance of the buildings in the background it can be assumed to be New York, while in the foreground we see geometrically sketchy dense traffic where extremely simply drawn cars move along a dotted line in a monotonous rhythm. In the next scene, the cars suddenly line up like soldiers to form a guardrail for a large limousine in which sits a "businessman" dressed all in white, as Vukotić describes him in the script, but it is clear from the film that he is someone who clearly has political and any other power. The "businessman" has a photo camera in his hand, which he has pointed towards the big bank building, but the button on the camera is not pressed by him, but by his uniformed servant. In the next scene in which the main character enters his office, we see an example of "creative placement", on an empty background only the arrangement of a few details, the desk in the foreground, the door in the background through which the character enters, creates an impression of spaciousness. A new effective sight gag follows, in which the "businessman" takes off his entire body, white and good, as a suit, under which his true self, black and evil, is

FIGURE 4.5 Concerto for Sub-Machine Gun (1958) by Dušan Vukotić.

revealed. Clearly, by parodying American genres, Vukotić also adopted visual codes in which the hero dressed in white is good, and the one wearing black is evil. By pressing a button, he opens the wardrobe where his men's disposable suits are laid out just like suits. He gives each of them violin cases (and we know what's in them from the beginning of the film) and one of them a photo of the bank.

That Vukotić is a master of cartoon pantomime is shown by the body language of the main character who, cutting off his own head with his finger, which is separated from the body for a moment, explains to the gangsters what their task is. The gangsters come in front of the bank in combat positions and surround the building while one of them places a note holder in front of him, in which he puts the photo, in addition to the handcuffs with the composition "Concert for Sub-Machine Gun". The bank guard, who in accordance with the principles of the cartoon pantomime momentarily transforms into a whistle, starts blowing his whistle and armed policemen appear on all floors of the building. The gangster-conductor repeats the beheading movement he learned from his boss and begins to conduct. Both in the soundscape and in the editing rhythm, the film takes on the structure of jazz. The shooting scene in which initially a large number of policemen fall like a bundle is impregnated with several visual gags typical of Vukotić, of which the one in which one of the robbers sneaks up to the bank walking along the line formed by a burst from his colleague's machine gun is particularly effective.

Outnumbered policemen nevertheless overcome the gangsters, from whom only the conductor escapes by bolting into the sewer opening. When the conductor appears before the boss after the failed robbery, he searches all his pockets and even puts his hand through his mouth into his gut, but the only thing he finds there are bullets. The "businessman" now sits down at the table and thinks. That his brain literally works like an engine is suggested by the fact that the contours of his skull are now represented as cylinders and gears in motion.

He now puts on his white, good edition once more and takes out other people-marionettes, those dressed in tailcoats, from the wardrobe. He is again in front of the bank together with the large, covered monument and while now his elegant servants form an audience applauding and cheering him, he unveils the large monument to the Goddess of Justice. The gangster-conductor is pushed under the monument like a postal envelope to be inflated back into his old form inside. With his special gloves, the gangster digs a tunnel and comes close to a safe guarded by a tangle of laser beams radiating from large mechanical eyes, which is a brilliant graphic-animation solution. At first, the gangster skilfully sneaks up, but one laser beam still catches him, but he, in another effective example of the principle of the cartoon V-effect, grabs and crumples it. Then he opens the safe and inserts a rubber hose into it and pumps money out of the safe in the same way as gasoline is pumped from the tank of a car, which is a new visual solution that confirms Vukotić as a genius of cinema cartoon. The police, thanks to that laser beam that finally unravelled and alerted them, discovers the robbery and, moving through the same hose, reaches the monument to the Goddess of Justice, whom they arrest and put behind bars.

The "businessman" is in his office again, this time by a pile of money, which he first dives into as if he is making love to it, then swallows all the money except for one banknote, which he gives to his remaining puppets, which causes a conflict between them. They shoot at each other and kill each other. The seriously wounded conductor, who is leaking paint and the ink from which he was drawn, which is another of Vukotić's cartoonist feats, shoots the boss with his last strength and wounds him. All the swallowed money oozes out of the wound while the "businessman" shrinks to eventually lose weight and begin to float above the capitalist city like a money-hungry spectre.

KRISTL: AN ANNOYED ECCENTRIC

If it were possible to make an objective history of the "century of film", encompassing the most valuable works of art (celluloid) film, and if it were possible to avoid American centralism and the so-called generic racism in favour of live-action, then the pantheon of film masterpieces would most certainly include several Zagreb animated films. When I say this, I think of such films as *Ersatz* by Dušan Vukotić,

Passing Days by Nedjeljko Dragić, *Satiemania* (1978) by Zdenko Gašparović, but primarily of *Don Quixote* by Vladimir Kristl (Figures 4.6–4.8).

The great advantage of this wonderful work is that it is one of those films that we do not evaluate on the basis of their belonging to the genre and even within the context of the times in which they came off. When it comes to *Don Quixote*, however, neither the fact that the film was made by animating drawings nor that it was created in 1960 has a crucial importance in assessing its value. *Don Quixote* would have been possible and as the film was made in the technique of object animation, drawing directly on the filmstrip, collage, it would be easy to imagine it as realized in any computer animation programme, especially today when, after the era of stop-motion, clay animation and the three-dimensional digital film, iconic animation suddenly resuscitates, this time on the computer screen.

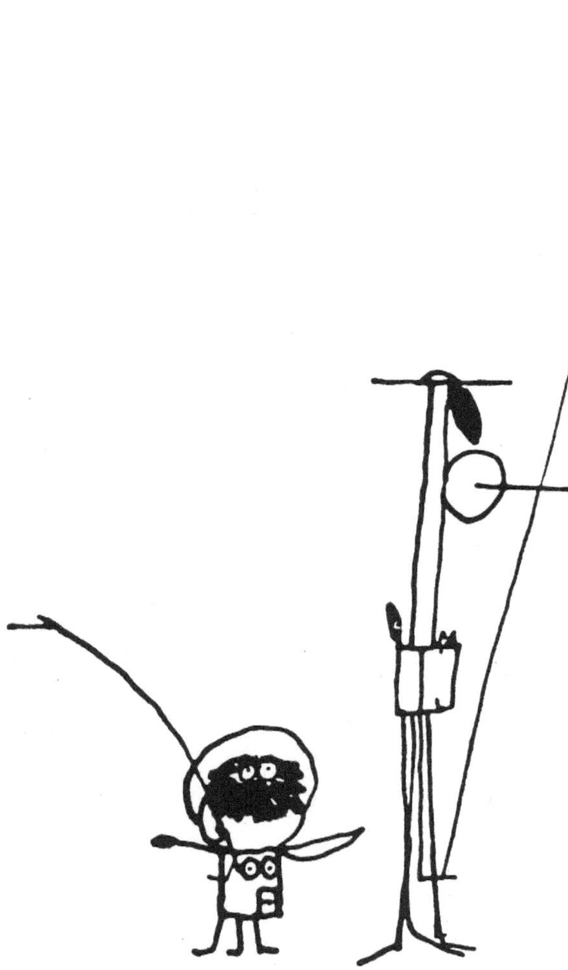

FIGURE 4.6 Don Quixote (1961) by Vladimir Kristl.

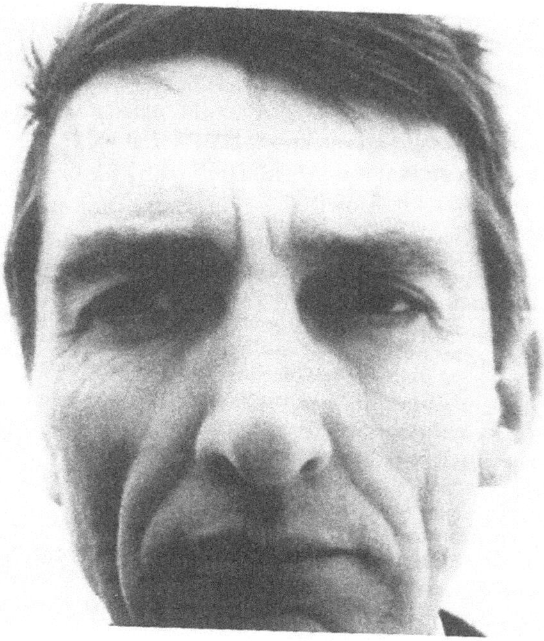

FIGURE 4.7 Vladimir Kristl.

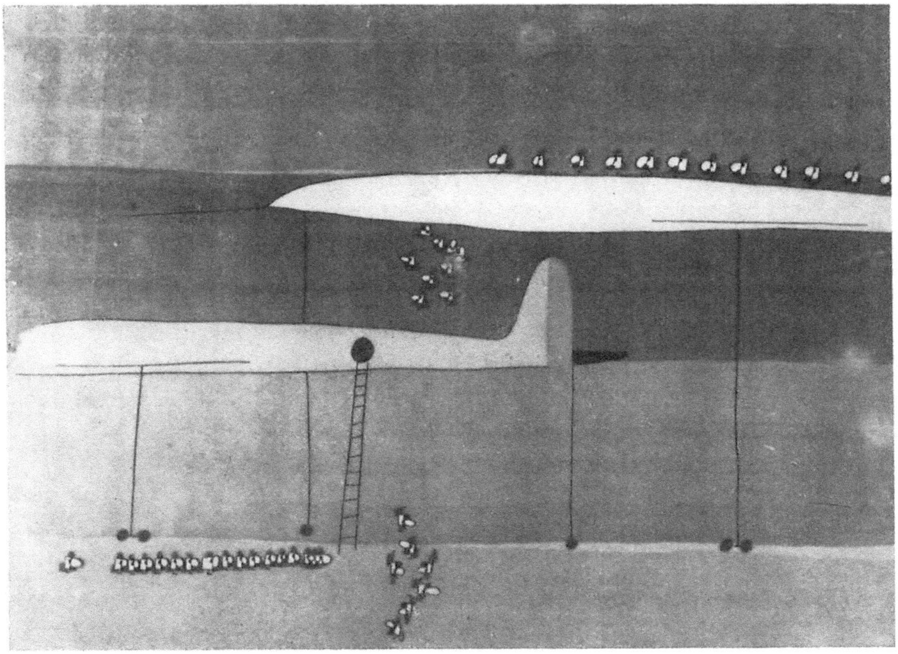

FIGURE 4.8 Don Quixote (1961) by Vladimir Kristl.

Just as in the case of such movies as, say, *Diagonal Symphony* (Viking Eggeling, 1925), *Night on the bald mountain* (Alexandre Allexeieff, 1933), *Neighbours* (Norman McLaren, 1952), *Reflexions* (Jerzy Kucia, 1979) or *Tale of Tales* (Youri Norstein) even *Don Quixote* is a work that communicates with a much wider time range than a year, decade or even the epoch in which it was created.

The value of this film actually was never doubted by the experts. So, for example when BILIFA organized voting for the best animated film of all time in 1980 the world's leading animation scholars gave their votes to MacLaren's *Blinkity Blank* (1954) and *Night on bald mountain* that shared the first place, while *Don Quixote* came at the fifth position.

Vladimir Kristl was born in Zagreb in 1923. Before and during his career as an animator, Kristl also participated successfully in several other artistic genres. He was a director, animator, actor, art director, cartoonist and an esteemed painter, one of the founders of the Exat 51 group, gathering representatives of geometrical abstraction, a totally unacceptable concept of art at one point in time. In the early 1960s, he left for Germany, where he died in 2004.

He started in the field of animation as the art director for the film *Jewel Theft* (*Krađa dragulja*, 1959, directed by Mladen Feman), but in 1960 he was allowed to co-direct *La peau de Chagrin* with Ivo Vrbanić, in which he used some of the material made from one another project, never finished *Magical Sounds* (*Čarobni zvuci*). Kristl immediately affirmed himself as an author who had not only mastered the technique of animated film amazingly quickly but also understood the medium in all its aspects and who had asserted himself as an artist with a personal understanding of animation.

Kristl wanted to innovate and individualize every detail of the process of making an animated film, to harmonize and adjust it to his personal understanding of the medium, regardless of the prevalent rules of the craft.

According to one testimony by his colleagues, Kristl dismissed even peg bar, storyboard and other standard procedures in the animation production since he thought that there must have been an easier way for tracing and registration of drawings. Kristl confused his cameramen several times when he in the middle of the shooting tore the background and ordered the cameraman to go on with shooting with only a part of what had been the background. The screenplay for *Don Quixote* confirms that Kristl considered this part of the film production process completely redundant even though some consider it fundamental. In a nonchalant 32 lines, for example, he states that the character of *Don Quixote* will be part of a joke involving "water and a horse", finding it unnecessary to elaborate on the gag. On another place, Kristl writes that Sancho Pansa will be involved in "other gags" not trying to describe specifically at least one of them. In a central scene of his future films, the one that comes after *Don Quixote*'s collisions with windmills, Kristl explains with the following words "We know what happened next". It is obvious that he was given that film because of the reward and success of *La peau de Chagrin* since this "scenario" for *Don Quixote* provided not the least understanding of his project.

Don Quixote is the first Kristl's film work that he directed single-handedly, which immediately brought him the first prize in Oberhausen, the most important award that came to the young Zagreb-studio up to date. But this prize was soon forgotten, partly because not long after that Vukotić won the most notorious film-prize in the world, an Oscar, partly because Kristl emigrated to Germany because of his conflict with the Studio's administration. In the beginning, the Zagreb film's management was unwilling to release *Don Quixote* at all because of the film's "incomprehensibility" and then decided to vandalize the film by putting a narration, which "explains" what is happening in the film, which understandably infuriated Kristl. When his next movie *The true man* (*Resni človek*, made in the production of Ljubljana's Viba film, 1962), an obvious satire depicting Tito as a prison guard that was totally banned which included the destruction of all copies his decision to become a dissident became final and he left the country never to return.

Even if today's radically changed historical circumstances diminished the importance of his conflict with the system in the former socialist Croatia and Yugoslavia one cannot but feel sorry for the unfortunate fact that Kristl on the doorstep of his 40s, at the height of his creative powers, went to Germany for god.

The myth of Kristl's eccentricity revived every now and then among Zagreb's animation circle, especially during preparations for "Animafest" since almost all artistic directors of the festival sought to bring Kristl to his hometown and organize his film retrospective and an exhibition. Needless to say: none of them has ever succeeded.

However, the fact that Kristl for decades successfully sailed through the German language ocean by building a very decent art career proves that he was foremost a serious professional, and that in his case, the eccentricity worked as a creative power. As far as his refusal to return to Zagreb, the fact is that one can feel disappointment and anger only towards those to whom he truly cares.

A MONOCHROMATIC VIEW OF THE WORLD

What Kristl basically did in *Don Quixote* was to reconcile two approaches to animation, narrative and abstract. Structuring a narrative line within a space of geometrically stylized visualization, Kristl integrates the dominant European and American animation traditions that preceded his work. If we freeze any of the frames of *Don Quixote*, we get an abstract image, however, this is not an abstract movie, but a narrative one. The grammar of this film primarily resides in the logic of geometry and the history of the two-dimensional representation of space, but its narrative structure is constructed in accordance with the conventions of the traditional American animated film, primarily "the chase cartoons".

Understanding always precedes drawing. Our hands do not draw what we see, but what is instructed by our thoughts. The thoughts may command to hands only what we understand. Drawing is thus the presentation of what we understand and how we understand it. All information gathered through our senses and experiences is translated into abstract codes by our thoughts. That is the foundation of all visual languages including written words. The stylized images indicate as it says by Sorlin, something that "enables us to get the world in perspective. We cannot think except in images which are models or derivation or reality" (1991). Even our ancestors drew in a way very similar to the abstraction by generalizing their experiences and reducing them to a common denominator and symbols. Consequently, the very precondition for the existence of any abstraction is some concrete experience from which the abstract is derived. That's why I rather disagree with Paul Wells when he claims the following: "The symbol in animation can operate in its purest form, divorced from any relationship to the representation of the real world, finding its proper purchase in the realms of its primal source" (1998). As I discussed elsewhere there are in fact no such things as symbols separated from its time-space context. Or if there would be something like that it could never have functioned as a symbol.

In his landmark study on visual storytelling *Understanding Comics*, Scott McCloud argues that our conception of reality is assembling pieces of the mosaic that we get through sensory perceptions and experiences. This modern advocate of Kant's philosophy claims thus that our experience of the world is incomplete since it is "a kind of faith based solely on the fragments" (1995). Since we always humanize each of these "fragments" as well as signs and symbols by giving them the human dimensions and characteristics, virtually every human communication has a high degree of anthropomorphism. Because of our obsession with ourselves, it seems to be enough to draw two eyes on the tree and we no longer see the tree but the man in the form of a tree. In his animated film *Les Joyeux microbes* (1909) Emile Cohl simply drew bacteria and germs in human form. Cohl was aware of the fact that the microscopic images of microscopic films seem unrealistic to us because they, unlike the artificial symbols, do not cause stimulus of our sensory experience. The existing insect world, in for example film *Microcosmos* (Nuridsanz/Pérennou, 1996), seems to us as "terra incognita", a completely different reality that appears as something abstract even if the rational part of our minds tells us that it is an objective picture of this very same world in which we reside. The objectivity of the camera is the objectivity of the machine, but the objectivity of our consciousness is "subjective", tied to human perception of reality. With those films whose content and form are something we have no previous knowledge of we can communicate only if we manage to attribute the characteristics of the world as we know it.

Due to the fact that two of animation's main means of expression are drawing (or any other man-made image) and the artificial movement, more often than in other types of film, the animation we encounter images that are outside of our real-life and conscious experience so that we recognize and interpret them in accordance with their "behaviour" on the screen. Kristl anthropomorphizes the simplest geometrical symbols, those from the primary layer of graphic simplification from which we can still discern some sense – squares, rhomboids and rectangles. He does this not only by coiling the cartoony round noses on them but especially through the animation resources, using expressive movements, and carefully elaborating the composition of a conglomeration of geometric symbols within the screen-space. Clusters of small squares moving from side to side, up and down or penetrating the depths of the camera and vice versa, functioning as "visual indications of the thoughts and emotions" (Balázs, 1970).

The key Kristl's characteristic is that he is an artist apparently exposed to two types of formative influences. On the one side, he is a modern artist, actively immersed in the most modern contemporary art trends, but also, on the other side, he is versed in the craft of Disney-like animation, which was something completely unknown, if not despised, for the most European avant-garde animator. His mastery of animation as a technique and a perfect sense of timing Kristl demonstrated in several places in the film, for example at the beginning of the scene with a "hiccups" riding of Sancho-character, which is a role model of a perfect sense of timing and rhythmic animation. Kristl's animation is distinguished even by furious gradations of tempo and use of conventions and codes already established in the animated film such as "(anti) gravity gags" like the one in which the square figure slips from the ladder, but it still remains in the air for a few moments and fall down only after "noticing" that there is nothing solid under its "feet" or when frightened Sancho turns into a red sausage etc.

Obviously, Kristl is very interested in organizing the movement of his "symbolical" characters. He personified a squares swarm that regroups, slides, hops, vibrates and pulses in successive intervals of implosion and explosion. In Kristl's shapes, there is no indication of human anatomy. The characters do not have the slightest hint of human anatomical features but are presented in the form of geometric sketch stuff. Animation is a phenomenon born in the Industrial Revolution with its fetishism of things and their "life". Thus, already the most likely the first ever created animated film dealing with the breathing life in ready-made things. These traits characterize the characters too: *Don Quixote* is presented as a water pipe with a beard and a hat, and his follower Sancho Panza is a simple egg with a hairy top and a hat. Both characters fit in the mechanical and geometrical world of the film, which is visible, for example, when *Don Quixote* picks up the old gramophone loudspeaker and uses it as a surrogate for an ear or in one another scene when he pours the contents of the bottle labelled "Aqua distillate" into his "head".

In an animated film time is an analogy for life, the space for the world. Animation penetrates in time and space making visible what is invisible and vice versa, what is visible becomes invisible. Kristl's treatment of time and space is in a direct connection with these principles; in scenes where *Don Quixote* and Sancho Pansa appear the whole background consists of a series of horizontal lines, while the scene in which the swarms of their militarized persecutors is shown the space is visualized as a two-dimensional plane divided in the middle by the vertical line of the street. Of course, this is not just a "way of drawing, but a way of looking!" (McCloud) because we see not only these two pictures but also the third picture that is a kind of blend of information, which results in a peculiar parallax effect as we viewers move between two spaces. The horizontal lines in *Don Quixote* function as a visual synonym for pastoral individualism, while the vertical lines represent the urban paranoia and collectivism growing out from the general acceleration that started already during the Industrial Revolution, which radically altered the human environment that at the modern time mostly composed by-products of technology, including the dominant one – the car. Already in the 1960s machines work as a substitute for our experience and memory and the car virtually becomes the protagonist of many films (sometimes even literally, as in Disney's franchise of bizarre films about the anthropomorphized car Herbie). Instead of the horizon that traditionally is elusive and placed far away, the modern animation abandoned the horizon and perspective and introduces diagrammatic simplicity since the modern consumer in the car quickly reaches the horizon and the speed doesn't give him any time to perceive details. In the new perception, the vertical lines presenting buildings in the modern cities are far more dominant than the horizon line. Such Kristl's modernistic update of the space and the film's overall simplicity and directness in expression create a feeling of mechanical coldness which is emphasized by the gamma and colour achieved by using aggressive and powerful parallel layers of paint.

The stage scenery is a very important element in the perception of this film. The precise arrangement of scenery and rhythmical movement of characters suggests the existence of a scheme in accordance with which the figures move, the decoupage that is set "below" the visible layer of the screen. Events in *Don Quixote* are obviously set on two stages, a city and something we could assume to be a natural environment because there are no indicators of urban surroundings. The first setting is packed with cars, road signs, whistles, fire-fighters, cannons, aeroplanes and signs, while the other is practically empty with natural elements such as a stone falling on *Don Quixote*, which he afterwards pushes uphill like Sisyphus. Kristl constantly relativizes the space, creating a feeling of constant instability by turning the scene "upside down", the upper line of the screen suddenly becomes the standing line simply by rotating the whole picture or by showing the horizon as a straight line in the middle of the screen.

In the film we have a third space, it is a "real" photographic image that appears in a point-of-view shot of *Don Quixote*, where he sees the photograph presented to the (un)reality and a live-action shot with windmills and sunflowers. In the context of the film the photography functions as a surface or a mere impression of things and beings, and its main feature is just that – superficiality. Photography functions as a synonym for our conscious experience, while animation and drawing present the bare body or even a skeleton, the very substance and structure of the picture itself as if viewed from the inside.

One another important element is the sound. Balázs concluded clairvoyantly that in the same way, the film image made us to see differently the film sound would make us to hear in a different way (Rohdin, 2003). However, film in general, and especially animation, did not fully use the potential of sound for a very long time. For decades after the discovery of sound film, the sound of the cartoons appeared to be mostly perfectly synchronized sound illustrations of the images, the so-called Mickey Mousing concept or was based on the already completed musical form where the animated images functioned as a kind of funny visualization of music. *Don Quixote* is the European version of the process that started in the US studio WB and continued in the UPA, where some great animators such as Avery, Cannon or Hubley put a lot of energy into activating the interrelations between picture and sound. These authors came to the conclusion that in animation there was no division of sound into diegetic and non-diegetic since the first one simply does not exist. Combining animated images with incongruent sound and music Avery created some of his masterpieces and the same did Cannon in his *Gerald McBoing Boing* and Hubley in *Rooty-Toot-Toot*, which marked a new era in the history of the medium. Sound background in *Don Quixote* is a collage of mechanical sounds, mostly congruent, while illustrating the swarms of personified geometrical symbols, whirling around a "town" in the grips of paranoia, a permanent state of war, chaos and overall anxiety, which is underlined by a sound background resonating with explosions, whistling, tyre screeching and some kind of a military march, which is the only musical motif in the film. On the other side, *Don Quixote* is "wired" with mostly non-congruent sounds. For example, his moment of weakness and indecision before the decisive battle is shown first through his pipe-body that "fractures" so he tries to encourage himself by reading a book illustrated with a photo that shows Dulcinea as a female aviator with a whisker. Browsing the book is accompanied by some sort of "tin sound" that in no way resembles the sound of paper. By using incongruent sound, Kristl underlines *Don Quixote*'s "factory error" – individualism and diversity in relation to his hostile surroundings of a neurotic city and its square inhabitants.

From the point of view of editing, the film is a mosaic, a collage, in constant transformation, collecting the pieces of time, rhythmic movements and geometrical images. According to the famous Hollywood rule, the best editing is that which we are not aware of and through which we see even what has not been verbatim shown in the pictures. At first glance, the editing in *Don Quixote* seems almost like a chase cartoon with its standard procedure of the linear directions of movement and connecting shots in accordance with the simplest rules of continuity. However, here we face a very complex editing procedure. Kristl confronts two "worlds" in separate scenes. Actually, there are only two scenes with a direct encounter between *Don Quixote* and his enemies. The first one takes place on the freeway when he uses a spear to "fish" square figures, at the second one is at the end of the film when the hero breaks out of pursuers' encirclement while they are shooting drill hat of Sancho, who is hiding behind his "shelter", a stroke of paint. Since we practically watch two movies whose events take place in two separate scenes formed in a very different range and texture and that between them rarely occur a direct contact, it is clear that Kristl relies on the properties of our mind to "fill" time and space gap between frames. Using such methods as zooming into the picture, activating of the frame of film images, subtle and subliminal flashes and metadiegetic implants, reduction and densification of space and time and the like, Kristl composes dramatic dynamics in an abstract form whose purpose is to provoke images created in our experience and memory, but also those that influence our instincts and subconscious.

Finally, as a direct consequence of Kristl's editing comes his animation method which can be described as arranging symbolic characters, creating a mosaic in the continuous transformation process, assembling pieces of time, segmentation of the space. Actually, animation is the basis for the total editing of the film: it is the finest weave of the entire montage complex that made possible such an amazing moving mosaic. Although every single frame of the film seems like an entirety for itself, when they are connected by the animation technique they transform into a new physical state, inorganic material becomes organic one, static becomes dynamic. It is through animation that Kristl's idiosyncratic drawing came to the fore; his intuitive topography created by drawing, fluctuation of characters, rhythmic bravura and a spectrum of colour in the background formed produced a harmonious, "cinematic dream on modern painting" (Sitney, 1990).

A true work of art always lives in the future. *Don Quixote* is primarily just that: an instinctive insight into the future. Kristl addressed the "ideal" spectator, an imaginary person who is versed in the conventions, trends, art history, and theory of animation, who possesses basic knowledge of spacioception and last but not least who is exposed to the media during most of his waking time. He found such a spectator in the future, in a media age that had been commencing at the time of the film's production. The ideal perception of the film *Don Quixote* is one in which the viewer can establish an interactive relationship with the film, something that became possible when the cinema came into our houses as video or DVD so we could watch the film in the same manner as we observe a building or a picture. Our experience gained through the senses today is just one fraction of our perceptions which are formed by the accumulated information and pictures from movies, television, music videos, digital pictures, video games, Hollywood, Internet … A modern human exists in a fictitious world most of his time because of the continuous presence of the media in our life; there are constantly some screens around us staring at us and we are staring at them. Media elongate, but even direct our view, media amplify our hearing but also make the selection of what we hear, thanks to the media, our perception is in a state of permanent transformation. In everyday, natural perception we see only the details that we, consciously or unconsciously, choose to concentrate on. In media it is someone else who chose for us so that our experience of the world is heavily influenced by what we are constantly exposed to – unknown people's choice of information and the image. From the one who chooses information, the modern human is increasingly becoming the only one who receives them. Boundaries that separate the physical and semantic, perception and recognition are almost gone.

VATROSLAV MIMICA: TWO ARTISTIC LIVES

"But Mimica didn't draw!", you can still hear the comment between the lines questioning the authorship of Vatroslav Mimica. Namely, he was neither a cartoonist nor an animator, so his films were mostly drawn by Aleksandar Marks and animated by Vladimir Jutriša. Let's remember that Mimica is not the only author who in his life dealt with various film forms or even the only one who was equally successful in each of them. There are many similar examples in film history, Frank Tashlin, George Pal, Wolf Koening, Wes Anderson, Mike Judge, Caroline Leaf, Piotr Dumala, Tarik Saleh… and so were his contemporaries and colleagues from the Zagreb studio, Dušan Vukotić or Vladimir Kristl. Should it even be mentioned that Walt Disney himself already at the age of 26 stopped practical work on animation, a field in which even before that he mainly relied on the exceptional competence of his associate Ub Iwerks. Disney's biggest opponent, Tex Avery, also did not draw his own films, it was done by the most gifted Preston Blaire as a member of Avery's crew. Neither Iwerks nor Blaire have ever realized their own work worthy of attention, although the former tried hard because drawing and animation are only one of the components of the final product that we call a cartoon (or some other animated) film.

The author, as the French New Wavers taught us, is that person in the production chain who is able to see the film before even one frame of it has been exposed. There is countless evidence that such an author was Mimica.

Of course, we will never fully know what his contribution is and what is possibly the merit of his gifted collaborators. For example, the question of whose idea it was to use linocut as a basis in the underrated masterpiece *Typhoid Sufferers* (*Tifusari*, 1963), which, for practical reasons, was massively used by partisan artists in their visual chronicles of war events between 1941 and 1945, will remain unanswered. However, the fact is that even such highly self-styled auteurs, such as Nedeljko Dragić, in collaboration with Mimica, made films more similar to Mimica than to his own worldview and aesthetics (See *Tamer of Wild Horses/ Krotitelj divljih konja*, 1966).

Finally, choosing the right collaborators is one of the most important competencies of a good director, regardless of the type of film he works in.

What sets Mimica apart from the company of filmmakers who worked in both animation and live-action is that, from today's perspective, it seems that he had two lives as an author. While it is quite evident that Frank Tashlin developed his concept of "human cartoon" in the films with Jerry Lewis thanks to his previous experience as an animator in the famous "Termite Terrace", the cartoon studio at Warner Brothers or that Wolf Koening in all his films remained a documentarian for whom animation served to record the "unfilmable", it is difficult to recognize Mimica-animator in Mimica-director of a feature film. Between, for example, his animated film *Alone* (*Samac*, 1958) and live-action *Prometheus from the island of Viševica* (*Prometej sa otoka Viševica,* 1964), it is difficult to find points of contact except that in both cases it is an author whose work fits into the most modern tendencies of both animated and feature films of his era.

Art history teaches us that art develops and grows in a dialectical process. As soon as an aesthetic model blossoms and matures, its antithesis appears in the form of a different concept opposed to the basic postulates of the established model – let's take for example the comparison of the Renaissance and early Dutch painting in the fine arts or Hollywood analytical editing and the French New Wave in film. In the same way, we can compare Disney's mature phase, which we colloquially call "cartoon realism", and the resistance to that aesthetic that arose in independent studios around the USA, especially in the famous UPA studio, which will very quickly spread throughout the world of animation, in which the Zagreb school also played a role.

Mimica's entry into animation came about through the scripts he wrote *On the Meadow* (*Na livadi*, 1957) and *Opening Night* (*Premijera*, 1957), the most important films of one of the first Zagreb cartoonist modernists, Nikola Kostelac. If we look at the historical development of Zagreb cartoons today, we will easily conclude that Mimica was one of the authors from whose works the modernist direction was generated, which will gradually dominate the production in Zagreb film and fight for the flattering name "school" in terms of the authentic aesthetics for which these films were globally recognized. This is even more impressive if we know that this entire phenomenon occurred in a country devastated by war and oppressed by economic scarcity, with an underdeveloped communication infrastructure and a low democratic culture.

Of course, one branch of the newly founded Zagreb animation had its roots in prewar animation production and caricatures and comics created under the influence of Disney's design model. Today we can see how hopelessly uninventive and imitative the films of authors were who applied Disney aesthetics, including those who would later gradually embrace modernism through a multi-year development process.

However, Mimica immediately accepted modernist currents. And he didn't just accept it, he became a global leader in that domain. That this doesn't sound pompous and excessive is evidenced by his films, which, apart from everything else, were highly professional in the technical sense. Sometimes obvious craft mistakes are justified by the author's tendency to experiment. But a mistake is not an experiment. Mimica's films were distinguished from the first to the last by a top professional level, although they all contained original experiments and modernist means of expression, such as the accelerated structure of connected scenes within montage continuity, unexpected metamorphoses, reverse narration from the end to the beginning, incongruent sound effects, reflexive playing with medium, nuances in timing with strategic pausing of movement, breaking through the fourth wall, optical games with perspective and in layout, sight gags etc.

In the novel *Flow My Tears, the Policeman Said* by Philip K. Dick (1974), that great SF writer predicts the appearance of 4D photography!!!! How a four-dimensional image could look like could probably only be explained by Dick's marvellous imagination, which we ordinary people can never fully understand. Every picture, even a photograph, including the picture we call 3D today, is two-dimensional. In the same way, English teacher Edwin Abbott played with an ageing two-dimensional world in his novel *Flatland: A Romance of Many Dimensions*, published as early as 1884. As it is an allegory where the story should be understood as a satire of social reality, then on a metaphorical level we can agree with such a construction, although our experiences and knowledge tell us that the world in practice cannot be two-dimensional. What is two-dimensional is the image of that world.

Nevertheless, art and artists such as Mimica do not necessarily pay attention to such things as logic and physical laws.

Mimica is one of the authors of the animated film who immediately and directly understood the very essence of the animated picture. There are no 2D and 3D, as is the common dividing line between types of animation today. A 3D image is one that has a photographic or photorealistic quality because it is a mathematically exact simulation of a real, three-dimensional space, while a 2D image is one in which the absence of the third dimension is more or less obvious. From his first steps in the medium of the animated image, two things were clear to Mimica: (a) space in animation is built with movement and (b) animation space lies between 2D and 3D. Namely, the very moment we draw a line on white paper, we have added a hint of the third dimension to the two-dimensional surface, because the line, that magical invention of human fantasy, by its very appearance activates the idea of space and opens the way from 2D to 3D.

Life takes place in time and space, so their relationships and mutual interactions are one of the central problems in art. The most important features of both time and space are that they are not stable because they are constantly in motion and subject to change. Movement in an animated film is similar to days in human life, it is a "collection" of individual images where only some stand out with their uniqueness, but we can understand the entirety of that life only if we study ordinary days, those that are forgotten or are drowned in the multitude of the usual. In order to illuminate life in an animated film, it is necessary to create movement, not imitate it. It is hard to imagine how revolutionary this idea was when the dominant understanding of space was stability and alignment with Euclidean three-dimensionality, and timing and movement were literally copied from nature with the help of a rotoscope.

In addition to accepting the idea of designing movement in animation, Mimica understood from the beginning that animation allows complete control over the mise-en-scène. The representation of flexible space that is unique to animation became a central characteristic of Mimic's approach to animation.

Mimica expressed his artistic view in his author's text "Reflections on film art", published in the magazine "Filmska kultura" in December 1963. For him, the meaning of film, that he defined as "epochal an invention as printing" because "what is recorded on film tape is the human spirit" and "the film tape is driven by poetry not by the projector engine". Mimica has no doubt that editing is the most important means of cinematic articulation of the author's idea and viewpoint.

It is interesting that in the same text, Mimica strongly opposes the "Euclidean conservative conception of today's conventional film", highlighting the cinematic space as the focal point of his aesthetic interests. A little further on, he is appalled at the "deep awe of the order of things" in Disney films. Rejecting that model as imitative, Mimica advocates the point of view of animated film, and of film in general, as "a visual melody that bypasses rational perception and enters directly into the emotional sphere".

It is therefore not surprising that Mimica's innovations take place primarily in the area of space and the contradictory relationship between reality and perception.

A characteristic of life is the dissipation of energy, a characteristic of a machine is its rationalization. In the movement of the machine, there is no aimless wandering, excited jumping or anything else that we associate with human qualities expressed in movement. In accordance with his civilization-critical approach to the human community as automated and holistic, with alienated individuals within it, Mimica sees the figure's movement as schematic and mechanical, thus expressing the general feeling of dehumanization and perversion of the modern world. Therefore, there are no characters in Mimica's films in the traditional sense; what we see as the bearers of action are usually anthropomorphic symbols of a certain philosophical idea. Movement should always be a change of position in relation to something, but Mimica often turns movement into an expression of man's futile efforts to find meaning, so it is unclear whether the movement achieved any change in the stage space.

When it comes to space in Mimica's cartoons, the first thing to notice is that there is no stable and unchanging scenography in them. Probably inspired by the ideas of Bauhaus, an artistic movement that was still very present on the European intellectual scene at the time of the creation of his films, Mimica and his collaborators already in their first films opened animation to new expressive possibilities. Particularly important in this sense is the work of Oskar Schlemmer and his effort to "reconcile the metaphysical and the mechanical" (Sutil, 2015), which is in some way the artistic materialization of the ideas of Ernst Hackel, presented in 1917 in his influential research on inorganic life, the book *Crystal Soul* (*Kristallseelen*). What we call inanimate matter, according to Hackel, is actually very much alive and is in a permanent state of movement and transformation, just like organic matter.

Accordingly, Mimica imagines space as something that is built, comes into existence and disappears. The matter is not divided into "living", organic which is endowed with movement and "inanimate", inorganic whose properties should be immobility and stability. Space does not exist as something given; every film creates spatiality anew. He therefore rejects Euclid's postulates ("if a=b and b=c, then a=c") and mathematical ideas about space as a cube that can be analysed using the laws of perspective. Instead of a cube, space can be imagined as a rectangle whose sides differ strongly, as a two-dimensional surface, as some other geometric form or an extremely irregular shape. Space is not understood as a given constant in advance but is constructed and integrated into the general formal and philosophical concept of individual film work. The idea of a space of variable shape results in the construction of a kind of "scaffolding" into which the other elements of the film work are incorporated. Such a method generates the belief that man's world is in eternal construction, creation and disappearance. The concept of space thus becomes the basis of the complexity of the film, which most often describes human civilization.

The configuration of the space is solved with the help of compositing, which can be defined as editing in the depth of the film image. Mimica and colleagues made great use of the possibilities of cel-animation technology, in which a scene is created by stacking different details drawn on transparencies, separated into levels (plans) and placed on a background painted on opaque material. Just as animation time is created by micro-montage of micro-frames (a method Mimica called "total montage"), space in animation is created with the help of compositing, not according to the logic taken from the perception of three-dimensional "Euclidean-Disney" reality.

According to Mimica's thoughts on montage, it is possible to make an analogy between the so-called analytical (continuous, invisible…) montage, typical of Hollywood, where the purpose of the montage process is to stimulate the viewer to mentally reconstruct a complete time and space based on the shown fragments. Thus, for example, what lasts 30 seconds on film, the viewer can experience a dramatic time that lasts a year, or based on several urban indicators, imagine the entire city. In the same Hollywood way, the Disney model uses montage continuity and compositing in order to create a stable and three-dimensional stage space.

Accepting and applying the modernist tendencies in the film of his time, Mimica uses montage, both on the macro-level – when interrelating film frames, as well as on the micro-level, where the film frames themselves are combined – to create time and created a space that is in a conceptual, not an analogue, relationship with human reality. As an illustrative example of such a procedure, his film *At the photographer* (*Kod fotografa*, 1959) can be used, where the space, given the anecdotal character of the narrative, is conceived as a stable scene, but compositing is used to fragment, collage and reshape the characters, here created with the help of "realistic" photographic images, which enhances the effect of wonder.

When creating animated films, Mimica seemed to adhere to Augustine's doctrine according to which "even when our senses deceive us and when we say that everything is perceived, we can still believe in our own doubts, and therefore in our own existence". And further: "Introspection, unlike the perception of external things and events, gives us certain knowledge" (Skirbekk & Gilje, 1993).

BETWEEN 2D AND 3D

Although he abandoned animation relatively early, Mimica left behind works whose value has not faded even a single human lifetime after their creation. I am primarily thinking of three films: *Alone* (1958), *The Inspector returned home* (*Inspektor se vratio kući*, 1959) and *Everyday Chronicle* (*Mala kronika*, 1962) (Figure 4.9).

Even at the level of the screenplay, written together with co-screenwriter Ivo Vrbanić, one can sense the rhythm and artistry of the film *Alone*, which can be seen from this short excerpt:

> *Wake up.*
> *It's morning.*
> *A ray of sunlight falls into the bachelor's room.*
> *There are objects around him.*
> *Children's voices are heard from the neighbourhood.*
> *The factory siren is blaring.*

In this film, sung at its time, Mimica creates a symbolic space using a multi-screen to suggest anxiety and disorientation, and sometimes with the great sets of Rudolf Sablić, which creates the impression of a fluid space in which the main character drowns like a non-swimmer. The figure of the single man is symbolically presented as a materialized sign representing a depersonalized man, a cog without his own identity, who is only required to adapt to the increasingly cruel mechanism of the

FIGURE 4.9 Everyday Chronicle (1962) by Vatroslav Mimica.

encroaching consumer society. The aggressive sound of the typewriter, materialized and underlined by abstract signs and letters in motion, as well as the deafening din of urban everyday life moves into the last oasis of freedom of a single person – his dreams. It is precisely dreams, represented by various optical means, that represent the layered human personality, so the return to reality, in which man is reduced to one dimension, is even more drastic.

Most of the critics who wrote about this film emphasized the theme of individual alienation and adaptability as the principles of a bureaucratized society. But today, when we can see the film several times in a row, and not just once at a festival screening, we can more clearly read the motive and message of this film, which is actually optimistic, and perhaps too romantic in its celebration of love. A single man, who we see in the office and when going to work ignores the girl, will find a solution and free his trapped soul in his dream. That solution is exactly a girl. A single person will be freed from alienation and constraint when he stops being single. In the abundance of bitter and pessimistic metaphors about man and humanity that came from the Zagreb studio, *Alone* is truly one of the rare optimistic flashes on the screens of that era.

The space in *The Inspector returned home* is conceived as a broken mirror in which distorted, "escherian" perspectives are constantly changing. The inspector, a polymorphic figure represented by a combination of collage and drawing, is in the middle of an environment created using iconic signs that suggest an urban milieu and a modern way of life. The inspector found a materialized fingerprint, a canonical indexical sign, suggesting the presence, but here more importantly – the absence of a man. Searching, we assume, for the owner of the print, the inspector moves horizontally, vertically, diagonally and in all directions, while Mimica does not represent the existence of the ground on which the character moves, literally spatializing the scene with its movement.

Another property of the animation space is suggested by exceptionally creative means, that it is filled with matter that is neither air nor water, but a substance with very specific properties appropriate to the inspector's world. When at the end the broken glass appears in the foreground, after which the screen is filled with blood, which causes the world of the film to rush into the world of the viewer, who suddenly finds themselves in a space that is confusing, incomprehensible and unstable, but still not unknown.

Mixing the space of the scene and the space of reality has been feature of animation since its inception, and the birthplace of animation is the theatre, not the film, which was forgotten under the influence of Disney aesthetics, so animation also insisted on an impenetrable "fourth wall" that separates the audience and the scene. But Norman M. Klein (2004) reminds us of this:

> Animation never required a fourth wall, neither in 1650 nor in 1950. Its proscenium had to appear fluid, to allow the viewer to enter the story; or for the characters to escape to the theatre. It is the art that transformed the baroque trompe l'oeil or anamorphosis into moving pictures. Animation developed in an era when the actor often spoke to the viewer.

Another interesting feature of this film is Mimica's abandonment of ambient sound, which the authority on film sound Michel Chion defines as sound that "closes the scene and inhabits its space, without raising the question of identification or visual embodiment of the source: singing birds, ringing of church bells". Instead, Mimica reaches for, in Chion's words, a sonic "super-field":

> I call the super-field the space created in films with multiple diegetic levels, ambient natural sounds, city sounds, music and all kinds of noises that surround the visual space and that can appear from speakers outside the physical boundaries of the screen.
>
> **1990**

Everyday Chronicle is undoubtedly Mimica's most significant animation work, for which he wrote the script together with Zvonimir Berković, another author who will establish himself as a live-action film director following the modern tendencies of European cinema. The film is supposedly inspired by a real event, when a Parisian journalist walked through the city with a monkey mask on his face, without any of the passers-by paying attention to him. The monkey is transformed into a dog in the script, which works better in the context of this film because the monkey evokes very different emotions than the ones Mimica wants to convey. If we have asserted that *Alone* left the door open to optimism and hope, *Everyday Chronicle* is one of the darkest films about the hopeless human situation that has ever been created in Zagreb studio, and as such it is comparable to the masterpieces of Polish black humour (or just "black") of the animated film – Lenice, Borowczyck, Giersz, Kijowicz, Czekala, Szczechura, Kudla, Kucia, Dumala or Rybczynski. The film, one could say, is more "Polish" than Zagreb usually is in that, apart from strongly expressed scepticism when it comes to faith in the possibility of human civilization, it is experimental on a technical level, something that Poles have always been inclined to do. It was not characteristic of most films of the golden age of the Zagreb School, which were mostly made in the cel-animation technique.

Everyday Chronicle takes place on the "big, gigantic conveyor belt of the city", as the film's spatial setting is called in the script. The film begins with an aggressive collage composition that, with sound, movement and tactile suggestiveness, creates an atmosphere of hustle and bustle, paranoia and commotion. By using real machine parts such as gears, screws and nuts, an impression of tactility rarely seen in animated films of the time is created. Futuristically designed vehicles move left and right, which are usually coded spatial indications that create a sense of orientation in the viewer. But in the very next moment, the viewer witnesses the relativization of the terms "up" and "down", directions and perspective. The vehicles stop, and the camera makes a U-turn to suddenly be met with a radical change of the whole scene which rotates 90 degrees, and what was horizontal (the column of vehicles) is now vertical. Mimica uses a flexible scenography with metamorphic image transformations in the foreground and background in order to activate the space in all directions, as well as in-depth. In addition to suggesting an unstable, rotating world by constantly changing directions, Mimica and his collaborators also come up with an ingenious technical solution. The main innovation consisted in physically separating the drawings of figures on celluloid sheets from the background through a type of multiplane so that the figures get shadows. This technical feat resulted in a plasticity and tactile sensation rarely seen in traditionally made cartoons. In such a physical space, extremely two-dimensionally stylized figures gain voluminousness and presence, so, using today's digital terminology, it can be said that the film is neither 2D nor 3D, but something in between.

This is the result of Mimica's work on compositing as a means of exploring the depth of the stage space by dividing it into segments but not to reconstruct the previous state, but to lengthen and deepen the stage space and thereby become something new and different.

A series of pedestrians pass through the space, moving in an abstracted, mechanical rhythm. They walk through something that sometimes seems like an empty space, and sometimes like a new, diagonal direction as if they are suddenly embarked on a subway train. In the middle of the city bustle, we see a blind man with a crowbar and his dog as an individualistic counterpoint to the dehumanized mass. A car accident and the chain crash that follows cause a collapse that will leave the blind man alone. The dog, which tries in vain to find the blind man in the chaos, ends up dying. Putting a black mark on the relationship between the dog and the blind man – the only humane aspect of the "running ribbon of the city", this tragedy leaves the viewer with a bitter taste, which was undoubtedly the author's intention.

Although the film also has certain weaknesses, such as employing subtitles to "explain" something in the film, which is not the best solution, due to the general narrative structure peppered with eloquent sight gags (like the one with the fallen head), philosophical seriousness, visual-technical spectacularity and innovative treatment of space, *Everyday Chronicle* must be included in any anthology of Croatian animation.

When Mimica turns to feature films, his collaborators Marks and Jutriša will become independent, but they will maintain an identical approach to space and the philosophy of animated film in general, so in a way their later independent work can be considered an extension of the aesthetic tendencies conceived in collaboration with Mimica, who was, after all, also co-writer of their greatest success – *The Fly* (1966).

STEINBERG'S INFLUENCE

If the domestic humour magazine Kerempuh influenced the first generation of Zagreb animators, then an American one, The New Yorker, especially the style of one of its authors, Saul Steinberg, strongly inspired several Zagreb animators from the second generation, the one that came after Vukotic, Mimica and Kristl.

Saul Steinberg's work impacted the development not only of the cartoon, caricature, comic strip and animation but of the visual media and culture in general. The drawings he made in his mature stage were sophisticated and unobtrusive in style, their main characteristic being a line of unchanging thickness used to express subtle philosophical thoughts and ideas in clear and simple form. Steinberg worked for The New Yorker for 60 full years, leaving the magazine a fascinating heritage ranging from cartoons, illustrations and cover designs to drawings based on his travels. Thanks to his strong feeling for form, Steinberg breathed new life into the art of drawing as such, producing works of such excellence that some art historians include him among the creators of modern visual understanding. One of them, E. H. Gombrich, in the essay *The Wit of Saul Steinberg*, especially praised Steinberg's ability to create "visual contradictions" and "conflict between incompatible thoughts", all shown with "extreme simplicity". Based on his analysis, Gombrich drew a logical conclusion: "There is no other living artist today who knows as much about the philosophy of representation as Saul Steinberg" (1996).

Steinberg used the beauty of line and simplicity of form to shape visual ideas in which he distilled the most important and most typical features of reality. He always composed his drawings with subtle graphic dissonance that approached the logical order of things with irony and used incongruous inserts or gestures to initiate long chains of associations about and allusions to the existential position of modern man and society.

Steinberg's influence on the animated film was enormous, which was also evidenced by a special programme at the animated film festival in Ottawa in 2007, entitled suitably *Animation Influenced by The New Yorker Magazine Illustrator Saul Steinberg* (1914–1999). George Griffin, who created the programme, included the following films, which, in his opinion, most clearly showed how filmmakers applied Steinberg's aesthetics in animation: *Brotherhood of Man* (Robert Bob Cannon, USA, 1945), *Adventures in Music: Melody* (Ward Kimball, USA, 1953), *Busy Day* (Gene Deitch and Saul Steinberg, USA, 1955), *Diagram* (Daniel Szczechura, Poland, 1966), *Everything is Number* (Stefan Schabenbeck, Poland, 1967), *The Characters* (Evert de Beijer, Netherlands, 1986), *Diary* (Nedeljko Dragić, Yugoslavia, 1974), *The Doodlers* (Kathy Rose, USA, 1975), *Curriculum Vitae* (Pavel Koutsky, Czechoslovakia, 1986), *Another Bad Day For Philip Jenkins* (Mo Willems, USA, 1994), *Feeling My Way* (Jonathan Hodgson, Great Britain, 1997) and *In Betweening America* (Candy Kugel, USA, 2001) (Figures 4.10 and 4.11).

However, with due respect to all the films selected, not one of them can be compared, in expressive strength and in the way in which Steinberg's minimalist narrative image was adapted and enhanced by movement, with Nedjeljko Dragić's masterpiece. As if the path along which the Romanian emigrant had started in the 1930s, on the pages of the famous magazine, had acquired its full meaning and final form in 1974, in the midst of the Balkan-Central-European ambience from which Steinberg himself had come. Dragić blended the scenes one into another and featured drawings of great American cities in Saul Steinberg's manner. The film was constructed as a visual essay full of allusive commentaries about the States – the empire of our times. For Jon Hallas, it was "Dragić's" possibly best film" in which "he (Dragić) breaks new ground. It is a record of his impressions, dreams and hallucinations over the period of a year, expressed in the form of visual images (1987).

DRAGIĆ'S HAZY PANORAMAS

Everything that Dragić did in his creative life is connected to the fact that he basically always was and has remained a cartoonist, regardless of what he was doing at a particular moment. His first great career step was publishing editorial cartoons in newspapers, and he turned attention to himself, among other things, through the collection of cartoons *Lexicon for the Illiterate* (*Leksikon za nepismene*) in which he visualized, in cartoon language, the basic concepts of Marxism. In that collection of intellectual captionless cartoons Dragić clearly applied Steinberg-like poetics, but also announced that he would advance and develop this poetics further.

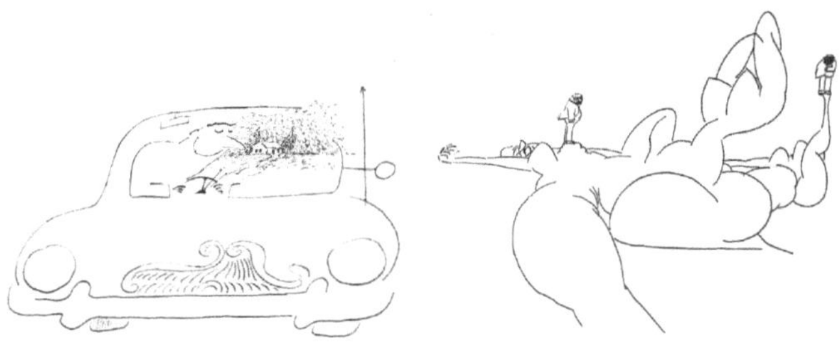

FIGURE 4.10 Diary (1974) by Nedeljko Dragić.

Dragić's cartoon expression is connected to movement, which is why he did not become a devotee of the philosophical restraint present in the drawings of Jean Jaques Sempé, Chaval or Bosc, the leading European cartoonists of the 1950s, although, like them, he quickly accepted the new linear style to which Saul Steinberg opened the doors wide. Dragić saw Steinberg's cartoons for the first time in 1957 or 1958, and realized, as he said himself, that it was possible to draw cartoons in a different way: "More than how to draw, Steinberg taught me how to think. To express thought by line", he told me in a conversation concerned with his work.

In editorial cartoons Dragić always tried to harmonize idea and expression through an ongoing process of simplification, while in animated films he wanted to harmoniously join this simplified drawing with movement. Instead of the frozen, pantomimic

FIGURE 4.11 Diary (1974) by Nedeljko Dragić.

movement of Bosc's and Chaval's figures, Dragić created his characters using a quick, lively line which always seems to want to break out of the paper, start moving and fly away. Moreover, as a cartoonist, Dragić is much more than an imitator of Steinberg because he built on Steinberg's style towards a more relaxed and spontaneous drawing, a kind of pictorial shorthand with a maximally reduced and simplified line, but one that nevertheless allows the expression of the most complex feelings and exactly suggests the character and even the emotions of the figures drawn.

Cartoons strongly influenced Dragić's manner of animation and narration through the animated image and in general the formation of all the preconditions that were to crucially determine the aesthetics of his animated films. Thanks to intuition and the ability to combine, Dragić breathed new life into Steinberg's taut and sharp line. Animation helped the simply drawn shapes and characters to obtain volume and movement.

Whereas most of his colleagues, when they turn to films, continue to be cartoonists only when they draw the pictures for the film, Dragić remained (and became) a cartoonist also when editing, scriptwriting, designing backgrounds and animating. In his films, cartoon-like stylization does not function only on the morphological level of the film's picture, like in many Japanese, European and American animated films. Instead, he intentionally moved away from the conventions of the live-action film and built strategies of editing, narration and humour adapted to the medium of the animated cartoon. For example, he hardly ever edited two shots according to the rules of film editing and framing but blended frame with frame in accordance with the associative nature of cartoon expression; his backgrounds are not mere settings, a place in which the characters move about, but become active participants in the entire process; his animation is not directed towards copying physical movement from nature but is a cartoon-like symbol of movement, just like the drawn character is a cartoon-like symbol of human.

His narrative process is one that is built on associations and where there is not necessarily a chronological order, but rather it is built as a summary of selected "pictures from memory" (as the title of his film made in Zagreb in 1989). In most of his films, Dragić expresses an extremely pessimistic view of human civilization, he is sceptical and even cynical when it comes to the possibilities of an individual man to do something for his individual freedom within the world he himself created.

After arriving in Zagreb film, he first collaborated on the projects of other authors as an animator and cartoonist, and after a few years, he got the chance to make his own films. Dragić became an internationally renowned animator with the films *Tamer of Wild Horses* (1966), *Diogenes perhaps* (1967), and especially *Passing Days* (1968). As a full-blooded film cartoonist, Dragić, in addition to the films that form the backbone of his oeuvre, also presented himself in his "mini films", actually animated cartoons in the form of a cumulative visual joke with an effective point. His first independent work *Elegy*, a 3-minute black humour joke about a prisoner who sees a narrowed picture of the world through the window of his cell, can be included in these. Dragić shows it so that the scene appears literally on the narrowed screen, and the only thing he sees is a flower. But when he is released, the first thing he will do will be to step on that same flower. Perhaps the most successful among his "mini-films" is the prophetic *A Way to your Neighbour* (*Put k susjedu*, 1979), where we see a man getting ready in a tailcoat as if to go out to the premiere, only to see in the last scene that he went to visit his neighbour – in a tank.

As with many other authors from Zagreb, Dragić's central method is the confrontation of a small, ordinary and average man with a panoramic vision of his surroundings. For example, in the film *Diogenes Perhaps*, the central character is a tramp with a bundle who makes his way through a mystical space full of mirage-shaped traps that provoke his (and our) optical logic, in *Passing Days*, a film that Holloway assesses as "the most powerful film work created in Zagreb" (1972) it is a peaceful citizen terrorized by the media, while in the film *Tup Tup* a similar figure is exposed to sonic aggression. While Vukotić and even Kristl in *Don Quixote* (1961) create a clear satirical panoramic vision of the modern world, Dragić's panorama is presented as something incomprehensible and elusive, extremely hostile to the small observer of the panorama, the man-line. To present such a collision, Dragić often resorts to the so-called functional whiteness, a procedure in which space is perceived as abstract as time by turning the character's entire environment into a white fog, which simultaneously represents an impenetrable wall and infinite depth. In one moment, it is a two-dimensional piece of paper on which characters are drawn to become a three-dimensional scene in the next. This concept in the tradition of Zagreb animation, a panorama of the world that is visible only sporadically, was introduced, as I assumed before, by Dovniković in *Curiosity* (1966), but Dragić upgraded it by adding to the humorous atmosphere the flavour of strong satire aimed at debunking media (un)reality that is often incomprehensible and invisible to the little man, but he is therefore perfectly visible, unprotected and exposed to it. As discussed, a particularly significant film in this context is *Passing Days*, in which the concept of a panoramic view is applied to an extremely pessimistic all-encompassing view (Figure 4.12).

FIGURE 4.12 Curiosity (1966) by Borivoj Dovniković Bordo.

DIARY – A CARICATURE OF REAL AMERICA

The panoramic view concretized at the level of a recognizable subject and object and materialized in the form of a fine animation weaving of images and scenes such as Dragić demonstrates in the film *Diary* (1974) led Horn to describe the film in his Encyclopaedia as "one violent stream of images, both figurative and abstract" (1976). Thanks to the nomination for the Oscar Dragić visited the States and made his animated travel essay, where New York functions as a synecdoche for America and the West in general. The cartoonist style borrowed from Steinberg functions not only as an artistic model but also as a representative of a certain perception. The understanding of the cartoonist as a "seismograph of the subconscious" is confirmed by Dragić in the BBC series Masters of Animation, explaining his starting point and the "reason for the film" to his colleague John Hallas:

> Given that I already had a lot of experience in animation, I wanted to make a film without a script and a storyboard. I wanted to make a film that is created the first moment an animator sits down at his desk and starts animating. Associations are then freely transferred to paper using the means of animation, a procedure similar to the "stream of consciousness" we have in literature. In the meantime, I went on a trip to the USA. As a visually extremely rich country, America left a strong impression on me and inspired me. I used those impressions from America as a vision, as my interpretation of impressions from America through animation.
>
> **1986**

The film begins with a scene of an almighty hand from one of the general emblems of animation from Cohl, Disney, Cavandoli, Trnka to Pärn and others. However, the context here is somewhat different. It is less about the "world" that the animator's hand creates, but about something much more as every day – it is the concrete hand of a man who writes (draws) a diary, which we understand by the fact that the hand writes that very title, in the tradition of Zagreb films and their eternal international ambitions, except in Croatian in English, French and German. The first drawing is a square of a comic book or a screen into which the camera plunges so that a sketchily drawn figure of a man walking in a lethargic rhythm appears from the whiteness inside the square. While walking, the figure metamorphically changes its appearance and shape, but this rhythm in the step with a certain sense of blasé in the movements of that "hero" is maintained until the end of the film. At one point, Dragić introduces freely thrown spots of colour that float around, after which the man flies into a literal quote from George Dunning's masterwork *The Flying Man* (1962), 12 years older, only to take the form of Mickey Mouse in one of the subsequent transformations. The idea of the entire opening sequence becomes clearer when the background flashes behind the walking man in the form of a panorama of a gigantic city, under the influence of which the exposed man constantly changes his form. Dragić's entire film is a play with colour and line in continuous change, each scene emerges from the previous one and drowns in the next one.

As a counterpoint to the city, a small square appears in the middle of the screen, an image whose content is an idyllic country house located in a natural setting. An hour later we see that this image is actually an abstraction, an illusion of a man driving a big car and smelling the image that soon disappears under the unbearable noise of the car that does not allow for imagination. In a lightning-fast frame, Dragić transforms to show the driver as Death with a scythe. The noise of the car enables a harmonious transition from the car to an equally noisy ship that approaches towards the "camera" to suddenly reveal the contours of New York while in the foreground is the same little man in an armchair who wants a little comfort and privacy, Dragić's favourite motif known from earlier movies. The man is soon eaten by a large, abstracted face that transforms into a series of angular lines that flicker on the screen, leaving us to try to recognize a face or shape in those hopping lines. By constantly varying between abstracted and recognizable forms, Dragić provokes our perceptive mechanism, making us maximally active and concentrated during the 8 minutes of the film's projection.

Again, a car is in the frame, driven by a mafioso-like driver with a companion he draws as a clichéd prototype of a prostitute. A car moving in the direction of the camera, occasionally transforming into a house, the driver's bedroom or the town hall, passing through a concrete labyrinth full of typical urban indicators, road signs, traffic lights, skyscrapers, overpasses, but also large three-dimensional letters composed of the words NO, YES, PROSPERITY which is another motif borrowed from Steinberg. In one moment, we see the entire scene of the network of highways connected in a complex loop in the middle from the top angle. When the car comes to the loop, it comes to life and, like a man-eating plant, it first swallows it, only to spit it out a few moments later. This is followed by another penetration into the interior of the car, which is shown to us as a posh salon in which there are blasé rich people, and among them is a figurine of a cartoon mouse and a cat. One human face is singled out and comes into close-up, only to be gradually reduced into simple crocs, in the interior of which a spot vibrates, which, after several attempts, comes out. After that, the figures in the fancy salon start kissing, the mouse and the cat do it for a moment, but they quickly remember who they are and start chasing each other, while the human figures left behind engage in orgies and group sex, shown with an effective play of abstract lines and shapes to end with a recognizable sketch of reclining female bodies that resemble a landscape on top of which a male figure has climbed.

The magic of animation metamorphosis makes everything melt again into a city, from the centre of which grows a large man-skyscraper on which is written WORK, BUSINESS, PROSPERITY. The man then shrinks, and the inscriptions on him are transformed into signposts that come out of the body, while simultaneously a mouse and a cat rush through the screen. The picture/page of the diary seems to open and Dragić, using animation penetration, introduces us behind the first perceptual layer into the lower level of the picture, which represents the bowels of the city, where the organism that drives it is revealed to us, represented by countless tangled pipes, cables and gears. Transparent square boxes containing uniform buildings and uniform people constantly fall out of the mechanism. The new zoom brings us closer to one of those boxes and now we see the scene of the square of a large American city presented in Steinbergian style; a policeman, a rabbi, women in flashy clothes and aggressive make-up, a man with a hat and dark glasses who looks like a caricature of Al Capone, a car with rotating lights and clearly a mouse still chasing a cat and a host of other figures, buildings, road signs and new Steinbergian three-dimensional letters which enter each other. Forms and shapes merge and melt into each other so that in the end the content of all that moves into the head of the figure drawn in profile at the beginning.

At one point, the inscription SUPER rendered in three-dimensional letters stands out and we, following that word, once again leave the head of the diary writer/drawer. Three-dimensional letters now occupy the space of the screen, forming an entire city. The fascinating animation-graphic scene is completed by busy people in suits and with business bags who have a wall clock instead of their heads, which leads to a feeling of claustrophobia, paranoia and general confusion, which is also contributed by the irritating soundscape. Dragić gradually reduces and condenses the image to a swarm of minimalistic drawn people, but in order to avoid any confusion as to which place on the planet we are talking about, one of them is designed as a hastily drawn Chaplin. We return again to the city of letters that now vibrate chaotically, building a composition of strong visual expression. The scene is combined with short inserts of people floating completely devoid of their own will like a squirrel in its wheel and a caricature scene of a man trying to escape from a chaotic hive, but he only manages to run in place, which is another almost literal application of Steinbergian figuration. From the swarm of letters, one "W" stands out, waving its arms like wings, flying over the faithfully drawn panorama of Manhattan before descending on that hyper-urbanized island like a nest. An hour later Manhattan sank into the water under the weight of the letter "W".

The letter "W" begins to deflate like a punctured balloon and the most diverse abstract shapes and forms come out of it, so the next few seconds of the film are quite like some non-figurative animation by, say, Norman McLaren, except that at one point the same mouse and cat rush through the screen. Abstract forms are transformed into a geometric transparent square that floats on something that resembles muddy water or sewage. We again see the melting of a series of different characters to return to a floating square on which a man sits as if on a desert island. An effective zooming back revealed to us that the whole scene, like everything we watched earlier, is in the body of the same man we saw at the beginning. The man lights a cigarette and continues his lethargic walk.

DOVNIKOVIĆ'S NAÏVE HEROES

Thanks to his long career, eagerness to travel to festivals and, of course, films, Borivoj Dovnikovic Bordo functioned as a synonym of the Zagreb school for decades. In one of his early films, *Ceremony* (*Ceremonija*, 1965), Dovniković already presented himself as a typical middle-European humourist with an inclination towards black humour. For the most part of the film, we are looking at a group of people enthusiastically assuming different poses as if they were going to be photographed. In the end, we see that they are standing in front of the firing squad, posing for their executioners (Figure 4.13).

Dovniković's characters were little, everyday, naïve heroes. As far as figure design and drawing technique in general were concerned, Dovniković, like Grgić and Dragić, was strongly influenced by Steinberg's purity and simplicity. Dovniković was somewhat older than his colleagues, so his drawing style kept plasticity and volume and the softness of line placing his graphics halfway between Disney and Steinberg. As an animator, he was relaxed, his drawings were copied from the paper on the celluloid with unequally thick lines which constantly pulsated on the screen creating lively and irresistible film images sometimes called "boiling line". All his films were drawn pantomimes whose humour was somewhat melancholic and bluish. Instead of dialogues, he used caricatured sound mostly authored by Miljenko Dörr, a genius sound technician whose oeuvre was more than comparable to the work created by Warner-Brothers' sound technicians Mel Blanc and Dawes Butler. Dovniković's stories always revolved

FIGURE 4.13 Ceremony (1966) by Borivoj Dovniković Bordo.

around a goodhearted, affectionate and naïve "little man" who would find himself in trouble because of something totally unnatural and illogical, or due to human wickedness. Drawn figures proved to be perfect "actors" which transferred with great precision the author's vision of an ordinary little man and his struggle to live an ordinary life.

In some of Dovniković's most important films his characters actually did not give up that easily. After having undergone molestation in the first part of the film, the character would experience a catharsis and transforms into a real fighter who refuses to be terrorized any longer.

His ordinary man becomes totally extraordinary.

In *Curiosity*, a man sleeping on a bench in a park escaping all kinds of disturbing the little man's slumber: soldiers, rebels, tourists, groups of children and many others who are trying to see, at all costs, what is hidden in the bag lying next to the bench and the sleeper. Finally, the little man escapes to a deserted area, only to make fun of his torturers by showing in an ironic closing scene that the bag is empty.

In *Learning to Walk*, an innocent and naïve figure of a man gets tired of following stupid rules imposed by those who are trying to teach him how to walk "properly". He transforms from a peaceful dork to a mighty fighter who chases away his tiresome advisors.

In *Second Class Passenger*, we see his usual little man in a train compartment where all kinds of irrational events take place. All that he wants is to travel in peace, however, he is terrorized by the conductor, police, postman with bad news, newspaper vendor shouting headlines, a man from the next compartment who is suffering from insomnia, a dog drinking brandy, a smoker which turns the compartment to a gas chamber and many other strange characters. His compartment becomes the battlefield of war between cowboys and Indians, he is even visited by the aliens. Specific caricaturist irony is revealed in the end when the Little Man, who seemed the only normal person in the compartment, reaches his station. We see that his luggage is full of alien animals, while the landscape surrounding his house corresponds to a scene from a horror film: dark gothic castle, cemetery, full moon, illustrated by an ominous soundtrack.

Krek (1968) is an anti-militarist anecdote ironically dedicated to all the world's corporals. A little recruit is coming to the barracks to serve his term. He encounters a ruthless corporal who tortures him with a steel military drill. In the recruit's bag, under his civil clothes, lies hidden a cheerful frog, an obvious "Schweikian" symbol of civil life joy and freedom. The recruit is forced to obey the corporal's senseless orders: physical training, rifle practice, marching, digging trenches, cleaning toilets and other demeaning tasks. However, as soon as the frog appears in the shot, the corporal vanishes. Instead of a saddening military ambience, the recruit and the frog travel to another reality, the world of freedom that Dovniković represented by attaching clips of postcards of western cities and tourist catalogues, which did not represent a mere counterpoint to the drawn reality, but also carried clearly understandable symbolism. The frog appears in the most unexpected places: under the recruit's cap, in corporal's boots, on the training course. Corporal hits it and kicks it, even shoots it, but the symbol of freedom is unusually tenacious. In the end, the corporal throws the frog into a deep well, fills it with bombs and then proceeds to slander his victim. The recruit's troubles continue until the end of his term when the indestructible frog reappears. Frog's legs are plastered, but it is still full of life's joy, just like the recruit who finally leaves the barracks and returns to freedom.

ONE DAY OF (EMPTY) LIFE

In all Dovniković's films from the 1960s and the 1970s there was a certain degree of optimism and hope for the little man. However, it has vanished from his later works. *One Day of Life* (1982) was the film in which pessimism overtook (Figure 4.14).

Jedan dan života (1982)

FIGURE 4.14 One Day of Life (1982) by Borivoj Dovnikovic Bordo.

The film's opening is irritatingly boring: in several consecutive scenes we are watching the same thing, following the life of a man going to work and coming home. Nothing else is happening. He goes to the factory, performs a meaningless job and furtively looks at his beautiful colleague for which his boss yells at him. Boredom is the only content of his life, which Dovniković emphasized using only several cold colours and accompanying it with depressive music.

One day, while tottering home, the hero unexpectedly runs into a man, much bigger and heavier than him. With the help of the brilliantly devised language of drawn pantomime used by the characters, we realize that they are old acquaintances, probably school buddies. The little man's daily routine unexpectedly and radically changes because the friend literally takes him to the pub. The two of them enter a typical Balkan pub full of cigarette smoke, men and women leaning heavily over their glasses. At that moment, colours and soundtrack change, both turning into something brighter. Friends sit at the bar and start downing rounds or drinks. Soon a drunken bum joins them, and they become a drinking threesome.

With every new round of drinks, Dovniković' adds some warm tones, both in the background and foreground. Animation rhythm quickens, while musical illustration starts to resemble popular folk music usually heard in Balkan pubs. The film's atmosphere assumes a wild stance, just like the one beating in the little man's head. The drunker he gets; the wilder is the atmosphere in the pub. Little man starts travelling with great speed between reality and fantasy owing to the apparent freedom procured by the alcohol. In a series of effective scenes, Dovniković combined situations in which we see reality, the little man drinking with two other drunken brothers and imaginary scenes illustrating his hidden desires. Suddenly he sees his boss. In his malignant hallucination, he hits him, but in reality, it is a small bum who gets hit on the nose. He also sees his colleague. She is naked and he takes off his pants intending to sleep with her. In reality, he is standing in the middle of the pub with his pants down, as the laughingstock of other guests.

He is making a full of himself, which is the only way to be free. "Schweikian" substance of absurd was reached with the help of alcohol, as is often the case in real life.

At the end of the film, we see the little man dead drunk: he is driving an expensive car, swimming in the sea of naked women's breasts (which is an obvious pastiche from an earlier Dragić's film), the whole town dances in the rhythm of folk music, the little man, in the size of King Kong, roams around the town. From above, we see a panoramic view of a picturesque landscape, endless open space, fields and rivers. Above all that little man is flying in the sky painted in screaming colours.

Here, Dovniković makes a sudden cut: again, we see the little man on his routine walk from his home to work, same dull rhythm and same depressing colours from the beginning of the film. The return to cruel reality is achieved with a sharp cut: yesterday's short-lasting happiness was an illusion created with alcohol. It was yet another day in which nothing had happened, and nothing can happen or change anyway.

Little man returned to his empty, doleful life.

A BLIND MAN WALKS THROUGH THE GRAND CANYON

One of the last major international successes of the Zagreb School in the former state came in 1978 with Zdenko Gašparović's *Satiemania*. The author's fascination with the music of the Swiss avant-garde composer Erik Satie combined with his rich visual culture resulted in an intimate autobiographical film made as a harmonious composition full of longing and nostalgia as well as erotic reminiscences. In the years that followed it would become a cult film among several generations of animation fans. Thanks to the fragmentary structure of the film, Gašparović also placed several witty caricature gags, the most successful of which seems to be the one in which he ironically comments on the idea of a small man who, with his comprehensive view, critically questions the big, wide world around him. In the beginning, we see a blind man stumbling in front of a completely white background, only to end up falling somewhere deep into the whiteness with a long cry. Only then, when the blind man is dead, does the background appear from the whiteness and we see that he was wandering through the Grand Canyon. Gašparović, who spent most of his career in the USA, obviously got the inspiration for that gag from overly ambitious cartoons based on global metaphors about major world problems, whose ideological background he presented in the form of a blind man who can't see where he's going. If we take the world around us and ourselves in it too seriously, is the message of this witty gag, we will end up being treated as a joke ourselves.

Satiemania was also one of the films that announced that the possibilities of classic two-dimensional "seven minutes" cell animation, both from Zagreb and others, were somewhat saturated, so already then, at the end of the 1970s, different aesthetic and conceptual concepts were strongly appearing.

Of course, the idea and practice of dealing with serious political and philosophical topics in the form of animated cartoons will continue to be present. Global metaphors and a panoramic, comprehensive view will no longer dominate, but this genre will develop in the last few decades in the direction of illuminating specific problems related to the life of an individual in a certain socio-political context.

5 The Tradition of Intermingling between Comics and Animation in the Zagreb School

CROATIAN COMIC STRIP

A more or less unknown fact even to renowned comic books experts is that during the 1930s, Zagreb and Belgrade belonged to a few world centres where superb comic strips were created. Comics were a new and exciting medium for the public at that time. Comic strips that evolved in Zagreb and Belgrade were of such high quality that they could easily compete with their American and European contemporaries, had there been linguistic possibilities for their rivalry.

The core of Belgrade's production of comics consisted of a group of very gifted artists who immigrated from the Soviet Union (among others: Kuznjecov, Solovjev, Navojev, Lobačev…), while in Zagreb, the leading role had domestic artists. The absolute leader among comic strip artists in Yugoslavia was Andrija Maurović, whose huge creative opus was one of the most original in the whole history of the medium. The period from mid-1930s to 1944, when he joined the partisan fighters, constituted the golden years of Maurović's career. From his first strip novel *Fiancee of the sword* (*Vjerenica mača*) from 1935, to three comic strips from 1944, *Tomislav*, *Ahuramazda from the Nile* (*Ahuramazda s Nila*) and A Grave in the Rainforest (*Grob u prašumi*), Maurović developed his inimitable graphic style. He had an incomparable feeling for shading, the ability to create a balance between black and white tones with grey halftones in every single frame, an instinct for creating characters in continual movement, with close-ups of expressive faces, and most of all, he was a skilful layout maker able to set up a dynamical relation between all the frames on a single page. In all of here mentioned he had no predecessor in the field of comics. A comparative analysis of Maurović's work would probably reveal that his true role models were filmmakers such as D. W. Grifith or Fritz Lang. Several of Maurović's important graphic novels looked as if they represented minute storyboards for some imaginary Griffith's film.

During the 1930s, at the time when radio celebrated its tenth anniversary, and while television was still more or less a fantasy, film was understandably the most popular medium. Owing to Maurović, the comic strip held the second place. His comic novel *Three in the Dark* (Trojica u mraku, 1936), a western written by the unconventional journalist Franjo Martin Fuis, ran in the daily Novosti. Their success was enormous, each morning buyers formed lines in front of Zagreb newsstands,

DOI: 10.1201/9781003375623-5

eager to read the new instalment and consequently print runs skyrocketed. It was unimaginable that a comic strip be this successful in any country in the world, perhaps with the exception of the United States. Maurović returned to comics during the 1960s when, among other things, he created six colour comics using the tempera technique, which at that time had no equal in the world (Figure 5.1).

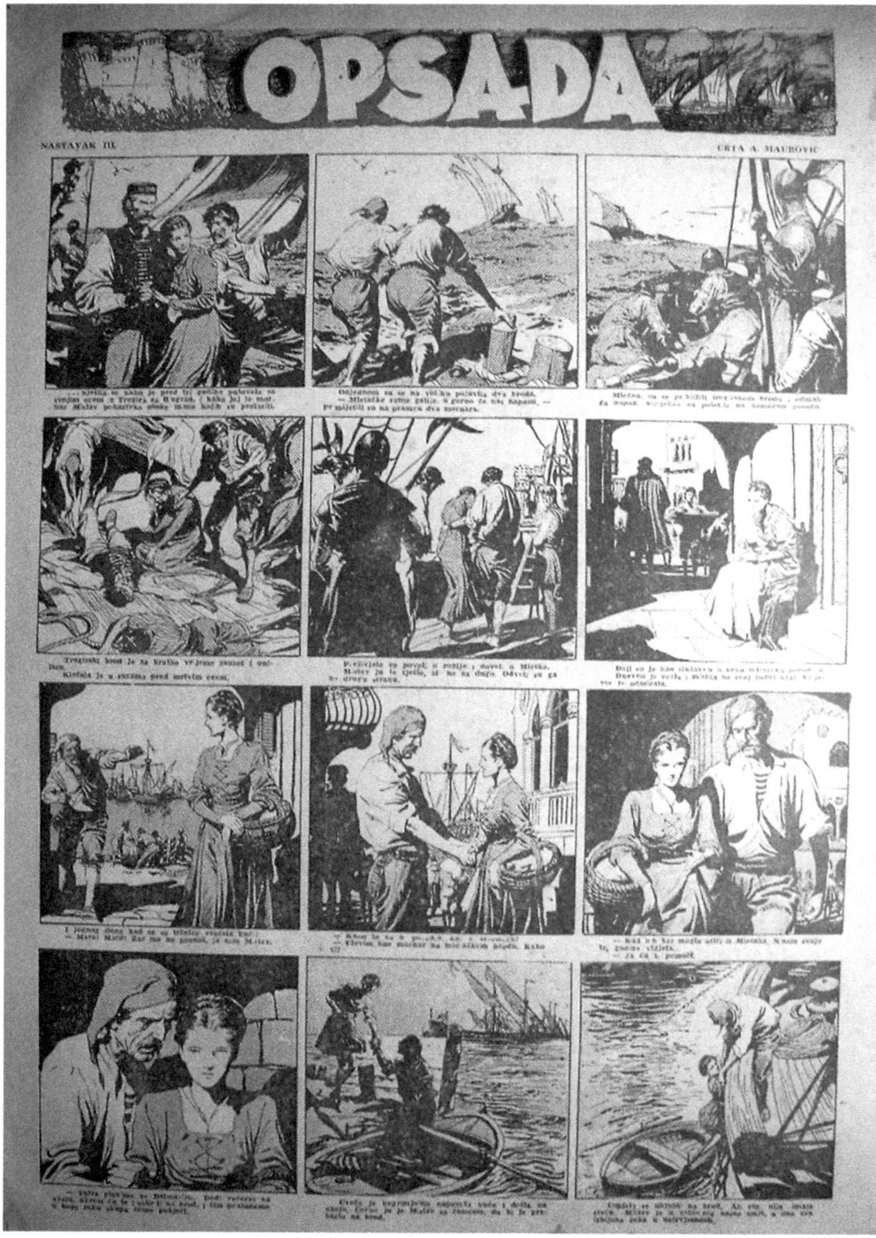

FIGURE 5.1 Comic page (1951–1952) by Andrija Maurovic.

Presence of the great artist and the immense popularity of comic books acted as a strong incentive for young people to start working on stories in pictures. The most gifted among them was Walter Neugebauer, a naturalized Zagreb citizen who came to Zagreb from his native town of Tuzla in Bosnia. He started his career at the age of 14 and immediately became, in the domain of caricatural comics, what Maurović was in lifelike figuration. As a young man already, Neugebauer had a phenomenal grasp on all the aspects of his trade. He drew in Disney style dozens of comic strips and published them in his own weekly magazine. Namely, during the years of war, he earned his bread publishing a non-political comics magazine Zabavnik, in which he also published comics made by other authors. Neugebauer followed the rules of the "round aesthetics" created in Disney's studio: the base of each drawing was a circle, and every character, be it human or animal, was constructed with circular, easily followed strokes, so that whatever we saw looked nice and cute. His line was soft and elastic, characters alive, caught in the movement, as if animated. We also observed the effort to use movement to achieve graphical and rhythmic continuity between the frames, so that the transition between the frames did not feel like a cut, as if each shot of the comic strip, the so-called key position, was drawn for the layout of some future animated film. He was also a proficient printer who knew how to get the best results from printing techniques, so that the quality of colour in his comic books was ten years ahead of its time. His comic books such as *Hungry King* (*Gladni kralj*, 1943), Dwarf Nosy (*Patuljak Nosko*, 1943) and Following Tarzan's Footsteps (*Tarzanovim stopama*, 1944) based on the book by Wilhelm Hauff and E. R. Barrows adapted in the form of funny scripts in verse by his older brother Norbert, besides marvellous foregrounds, also had studiously elaborated scenery.

A logical outcome of this was the fact that the same Walter Neugebauer was the key figure in the group that, after World War II, founded Croatian and Yugoslav animated films (Figures 5.2–5.5).

A CENTURY OF DISREGARD

In this study, comics are considered a medium and an art form absolutely equal to all others, literature, painting, film etc. However, this was not always the case. For more than a century academic art historians held a monopoly in visual studies, which resulted in the inconceivable disregard and marginalization of a whole verbal-visual medium – the comic strip. In addition to being a powerful storytelling tool, comics played an important role in the constant advancement and broadening of the boundaries of human expression, communication capabilities and diversity of imagination and thought. The great spiritual potentials amassed during their historical development are today mostly still unknown and unresearched. Having been ignored for so long, comics are still a medium whose significance is inversely proportional to the status they are given in most of the world. Comics have led to such a change in the visual reality of our world that they can, without exaggeration, be seen as a medium that links two eras of civilization – the print-dominated era, and that which is usually called the civilization of the image, meaning films, television, computers and the like. What is more, people are not usually aware of the extent to which comics have changed our understanding of visual art and advanced our ability to use visual symbols.

FIGURE 5.2 Hungry King (1943) by Walter Neugebauer.

Therefore, it was after the 1970s and the advent of semiotics as an established scholarly discipline, and especially after the 1990s and the expansion of the image-mediated media, the visual turn and the century-overdue establishment of comics scholarship, that the scholarly public discovered many facets of the comic strip.

Another medium, which directly originated from comics and was based on them, shared a similar but less drastic fate – this was the cartoon film, a subspecies of the animated image that had been the dominant form of animation for many decades. To paraphrase a Croatian film scholar Ante Peterlić, for whom the animated film was a boundary region between cinematography and painting in the same way in which "opera stands at the meeting-place of drama and music" (2010), one might say that the boundary region of cartoon film in fact connected film and comics.

FIGURE 5.3 Cover page for Dwarf Nosy (1943) by Walter Neugebauer.

Technology has a crucial impact on form, and after the end of the nineteenth century, the living image developed along two branches: on one hand, towards the moving photograph or the film, and on the other, towards the moving drawing, image or object, that is cinema animation. The 1960s to the 1990s brought the increasing development and presence of the morphology of the animated image, which became more three-dimensional and photorealistic. This process got its full meaning in the

FIGURE 5.4 Dwarf Nosy (1943) by Walter Neugebauer.

new century when digital 2D and 3D animation began to completely oust film technology. During the film period of the history of animation, however, the comic strip, caricature and editorial cartoon were dominant points of origin and direct sources for the aesthetics, graphics, communication conventions and codes of animation.

FIGURE 5.5 Cover Page for magazine Zabavnik (1944) by Walter Neugebauer.

I have already discussed, in other places, the expression and depiction of movement in modern visual language, which advanced as it moved from medium to medium, for example from cartoons to comics to animated films and other forms of cinema animation, right down to digital animation. The development of the human spirit includes several huge and rich chapters about the graphic-visual media of the cartoon, caricature, comic strips and animated film, but none of these exist in the text-books of official art history, as if image research in the larger part of the twentieth century had been done by people who were blind.

This state of affairs did not begin to change, as we have said, until the end of the last century, and today animation and comics scholarship has become almost common, if only in the most developed countries in the world, where its international affirmation began in the 1990s. The study of animation resembles archaeology, a kind of excavation of the image, in the era of media, since literally whole ages, long historic periods, immense lifeworks of authors and numerous important works have not yet been analysed or have been completely forgotten, even lost to humanity forever. Tragic examples, among others, are the first ever feature-length animated film (*El Apostol*, Quirino Christiani, 1917) and the first animated sound film (*Peludopolis*, Quirino Christiani, 1931), which were destroyed in a fire, and the works of Helena Smith Dayton, an artist and dramatist from New York, who in 1917 directed her own stop-motion animated version of Romeo and Juliet using clay dolls dressed and adorned with human hair. After the successful showing of this film, Helena Smith Dayton made several more short films in the same technique, but none of them exist any longer. There are even animated films that still exist in some archive or another place which are unknown because of cultural centrism, the above-mentioned marginalization of the animated film, and simple negligence or lack of attention given to it. This is the case with the masterly achievements of Chinese animators from the Shanghai studio, for example, which are a blind spot even for experts.

We will find a large number of such archaeological excavations even if we restrict ourselves to Croatian animation. They would, for example, include the life and artistic biography of Bogosav Patanjek, who used to work as the chief animator in Chirino Cristiani's studio in Argentina during the 1930s. Petanjek's animation style, consequently, developed under the influence of Christiani's comics. For his part, he will encourage younger authors from the first generation of the Zagreb School, who did both comics and animation for many years, as did Dovniković; Delač, Reisinger and others. They belonged to the cartoonists recognisable for their links with comic magazine Plavi vjesnik, an important but internationally poorly known branch of the European comic strip, which in its post-war period slowly broke away from the conventions used in the dominant American comics, in search of its own expression, style and form. Challenges of this kind faced by European cartoonists culminated during the 1970s in what is known as the French-Belgian School of the 1970s, the golden age of the European comic strip, whose Croatian answer appeared in the work of the cartoonists of Novi kvadrat (The New Panel), a group of authors whose importance reached cult proportions, but in the work of others, as well. Some group members like Krešimir Zimonić and Joško Marušić left their mark in the tradition of Zagreb animation with films strongly impregnated with the language of comics. Another interesting profile was Milan Blažeković, who made three full-length animated films based on the style he developed in his comics.

COMICS AND FILM: THE NARRATIVE IMAGE

David Kunzle is an exception among twentieth-century art historians, one who did not ignore comics but even wrote authoritatively about the history of that medium in the western civilization. His meticulous studies were a keenly awaited alternative to the various dilettante histories of comics full of complete nonsense, and "facts" such as that the first comic strip was made in America in 1896. Kunzle consistently applied the scholarly methods of art history in his study of comics, showing their deep roots in the cultural history of Europe and America. Analysing the work of William Hogarth, the great British seventeenth-century caricaturist and graphic artist, Kunzle (1990) wrote about the movement before movies, which, he said, took place in the golden age of the editorial cartoon, in the nineteenth century (1973). In his view, Hogarth synthesized the basic components of caricatural expression which had earlier been separate, such as: (1) comic faces, varied either according to character and social type or in a grotesque, arbitrary and virtually autonomous fashion, and (2) expressive postures. Kunzle also wrote about the narrative image, which differs from the representational image because it lays greater emphasis on movement (time) in the composition (space).

To use a comparison from the technological language of animation, the representational image would be the final, key phases of a movement, the so-called extremes or poses, while the narrative image would show the in-between phases, the moment in which movement is captured in the process of change and metamorphosis, an image allowing us at the same time to picture what preceded it and what is to follow. Considering its role in depicting narration, expressing movement takes two aspects: (1) the continuous rhythmic movement that carries the story forward and links visual experiences between two panels in a strip or two shots in a film, following the general narrative and its chronological structure, and (2) the visualizing of movement within the framework of each individual image, each panel or each shot. A special place belongs to morphing, which is often used in animated films. It is an imaginary transformation of one form into another through several consecutive transitions, in which the initial recognisable form A melts into a series of semi-abstract forms and ends up as the recognisable form B.

Therefore, although the narrative image primarily began as a way of showing a humorous or satirical approach, it was soon, already in the work of authors such as Doré and Cham, assimilated into the domains of the dramatic, historical, psychological and propagandist, which laid the foundations for the further development of image-based narration and its branching into various media, especially comics and films. Despite the key difference between them, since films are dominantly temporal and comics are basically material, what directly connects them is the narrative image as well as the fact that both film and comics are pictorial visions of the world or worlds. The visual is always dominant. If we eliminate the sound recording, what remains will still be considered a film. If we eliminate the picture, it will not, what remains will be called – radio. Or, to put it very simply, a film is narration using (dominantly) a picture. The same is true of comics, which, as we know, can exist as pictures without words (silent comics), but words without pictures are called literature. Both the media are based on narrative images, and their interconnection and blending through the animated drawing, painting or sculpture are becoming increasingly important in our age dominated by digitally produced and distributed images.

Although definitions must be made with care, as we have seen, we will not be at too great a risk if we define comics as the static and films as the moving narrative images. This solves the major conceptual want of precision in media-centred technology-based interpretations of the film, which look at the film as a photographic recording on a celluloid tape, projected on a screen. For example, Émile Reynaud's works were films in the semantic sense although they did not include a single form of the photographic process. The same is true of the great deal of digitally produced moving images, which has in quantity probably already reached that based on photography.

The connection between comics and films is more than obvious, natural and logical, which especially comes to expression in the work of many important authors who engaged in both the media at the same time. Thus, even the important animation historian Donald Crafton, whose refusal to see links between comics and animation cannot be accepted, in some cases, for instance in the work of Winsor McCay, nevertheless recognizes that "although the word 'cinema' is often carelessly used to describe comic-strip art, here is one case in which it seems justified" (1998).

In his study on visual narration Scott McCloud is very specific and sees links between comics and films in five crucial elements of narration technique, which appear in both the media: (1) Choice of Moment: Deciding which moments to include in a comics story and which to live out. (2) Choice of frame: Choosing the right distance and angle to view those moments and where to trim them, (3) Choice of image: Rendering the characters, objects and environments in those frames clearly. (4) Choice of word; Picking words that add valuable information and work well with the images around them. (5) Choice of flow; Guiding readers through and between panels on a page or screen (2005).

It must also be remembered that right from the beginning both films and comics were subject to commercial and consumer codes, which means that they served two primary aims: (1) to entertain as many people as possible and thus earn as much money as possible for their producers and agents and (2) to play their role in the preservation of the social status quo.

But just like in some other forms of expression, some of the most important advances in the development of the narrative image in comics and cartoons, and also in films and animation, were made by resisting commercial codes and departing from the given conventions and aims.

THE BRANCH OF SIMPLIFICATION

Norman M. Klein defined animation as an immanently modernist medium and singled out four key elements confirming this: (1) abstraction, (2) reflexivity, (3) defamiliarization, (4) graphic design (1993). Looking back, we see that animation assimilated all these four elements as they flowed from medium to medium and that all of them came from comics and even before that from editorial cartoons. Indeed, even a cursory survey of cartoon and comics history clearly shows that modernism was discovered and then forgotten many times.

One of the most fascinating human inventions is the line, which has existed as long as the human intelligence and spirit. It is also one of the basic phenomena of our existence, something that usually goes unremarked because this perfect substitute for the weakness of our power of perception, this way of representing nature by something that does not exist in nature, seems completely self-evident. More or less like geometry, that most obvious signal of the presence of civilization, without which there would be no technology, science or art, and which would, like many other things, not be possible without the line. Or, to put it another way, a large part of what we see around us and what we experience as a human civilization were first-line drawings.

In his excellent book of illustrated essays *When you Draw Horses* (*När man ritar hästar*, 2010), the Swedish artist and intellectual Claes Jurander writes about the miracle of the line, which is the product of man's pure spirit and intellect. Jurander expands the theory of the Danish communicologist Tor Nörretrander, who considers that the basic quality of human intelligence is not the ability to consume information but to reject it – Nörretrander calls this *exformation*. Our brain can process only 75 bits per second of the approximately one million bits our environment is constantly bombarding us with. Selecting, Jurander calls it sieving, what we will pay attention to, and discarding the enormous amount of what is unnecessary, is what we call perception, in other words, making sense of the world that surrounds us and that we are looking at. The line expresses exformation in a visual, i.e. material form, enabling us to record and pass on to others what we saw and how we experienced and understood it. For Jurander, the line is undoubtedly primarily a language whose "aim is clarity, to transfer in material form what a person thinks and feels" (2010).

There are no two cartoonists with the same styles. Besides its other properties, the line is also a material expression of human uniqueness which lies at the foundation of every artistic personality. Innumerable examples prove this, such as the difference between the calm, exact and steady line in Saul Steinberg's graphic acrobatics, André Francois's line variations, Ronald Searls's or Ewart Karlsson's fluid line of three-dimensional impact, Chaval's or Bosco's restraint and the pantomimic movement of their characters and, of course, the works of the Zagreb masters.

Long ago Rodolphe Töpffer, whom some people consider the father of the modern comic strip, made theoretical and practical studies of the language of the line, searching for and inventing graphically economical ways to effectively integrate text into pictures. In *Essays on Physiognomy* (*Essais de physiognomonie*, 1845), Töpffer wrote about gesticulation and mimicking as kinds of coded visual language representing movement and tried to develop an iconic classification of basic human moods shown graphically through simplified renderings of the human face. During the 1900s Töpffer's attempts were affirmed through their use and establishment in mass-produced comic strips: the caricatural style of drawing, the reciprocity and equality of picture and text, and, most importantly, visual-sequential narration. But even though some of his contemporaries, such as Goethe, wrote about Töpffer as a genius, almost a century and a half was to pass before his work was evaluated or even understood. Kunzle published a monography about this great visionary of the visual, while E. H. Gombrich proposed that the antropomorphization of the line, that is, the fact that we give life to a human face the moment we recognize it in a line, should be called "Töpffer's law". The Swedish scholar Helena Magnusson founded much of her doctoral dissertation *Narrative Pictures* (*Berättande bilder*) on Töpffer's works, emphasizing his contribution to the invention of various lineal ways of representing movement, speed, haziness, shaping photo effects and simultaneous succession (movement represented by showing the same figure several times within one picture). It is important to remember that the comic strip originated in the editorial cartoon because what had been taken over from the cartoon, such as deformation, explanation, emphasis and stylization, was further developed in comics and assimilated in films "as narrative norms and conventions that had already been defined" (2005).

Kunzle especially accentuated the role of another early cartoonist and comic-strip artist, the German Wilhelm Busch. He is credited with creating some of the basic conventions for the visual representation of movement and emotions which we today consider self-evident, such as various kinds of accessory lines suggesting movement or oscillation (air currents, impact lines, speed lines, patterns of oscillation), the visualization of heat (melting) and cold (freezing), the most diverse physical transformations of the human body, exaggerations and deformations that express particular emotions, the visual code for human speech (the bubble), visual conventions for showing music, page layout and various kinds of framing codes and so on.

The great caricaturist Grandville, just like Töpffer, also sought to develop the narrative image (Kunzle, 1990). In 1844 he wrote a manifesto seeking freedom for the picture and its liberation from the tyranny of the word, i.e. from the caption, which was de rigueur in the first caricature magazines La Silhouette (founded in 1829) and La Caricature (founded in 1830).

The aims expressed by Grandville and other like-minded artists resulted in the late 1880s in the development of the cartoon as an independent form of expression, which gradually broke away from the visual representation of the gallery type and verbal/written humour. A new kind of modern cartoon came into being, first in Europe and then also in the USA, without text and with recognisable characters, a kind of graphic aphorism that relied on incongruent combinations in the picture, increasing generalization on the thematic level and simplification in visual stylization. An especially important feature in visualization was a departure from the classic laws of perspective that had for a long time also been applied in cartoons. In the modern cartoon, the drawing was seen as a two-dimensional interpretation of a particular idea, with an increasing accent on the role of the line. Having thus discovered the narrative image, cartoonists no longer needed words, and at the turn of the century, the captionless situation cartoon was definitely established, which was probably the peak in the development of this form of expression.

An important branch in the development of the cartoon is the expression of strong meaning rendered with visual minimalism and general graphic simplicity based on the less is more principle, where the viewer must make an effort to identify the whole from fragments shown in a completely stylized line drawing. In this case looking at the drawing and the visual pleasure this provides implies deciphering codes, interpreting suggestions and filling voids in something that is only implied in several strokes. The modern situation cartoon had an especially strong influence on animation in the films made in the USA after the mid-1940s and in Yugoslavia after the 1950s.

Several factors contributed to the appearance of this minimalistic trend, the most important being currents in style and the general approach to visual form in art, such as Cubism, which preceded Art Deco, or the influence of Japanese medieval art, which the European public discovered at the end of the nineteenth century.

The magazine Simplicissimus, founded in 1896 by the cartoonist Thomas Theodor Heine (1867–1947) with the help of the publisher Albert Langen, played an important role in this entire process; it was perhaps the greatest contribution to caricature and situation cartoons from the German-speaking world. Heine was one of the main contributors to the magazine, making outstanding caricatural portraits of Al Capone and the young Adolf Hitler. He supported an intellectual style in published contributions and encouraged an ironic view of important public issues so that writers such as August Strindberg and Anatole France wrote socially engaged articles in Simplicissimus. Even when the magazine actively joined the propaganda war against France and Britain during World War I, it mainly wrote for the educated middle class. Under its famous logo "die bissige Bulldogge", created by Heine, the magazine primarily aimed its satirical sting at the militaristic class, not even sparing the Emperor himself. In the late nineteenth-century Munich had become a metropolis dominated by middle-class liberals who, in public and cultural life, functioned as a counterweight against the "militant, pompous figure of Emperor Wilhelm II in Berlin", to quote the cartoon historian Fritz Arnold in the catalogue of the retrospective exhibition of cartoons from Simplicissimus. Arnold gave great importance to the tolerant atmosphere and cosmopolitan spirit of contemporaneous Munich, which received artists from other places with open hands and gratitude, including those from non-German-speaking regions.

Besides Heine, who was to some extent close to Cubism, the magazine also featured the work of George Grosz (1893–1959), a former Dadaist who opposed Fascism openly and without reservations and of the Norwegian Olaf Gulbransson (1873–1958), who became the central figure in the magazine and whose minimalist style Hillier described as "cold resoluteness and complete confidence" (1970). His style of drawing had obviously developed under the influence of Art Deco, the Japanese medieval woodcut and the expressionist dynamism of Edvard Munch. Gulbransson's drawings, executed in a line relaxed in stroke and elegant in purity, in time developed into maximum minimalism where all details except the most indispensable were omitted, so that the finished drawings gave the impression of having been created in a moment. They make viewers call upon their own reserves of ideas and memorized pictures, which they project into the empty areas of the drawing and in that way, in fact, complete it. The beauty of the simple line is best expressed in Gulbransson's convincing minimalist portrait caricatures, where only several strokes were enough to portray recognisable features, from Ibsen's to Hitler's.

Another special aesthetic feature of Zagreb cartoon is a strong inclination to minimalist figuration, which sometimes places viewers in the situation of having to identify the whole and in general build their art experience from fragmentary visual information shown in simplified stylization. That aesthetics and poetics cannot be completely comprehended without understanding the context of the simplified, intellectual cartoons of the kind nurtured in Simplicissimus. Thus, the key to understanding (also) Croatian editorial cartoons, caricatures, comic strips and animation must be sought in the broadest approach to the development of the narrative image, in the dynamism with which ideas passed from one medium to another and also within each of the media.

THE NEW YORKER AND THE ANIMATED FILM

After the terrible erosion of German culture caused by the Nazis, the price of which Simplicissimus, too, paid because many of its contributors emigrated and the magazine simply stopped coming out, the main work on the further modernization of the narrative image continued in the USA. The contributors to Vanity Fair espoused the minimalist caricature, for example, the Mexican Miguel Covarrubias and Al Hirschfeld, who gained fame by showing famous Hollywood profiles in a simple, calligraphic line. The American cartoon also flourished after the 1920s thanks, among other things, to distribution through syndicates. These had earlier greatly influenced the rapid spread of comics and had then also begun to distribute cartoons, enabling the sale of one cartoon to several newspapers and securing millions of viewers for the cartoonists and the possibility of going professional.

The most important event for the American and world cartoon was Harold Ross's foundation in 1925, in the new cosmopolitan metropolis of New York, of The New Yorker magazine, profiled as a somewhat snobbish, left-wing, liberal weekly combining satirical literature and sophisticated cartoons. In Europe, the leading elite among visual artists supported and practised the idea of animation as rhythm in colour, which was a welcome tributary to the broader currents of avant-garde art. America differed from Europe inasmuch as the first animators were semi-educated (neither Disney nor Iwerks had graduated from secondary school) and their only accessible and reliable reference material was newspaper drawings, especially cartoons and comics. Thus, the point of origin for American animated films was the kind of narrative image fostered in comics and cartoons, which was more modernly profiled under the strong influence of The New Yorker.

Soon after its foundation The New Yorker developed its own style and views, which greatly differed from those in other American humourist magazines. In the beginning, its contributors, for example Bill Gropper, were still under the influence of classical cartoonists like Daumier and Steinlen or the American illustration star Thomas Nast, but already in the first year's cartoonists such as Gluyas Williams appeared, who was obviously inspired by the collected yearbooks of Simplicissimus. His approach helped create The New Yorker type of cartoon, a sophisticated and slightly abstract humour that usually focuses on the average person's difficulties in negotiating the existential maze of modern life.

The New Yorker's cartoonists concentrated on jokes about human shortcomings and avoided direct political satire, using subtly sarcastic humour to depict average everyday life and trivial situations. Their ironic approach dealt with all the aspects of the capitalist culture and the American apolitical lifestyle, the values of the consumer society and man's increasing dependence on the machine. They showed a very complicated context in drawings that were simple and easy to read, sometimes armed with a short caption that logically corresponded with the message of the drawing, sometimes showing captionless cartoons with the punchline in an anagram, slight exaggerations and deformations, incongruence and the irrational structuring of elements.

The work of many of the magazine's cartoonists soon became a source of inspiration for the makers of feature and animated films. One of the most outstanding of these was Charles Chas Addams, known for his love of horror humour, especially in the black-humour series of cartoons featuring the diabolical family to which he lent his surname, and which appears in many of his films. Besides the macabre chronicle showing the life of the vampires, witches and werewolves in the Addams family, his speciality was creating a comic situation through the use of incongruity, or as R. C. Harveys said, "cartoons of incongruous comedy". What is probably his most famous cartoon was first published in 1950. It shows a skier climbing up a ski slope and looking in confusion at another skier who is skiing down the slope: a tall tree is standing between the tracks his skis left in the snow.

The former jazz pianist Peter Arno, although cultivating a rather classical art style, introduced cartoons to the atmosphere of nightclubs and the glamorous pin-up girl in the company of an ageing millionaire. Rössel, who wrote one of the first European books about The New Yorker cartoons, concluded his analysis by saying that life in the materialistic culture of the US dollar-empire is a constant race for money, power and sex. Love has become a kind of business. (1955) Arno's eroticized settings and his ironic approach to puritan norms function as a frame of reference for Tex Avery and his series of films about Little Red Riding Hood and Snow White, made in the 1940s for MGM.

James Thurber was a New Yorker cartoonist who most directly influenced the animated films of his time. Despite very limited abilities in draughtsmanship, Thurber was able to create extremely complex narrative images. One of the most original animated films in the 1950s, *The Unicorn in the Garden* produced in the modernistic UPA Studio, was based on a picture book by Thurber. Another New Yorker cartoonist, Sam Cobean, who began his career as an animator for Disney, inspired Chuck Jones, who borrowed Cobean's graphic style and figuration in the famous film *One Froggy Evening* (1955), produced by Warner Bros.

The case of Otto Soglow, one of the magazine's contributors, was especially interesting. His drawings were in extremely reduced stylization and with an outstanding feeling for depicting body language, sometimes shown on a single panel, sometimes in a strip without text covering an entire page. His greatest success was the strip series *The Little King*, which began in 1934 as an occasional contribution to the magazine and was soon purchased by King Features Syndicate, the largest comics-syndicate founded by the newspaper magnate William Randolph Hearst, which distributed it to many daily papers in the USA and Europe. Many comics analysts, for example Goulart and Horn, said that in time Soglow's drawings in the strip about the childlike king became so reduced and schematic that they could not be described otherwise than as a pantomime strip.

Soglow's strip became the basis for a series of animated films produced by the Van Beuren Studios in the 1930s. It was not simple to create a film based on that strip because, as Maltin also said, "the hero of the film is low-key and expresses himself in sophisticated pantomime – which is not the best characteristic for the star of a film cartoon" (1987). The animators who worked on the series, such as Vernon Stallings, made great efforts to preserve Soglow's minimalist style and the *Little King's* main characteristics; the films, just like the comics, were without words and the humour was based on the same premise about a king whose childlike behaviour makes him completely out of touch with his pompous environment. The only visible departures in the animation medium from what could already be found in the strip were softened slapstick humour and visual gags based on optic incongruity. The animated series about the Little King did not come even close to repeating the success of the character on the pages of newspapers, probably because the films seemed literally like a screened strip, despite the elegant animation which sometimes included animating not only the middle ground but the background, as well.

THE REFLEXIVE COMIC

In addition to the New Yorker, another American magazine strongly influenced the global development of cartoon animation – Mad magazine whose contributors distinguished themselves with their propensity towards reflexivity. Actually, in comics studies, reflexivity is frequently examined in the example of Mad magazine, which especially impacted American culture in the 1950s and 1960s. This magazine, whose importance reached cult proportions, right from the beginning predominantly focused on parody strips, which usually varied reflexivity in procedure and contents. Analysing the work of Harvey Kurtzman, one of Mad's leading authors, Maria Reidelbach sees his method and approach as a combination of the wild and untamed, but nevertheless artificial and harmless violence of animator Tex Avery, and the polyethnic dialogue and play with logic of George Herriman's comic strip *Krazy Kat* (1991).

The contents of Mad in its great period inspired animators, which can be seen in Warner Bros. production, especially in Chuck Jones's masterpiece of the reflexive animated film, *Duck Amuck*, 1953. It also enabled the appearance of the reflexive newspaper daily *Sam's Strip* by Jerry Dumas, jointly signed by himself and Mort Walker, which was probably the peak example of this kind of comics. It came out in American papers between 1961 and 1963, distributed by King Features Syndicate, with a total production of 504 daily strips of four panels each, which is considered an unsuccessful market project by American standards. As Walker's assistant on major commercial comics such as *Beetle Bailey* (from 1950) and *Hi and Lois* (from 1954, head artist Dick Browne), Dumas and his employer created *Sam's Strip* for relaxation, as a kind of internal joke in their small studio. Sam is aware that he is a cartoon character employed as the strip's hero, and he talks to his public from this position, complaining about the artist, commenting on current events and, what is especially effective, re-examining the strip's aesthetics and semiotics. The strip is full of jokes about motion lines, word balloons, panel borders and other strip codes. Sam, for example, has a cupboard full of used balloons, exclamation marks and question marks that he sells at half price, he sucks in the clouds of dust that appear behind him when he runs, appears in the closeup to "come into closer contact with readers" and in one daily strip, he complains that "he has run out of ideas today" and the bulb in the balloon above his head is dark. The supplementary character in the strip makes a point of explaining to Sam that he did not pay his electricity bill for that month. Sam tells readers that there is a hidden device behind each panel, and the last panel is slightly turned back to show the wheels of the device behind it. In another tier all the three first panels are empty, and the last has the title "closed for renovation".

Just like in Jones's animated masterpiece, or earlier in Fleischer's *Out of the Inkwell*, the strip about Sam abounds in gags based on the direct contact between the strip character and his author. In one panel we see an aeroplane drawn with great technical precision, and in the next, Sam explains that he is going on a trip so he hired an engineer to draw the plane because the artist Dumas could not do it. When Sam's figure appears in the middle ground in the panel, his conclusion is that the "stingy Dumas is saving on ink by drawing him smaller". Some tiers show a caricature of the artist, whom Sam on one occasion, dissatisfied with his appearance, asks: "Why did you draw me like this?" "Who do you think I am, Michelangelo?" comes the answer.

Another frequently used procedure is interaction. The four panels of the strip are Sam's property, which he can, if necessary, lease to other strip-characters, ask for their autograph (Blondie) or what kind of ink their suit is made of (Dick Tracy). Finally, an important dimension of the strip is Sam's comments to the public, which are a daily update on important political events with episode characters including John F. Kennedy, Nikita Khrushchev, who always holds a shoe ready in his hand, General De Gaulle, with Sam's comment that the artist is lazy and does not feel like drawing backgrounds, so the General is using the strip as a short-cut to the cover page.

Readers' reactions were enthusiastic (fewer) or enraged and aggressive letters and threats to the editors (the great majority). It is difficult to understand why a small daily newspaper strip was so aggravating for people that they were not simply able to ignore it, which is confirmation of a kind that the strip had succeeded in its basic intention. A person uninterested in crossword puzzles will never write a letter to the editor demanding that they should be eliminated. Since papers received vast numbers of protests against the publication of *Sam's Strip*, one by one they cancelled their subscriptions and on 1 June 1963, King Features decided to stop the strip's production and distribution.

However, *Sam's Strip* had a great influence on the later generation of cartoonists and it can be identified in works ranging from Hurt's to Crumb's. In time the strip acquired cult status, and in 1980, when the New York offices of King Features were broken into, the only thing stolen was the originals of *Sam's Strip*.

History was in a way repeated about ten years later in Zagreb, in connection with Nedeljko Dragić's comics *Tupko*.

TUPKO: A CARICATURE OF A COMIC

The central principle of reflexivity, calling attention to oneself, and re-examining one's own decisions, is a basic procedure in some of Nedeljko Dragić's films, especially in *Diary* and Pictures from Memory, and he also practiced it in his daily comics *Tupko*. Reflexivity can be understood as a consciously chosen stand that universal knowledge is impossible because the central part of our subjectivity – the unconscious – is not accessible to our consciousness. Therefore, authors are simultaneously the creators and the critics of their own work, constantly re-examining their mental condition and how it affects their creativity, and also its feedback influence on the creators themselves. It is reflexivity that makes Dragić and his work feel so modern even today.

Nedeljko Dragić holds a special place in the interaction between the Croatian comic strip and animated film. At first glance he seems to have been self-made because he was not even partially under the influence of Plavi vjesnik nor did he belong to the Novi kvadrat generation; instead, his comics are sometimes, for some reason, called a meta-comic (which is incorrect) or an anti-comic (which does not make sense). A better name for this sub-genre would be a pro-comic because its parodic or satirical deconstruction of aesthetic convention is not aimed at the destruction of the medium but at its enrichment.

In the wave of experimentation with the strip form, its means of expression, codes and overall semiotics, Dragić, I dare say, reached the very top, besides several American authors, primarily above-mentioned Jerry Dumas. This most of all comes to expression in *Tupko*, but in some other works, as well. *Tupko* was first published on 3 January 1970 in the daily Večernji list, where it came out with interruptions for one and a half years. Editor Danijel Jelinić deserves great credit for this truly bold editorial move because he continued to publish and support Dragić even in periods when his strip was exposed to the strongest criticism of colleagues in the editorial office and of readers. Just as in the case of his American predecessor *Sam's Strip*, *Tupko* confirmed that man is a being (or slave) of habit and convention. This is why we react so dramatically to change, semantic shift, breach of the norm, irregularity or, in these cases, the radical challenging of strip codes. Every new daily strip increased the number of angry readers of Večernji list threatening to cancel their subscriptions and heated discussions were often led about it in the editorial office. For the youngest generation of strip lovers, however, *Tupko* acquired cult status and became the greatest ideal in the uninhibited and liberated understanding of the medium.

Several unexpected feats prolonged *Tupko's* life. In its issue of 22 July 1971, Večernji list had the honour of informing its readers that *Tupko*, "Nedeljko Dragić's popular strip" published daily by that paper, had "won first prize at the distinguished international festival in the Canadian city of Montreal. The award is even more important as the festival is held on the American continent, in the homeland of comics". This was a truly important achievement because the International Salon of Cartoons in Montreal was the most distinguished contemporaneous world event of its kind, which ceased to exist after the death of its founder, the great Canadian cartoonist Robert LaPalme. Furthermore, at the proposal of Vera Horvat-Pintarić, *Tupko* was shown in an elite gallery in Graz in 1975, at the exhibition called *Identity, Given Identity and Alternative Identity*, which researched visual art. Dragić exhibited a witty experiment consisting of three large pictures hanging on the wall at human height. The first showed Tupko entering the panel, the second and third showed him carelessly wandering about, and the fourth "picture" was a mirror of the same size to which an angry Tupko was stuck, with a bubble showing him saying, "Get out of my strip". This was one of the first times that a maker of comics and animated films had been allowed into the forbidden area of gallery premises. Tupko's international success also included the publication of selected tiers in the specialized Italian magazine Comics with a foreword by Horvat-Pintarić, who looked on *Tupko* as "the animation of rectangular sheets".

How did Dragić, who insists on representing himself as a self-made artist and one who primarily relies on his own instinct, arrive at such a modern approach? The preconditions for interpreting the creativity of such an, at first glance, indigenous artist rest on the interaction of three circumstances: (1) the environment in which he found himself, the Zagreb School of Animated Films in the full power of its creative potential, kept pushing Dragić forward, (2) his fervent interest in editorial cartoons, caricatures and comic strips, (3) the established generation of traditional comics authors in Croatia, whose inheritor he was, and, of course, (4) talent.

Thus Dragić, despite his alleged lack of education, emerges as an author with a high knowledge of the basic principles of semiotics. He effortlessly plays about with the convention of reading from left to right, for him the surface of the strip's panel is no firm stage area but an irrational setting basically characterized by change and adaptability. He knows perfectly well, for example, that there is no image without a frame. The definition of composition, as the distribution of the pictorial elements within the frame, is equally important in comics and in films. In comics, the panel border developed as a specific code where the regular rectangular shape is used to describe reality, and an egg-shaped or cloud-shaped border indicates dreams or introspection; four equal panels of unchanged content suggest the inevitability of the passage of time, because, as already noted by Mitry, panels are not equal even when they show the same static object lit by the same lighting (1997). Sometimes the panels are uniformly distributed and balanced in a tier, but the angles from which the content of the image is observed differ, a procedure that Dragić was especially fond of in *Tupko*.

Already in *Elegy*, an early film from 1965, Dragić had separated the screen frame from the frame surrounding the world of the film, and many cartoonists and animators approached the image frame, the entrance to the world of the art work, as a challenge. The Dutch animator Paul Driessen was an especially persistent experimenter in this field.

Dragić tailors all the other basic rules of academically understood composition to suit his needs, too, sometimes behaving as an expert and sometimes dispensing with them to achieve a particular effect. He ignores the principles of perspective and self-confidently destroys the rule about the placement of focal points in the composition, which says that objects placed on the right side of a picture are experienced as heavier than those on the left side; he breaks the principles of avoiding movement from right to left because this forces the character to overcome resistance, of accentuating figures by isolating them, or making the image compact and balanced by concentrating on the composition centre.

All these conventions and rules have sunk so deep in our consciousness, way of thinking and looking that, when Dragić plays about with them, we experience the images in his comics like the aftermath of an earthquake (an "image-quake"?). Everything is unbalanced, shifted, disturbed and the depth perception and proportions among the objects and characters suddenly seem like illusions that jerk us out of our passive and indifferent habit. This is the reason why that aggravated mass of people did not want to see a disordered strip of that kind in their favourite daily paper. Dragić applied his visual ideas in all the media he worked in, and he already tested quite a lot of them in his first ambitious film project *Diogenes, Perhaps*, which Croatian film critic Hrvoje Turković wrote about in a review published for its early showings, calling the film a "kind of Alice in the land of absurdity and paradox, a land of living dreams, which are not even dream images of what is real in our everyday life: its subcutaneous nightmares and anxieties (1968)". However, there were no enraged reactions in this case because the animated film then held an elitist position. Here, too, Dragić showed himself as a filmmaker with a perfect command of condensing images, i.e. attempting to express as much as possible with as few elements as possible. He was a master at condensing dramaturgy and at almost nonchalant editing, all of which resulted from his cartoons, where he had effectively used editing to connect two or more shots in a single image.

Finally, the reflexivity of *Tupko* perhaps came as a result of Dragić's understanding of cartoons, comics and animation as three formal variations within one overall concept.

BLAŽEKOVIĆ: FROM COMICS TO FEATURE ANIMATION

Dragić's close associate Milan Blažeković, an author who realized as many as three full-length animated films, also came from the comics tradition. But the aesthetic basis on which he built his opus is significantly different from Dragic's.

As we said, along with American independent studios, above all the New York animation studio with the pompous name UPA (United Pictures of America), the most vital alternative to the Disney model during the 1950s and 1960s was offered by a group of cartoon authors from Zagreb whose work would become a film-historical term known as the "Zagreb Cartoon School". However, the foundations of that "school" were laid by loyal Disney followers, a competent animator who acquired his knowledge in Argentina, Bogoslav Petanjek and an exceptionally gifted cartoonist, Walter Neugebauer. As I wrote earlier, his first cartoon film *The Big Miting* extremely important for the later development of Croatian and then Yugoslav animation, was realized under the great influence of Disney's understanding of animation. Namely, the people (Neugebauer, Kostelac, Marks, Kristl, Jutriša, Vukotić…) who will later form the core of the "Zagreb School" gather around the project. They will be joined by Milan Blažeković, who entered animation as a high school student in shorts and never left it.

Blažeković was therefore present at the very beginnings of the creation of the "Zagreb School", acting as a caricaturist, cartoonist and then as a collaborator on more than a hundred films that were produced in the Zagreb studio; he was an in-betweener, animator, director, head designer and supervisor. No matter how much the "Zagreb School" will develop in the direction of moving away from Disney conventions and searching for its own formal and substantive expression, in Blažeković's entire work there is a constant striving towards the synthesis of Disney's global model with domestic tradition, culture and humour.

This is actually what makes his work a unique phenomenon within the entire history of the "school".

Constantly in the rift between his primary vocation, long feature film in the Disney style, and the environment in which he lived and worked, Blažeković created films a la Zagreb with a Disney flavour and vice versa. It is interesting that his path to the longest film form led through – the shortest. In his ads, trailers, work for television and especially a series of mini-films, he sharpened his animation nerve, perfected his sense of timing and visually expressed humour. Blažeković is one of the prominent profiles of the Zagreb School who actively participated in the very beginnings of media culture in Croatia and the former Yugoslavia. He was one of the first to practice applied television animation, bringing to life, for example, the teddy bear Mendo Mendović, based on the comic strip character drawn by his colleague Borivoj Dovniković in the immensely popular magazine Plavi vjesnik. In Zagreb film, he worked on the co-produced series Inspector Mask and the internationally successful Professor Balthazar, where, although within the matrix outlined by the main author of that project Grgić, he achieved notable achievements as a director or screenwriter of individual episodes and an animator (entrusted, among other things, with the animation of heavy animal characters such as crocodiles or hypos).

However, a particularly interesting part of Blažeković's oeuvre are the one- or two-minute films, the so-called mini-films that enriched the Croatian animation tradition and often a breath of fresh air in the festival programmes, eliciting bursts of laughter and storms of applause. The meaning and goal of those Blažeković films as well as the "minis" made by his colleagues, for example, Dragić, was exactly that – humour and laughter. Mini-films are a form of humour that directly grows out of the newspaper genre of wordless cartoon-comics. Made in a unique graphic configuration and maximally compressed time, Blažeković's animated cartoons are most often based on the creation of humorous situations that produce a confused man who finds himself in them, which is funny to us. Sometimes minis are based on the ordinary behaviour of characters in unusual situations, that is, unusual behaviour in ordinary situations. Blažeković often takes over and animates standard clichés from cartoons such as the leaning tower of Pizza, a big and a small man, Icarus who (un) successfully tries to fly, a big fish that eats a small one etc. On the most well-known cartoon cliché, *the man on a desert island*, is founded an entire series of mini-films *Largo Island* (1972).

Animation enriched cartoons and comics with two important elements: movement and time. The animated drawing proved to be an ideal means of bringing alive the so-called impossible situations from cartoons and comics. Live-action pictures would have a difficult time showing, for example, a truck going through the eye of a needle while the animator can simply draw it. Or when Blažeković's hermit pulls out a cannon out of nowhere and sinks a ship passing by the island.

The time that an animated cartoon has at its disposal enables the viewer to play with expectations and anticipation. In every situation that is presented to us, there are accumulated expectations, starting with the simplest ones, such as that we will see this and that from the corner or that the traffic light will turn red after the green one. If there is a person waiting around the corner with a raised bat or if the signal is broken and someone waits for an unreasonable amount of time, we are already on the verge of a humorous situation. Sometimes the humorous point is achieved by fulfilling expectations, as when the crooked tower in Pizza finally collapses in Blažeković's minis. Blažeković plays successfully with so-called off-space, zooming in to reveal some detail at a favourable moment, a detail sometimes extremely caricatured by disproportion or by simply human clumsiness.

And yet, in spite of all his short-film author's and commercial projects, Blažeković deserves his prominent place within the Croatian animation tradition primarily because of his feature-length films.

The *Elm-Chanted Forest* (*Čudesna šuma*, 1986) probably represents the very peak of Blažeković's career and certainly one of the important events in the history of Croatian cinematography. Blažeković managed to harmoniously merge two animation traditions. The longer duration allowed more characters, whereas the visual quality of the movie screen was enriched with deep and massive scenes. The drawing was accomplished with full animations in the so-called O line, although the visualization was reminiscent of the Zagreb School films, particularly since the film's main human character was surrounded by animal characters designed in a Disney manner. Blažeković did not hide his preferences and the film is full of tributes to Disney through the stylization of characters such as Mate the Bear, who is clearly inspired by the bear from *The Jungle Book* (1967), to details such as the rabbit thumping the ground similar to the rabbit from *Bambi* (1942). An ecologic subject and a warm, humane story about the painter Paleta who gets lost and ends up under the Magic Oak, where he acquires the ability to talk to animals, served Blažeković to show exceptional imagination in creating striking characters. Wizard Stick, Emperor Cactus, the water king, talking mushrooms, a snail that is very rarely an animated character and others remain in the memory for years after seeing the film. Situational humour prevails, like in Blažeković's cartoons and comics, however in the film he used experiences from his mini-films and made use of the fact that the characters were drawn, so the film is enriched with witty visual gags and caricature solutions, such as in the scene when the painter draws Mate as an athlete, but moments later his body on the painting turns all soft and saggy.

Blažeković's second full-length film *The Magician's Hat* (*Čarobnjakov šešir*, 1990) is a sequel to *The Elm-Chanted Forest*, but this time without the painter Paleta or any other human character. The film is a kind of modernist fairy tale dealing with ecology and particularly with the relationship between man and the city. Blažeković compiles motifs from classic fairy tales, such as the magical sword in a stone that becomes the wizard's main weapon but also provides some original solutions, for example, the fire-throwing dragon is shown in the film as a character on the side of good. The film has somewhat simpler visuals and has narrowed animation compared to *The Elm-Chanted Forest*, which is the price of the troubles that accompanied the production but also the trendy animation of the 1980s, when, in the pre-computer era, special animation effects were made by excessive use of airbrush.

Finally, Blažeković's trilogy of full-length cartoons closes with an adaptation of a classic work of Croatian literature for children *The Amazing Adventure of Apprentice Lapitch* (Čudnovate zgode šegrta Hlapića, 1997) by Ivana Brlić Mažuranić. The film about Lapitch is a fine work by a mature author, where Blažeković decided to place the entire story into an animal world (Figures 5.6–5.8).

FIGURE 5.6 The Amazing Adventure of Apprentice Lapitch (1997) by Milan Blazekovic.

ZIMONIĆ'S POETIC SF

The end of the 1970s and the beginning of the 1980s can generally be marked as the great era of European comics. The leading direction of European comics from that period, the so-called the Belgian-French school is considered a revolutionary phenomenon in the history of the media for many reasons. This, of course, is not only because European comics were approaching the market success of Japanese manga and different comic traditions created in the USA but also, what is particularly important, for the first time in western culture, comics was beginning to be understood as a serious form of expression. The central figure of the Belgian-French school was Moebius or Gir (depending on which work he signed), the artist who founded the so-called the heavy metal graphic style in the drawing and the complex intellectual layout of each page and whom among others Federico Fellini described as "the Almighty God", putting him on the same level as Picasso and Matisse. Of course, the school was created not only by numerous French-Belgian great authors but also by a whole series of other comic artists of personal poetics and vision, including those who come from outside that geographical framework (Pratt, Toppi, Battaglia, Hernandez-Palacios, Weinberg, De la Fuente …).

FIGURE 5.7 The Elm-Chanted Forest (1986) by Milan Blazekovic.

Of our special interest is the Croatian comic group Novi kvadrat, some members of which have become globally recognized for their graphic exhibitionism, penchant for harsh satire and dark humour, but also for the fact that they came from what was then called a "communist" country.

The French-Belgian comic was distinguished by an extremely realistic treatment of space and figures in motion, a free presentation of eroticism and all this was enriched with a kind of graphic pyrotechnics in the form of shading and colouring. The rich possibilities of comic expression are freed from the conventions of traditional newspaper comics: the comic panel is treated as a sequence that represents a segment of a wider development or event, and panels are no longer reduced to

FIGURE 5.8 The Elm-Chanted Forest (1986) by Milan Blazekovic.

chronology only but follow the logic of character development, spatial, temporal, psychological or plastic elements are combined by complex montage procedures performed on the entire page and therefore these comics were mostly published in albums instead of traditional strips in daily papers.

In addition to the innovative approach to frame and page montage, these comics stood out for their risky narrative techniques and were often imbued with intelligent and harsh satire that expressed and nuanced the left-wing ideas and existential pessimism of their authors. Dystopia dominated the genre and thematically, while alongside science fiction classics like Dick or Lem, the obligatory reading of most Franco-Belgian comic authors were neo-Marxist philosophers such as Marcuse and Lefebvre. Probably series *John Difful* (Moebius and Jodorowsky, 1981–1989) can be taken as the central work of the entire Franco-Belgian comics legacy, a kind of cross between soap opera and social satire that expresses absolute disbelief in the future of human race.

The most ambitious attempt to apply the aesthetics of the French school in animation was the full-length animated film *Heavy Metal* (Gerald Potterton, Canada, 1981), based on several well-known comic books. The influence of the "heavy metal" school of Franco-Belgian comics during the "convergent" years from the end of the last century and the beginning of this century spread globally and beyond its medium, and today it is most present as the prevailing iconography in video games or 3D-animated films such as *Final Fantasy* (Sakaguchi/Sakakibara 2001, sequel 2005) while it has almost disappeared in its original medium, comics.

It is interesting that today we no longer see that iconography as a look into the future that feels like it has come and gone – but as a nostalgic look into the past.

Krešimir Zimonić was the first comic author of Novi kvadrat who established himself among the public of the former state. During the 1970s, a wave of increasing interest in comics swept over Yugoslavia as well, so film and comics critic from Belgrade Žika Bogdanović managed to launch the magazine Pegaz, which published serious studies and research on comics, bringing together domestic authorities in the field with translations by relevant foreign authors (Ecco, Molliterni, Moren…). In 1976, the magazine published Krešimir Zimonić's ambitious comic, the poetic SF *Luna*, accompanied by an interview made by his later world-famous colleague Mirko Ilić.

Zimonić, which is already evident in his first work, is a supporter of a kind of combination of the fantastic and fairy tale with science fiction. On the thematic level, except in shorter, one-tabloid comics such as *The Last Man in the World* or *How Social Realism Was Created* (based on the script by Mirko Ilić), he was not inclined to dystopian or satirical discourse to the extent that most of his generational colleagues in Croatia and Europe.

Although the narration is somewhat unrefined and the characterization of the characters sketchy, Zimonić presented himself from the very beginning as an author who, given his youth, has an astonishingly sovereign command of sophisticated graphic-montage expression. The choice of the frame itself, the placement of the figure within it, the relationship of the frame with other frames and within the entire page, the plan of action and the setting of the page, as well as the choice of details in each image to guide the reader-viewer in the desired direction, is something for which this author shows an innate gift. In addition, when expressing emotions graphically, Zimonić relies on bodily movement, whether it is about basic, general emotions common to all human beings regardless of their origin, culture or age, but also emotional individualism related to specific characters within the diegesis of an individual comic. Unlike facial expressions, there are no "primary" body movements of any kind from which all others are "secondary" derived. Mastering body language means solving four problems: (1) transmitting various types of signals by placing the human body in a certain movement or pose, (2) using anatomy as a means of expression, (3) gaining knowledge about semiotic and perceptual mechanisms that determine the relationships between certain physical actions and the message it represents and (4) creating a personal visual strategy for presenting the relationship between gesture and communication in each comic sequence. It was his tendency to treat the body in motion as a symbol or in the process of metamorphosis that eventually led him to the animator's lightbox.

If we don't count his earlier work on animation as a collaborator on the project *The Plague House* (*Kugina kuća*, 1980), Zlatko Pavlinić's essentially animated illustration of a macabre poem by Zvonimir Golob, where the animation is quite static, performed mainly by toning and less by in-betweening, Zimonić's first and to this day his most mature film the work *Album* (1983) grew directly out of comics and is one of the most suitable examples that argue the thesis of the closeness of the two media.

ALBUM: (RE)CONSTRUCTING AND (RE)INVENTING LIFE

Zimonić's concept is based on metamorphoses as a means of connecting separate pictorial units into one continuous sequence, here they are photos from an album, which by its very form resembles a comic in which one life is embedded. The significance of this truly important film for the history of Croatian animation can be broken down into several elements, each individually testifying to the organic connection of this work with the medium of comics:

Visual morphology: At the turn of the 1970s and 1980s, we suddenly have a whole series of films that are no longer based on cartoon images, but have their origins in underground illustration, Central European graphics and posters or, as in Zimonić's case, French-Belgian comic. The fact is that Zimonić perhaps most radically jumped out of the rut of the traditional style of the Zagreb school, a process in which some other important authors (Marušić, Štalter...) were involved and which was accelerated by the appearance of the film *Satiemania* by Zdenko Gašparović. Thus, in one scene, Zimonić quotes Gašparović verbatim, whose success somehow freed up a space where he could freely enter with his understanding of the media.

Narrative discourse: If on the visual level, the characteristic of the film was a departure from the cartoon morphology and the use of comic figuration, then on the narrative level, it is a total turn from global metaphor and anecdote to a more complex storytelling process. More than in any of his other animation or comic works, Zimonić in *Album* draws from the fountain of life, which is already visible in the choice of scenographic solutions that are inspired by the landscapes of his native Slavonia, as well as in the construction of the narrative structure, which is based on the aforementioned similarity between photo albums and comics. At the beginning of the film, we see a woman, the central character of the film, reading a comic book of her life, an album with photographs that she mentally revives and connects into a whole. So, what we are watching is actually a psychological study of that character and at the same time an essay on transience presented in visual form. The constant change of appearance, philosopher Bergson believed, the irreversibility of this phenomenon, total individuality within a closed system – these are external indicators (regardless of whether real or apparent) that separate a living creature from pure mechanics.

> We would say that life is a type of development in time and at the same time a complication in space. If we look at it from the perspective of time, then we are talking about the continuous development of a creature that is continuously aging. If we observe it from the perspective of space, we will notice the coexistence of elements that are intimately connected with each other and to such an extent and so literally created for each other that not one of them can belong to two organisms at the same time. Every living being is a closed system of phenomena that are unable to function within another system.
>
> **1987**

Zimonić materializes Bergson's idea using the animation method of accelerated metamorphosis, the condensing of time that allows us to visualize long-term life or historical processes in one uninterrupted continuity. For him to succeed, he relies on an entire iconographic arsenal with which he introduces harmony into the storm of life and presents the circumstances of growing up and ageing, where imagination and fantasy are just as valuable as memories of real events that the photos from the album associated. Imagination, the mental world and the real, physical world harmoniously merge, presenting this person to us as a separate world.

Communication of an idea through illusory movement: Every animator creates movement – he or she communicates through movement. Basically, from the point of view of its experience, there are two types of movement: (1) perceptive, i.e. movement that is the result of the movement of the world, and (2) non-perceptive, i.e. our subjective experience of change in space. As a traditional animator, a connoisseur of "handmade" animation, Zimonić simply excels in some places by applying his experience from comics when it comes to compositional variations and the movement of the human and animal body. His fascination with Muybridge's horses in motion is also noticeable, which works especially well in perhaps the most memorable scene of the film, the one when the horse blows away the wrinkles from the woman's face with its powerful gallop.

Visual symbolism: Zimonić made a huge effort to create an image, a symbol, an iconic material that will not be caricature-metaphorical in the tradition of the studio in which he produced the film, but more poetic-imaginative, such as nuances of green colour, erotic scenes with Freudian symbolism, rain and horses, metamorphoses and merging between scenes, the purpose of which is to show the complexity of male-female relationships and the materialization of duration through the mentioned thickening of the space between the thumbnails of the comic, i.e. the album.

Treatment of time: The time and space of a narrative picture in a comic are often one and the same thing – as long as you look at it, as long as it lasts. Timing, movement of the illusion camera and editing in the film are something decided by the filmmaker. *Album* is actually an attempt to adjust the logic of reading the author's own comics. The fact that a new, thoroughly reworked and final version of the comic book *Album* appeared two years later is evidence of the film's impact on comics.

Reception: For the film *Album*, Zimonić experienced enormous success, first winning at the national festival of the former state in Belgrade, and then winning the first prize in Annecy as well as at several other festivals. Measured by international breakthroughs, it is actually the most successful film of the Zagreb School in that entire decade.

Of course, the film did not go unnoticed by critics either. From today's time distance, the fact that Zimonić defeated the now globally famous Tim Burton, who with his first major international breakthrough, the puppet-film *Vincent*, was also nominated for a debut award is particularly valuable. The success becomes even more significant if it is known that it was one of the festivals with the highest quality programme in history thanks to the fact that it was a big animation year. For example, the main prize went to Jan Švankmajer for the master-piece *Dimensions of dialogue*, which in 2010, in a vote of 25 members of an international jury of experts, declared the best animated work created in the last 50 years. Apart from that, other films shown at the time such as *Trapez* (Bonan), *One day of Life* (Dovniković), *The Snowman* (Jackson), *Once upon a time* (Nazarjev) undoubtedly belong to animation works of lasting value.

After this project, Zimonić realized the films *The Match* (*Utakmica*, 1987), a satirical discourse that today is read as an expression of the Zeitgeist in the country where it was created, which began to collapse, and *Butterflies* (*Leptiri*, 1988), a beautiful animation composition whose nocturnal scenography and gentle melting create a feeling enjoy every time you watch this movie. The film seems like a kind of update of the *Album*, this time enriched with the drawing sensibility of the film's collaborator Magda Dulčić. None of these projects can therefore be denied their value, even though none of them repeated the success of *Album* (Figures 5.9 and 5.10).

FIGURE 5.9 A page from Album (1979) to be an animated film by Kresimir Zimonic.

FIGURE 5.10 Comic page by Kresimir Zimonic.

6 The New Wave of Croatian Animation

THE LONG SHADOW OF THE ZAGREB SCHOOL

As we saw in the previous content, the great international breakthrough and the objective value of what was created in the Zagreb studio between the late 1950s and 1980s was mainly based on the highly mastered technology of so-called cel-animation, stylized movement and global metaphors that expressed resistance directed towards the arms race, a possible nuclear war, and other fears and anxieties about the future that marked an era commonly called the Cold War. All this was personified by the figure of a small, everyday man, who in the form of humorous anecdotes resolutely propagated the idea of neutrality, independence and a big No to bloc politics.

Like any model, it has exhausted its capabilities over time. Already in the 1970s, the classic "seven-minute" cel-animation began to resemble a told story and stagnate in relation to other, new techniques, in which enthusiastic and innovative animators created their original works, penetrating more and more into the depth of the screen and hinting at what we know today as 3D digital film. Of course, cel-animation, in the form of its surrogate in a computer program, will remain an important animation technique, the way it is, for example, watercolour in painting, but it will never again be dominant to the extent it was at the time when Vukotić and others were glowing and set fire to world festivals, and the most respected film authorities of the calibre of John Grierson or Georges Sadoul wrote about the Zagreb cartoon as one of the most interesting phenomena in the world of cinema.

As we could see, the core of the Zagreb School was made up of newspaper cartoonists who, even as film directors, basically remained caricaturists, cartoonists, comic artists and illustrators, who showed no interest in puppet-film, plasticine animation, objects or animation techniques based on the use of computers. However, it would be completely wrong to describe the whole phenomenon as something monolithic and limited only to the production of satirical narrative films within a flattened two-dimensional space. The Zagreb school or the Croatian animation tradition, which seems to me to be a better label because it includes what was created in the Kingdom of Yugoslavia as well as in independent Croatia, did not exist only in the genre of global metaphor expressed by cartoon, although this is its most recognizable and, due to several circumstances that I tried to say something about here, dominant discourse.

Zagreb's animation tradition has nevertheless branched out into individual parts, some of which were often unfairly marginalized because it was difficult to fit them into the "mainstream" of Zagreb cartoons whose main representatives (Dovniković, Zaninović, Vukotić, Dragić, Grgić, Marušić, Blažeković, Pavlinić...)

DOI: 10.1201/9781003375623-6

in the majority films operated within the dominant model of a small, two-dimensional man with a round nose who observes and interprets the panorama of the big world from his ideological dome. Their films were anecdotes with clever characters and funny final points while messages usually were concerned with global problems of humanity.

But not all Zagreb authors shared such a worldview and aesthetics, so a good number of them deviated from anecdotes in content and caricature-satirical graphics in expression and tried to join new forms and different thematic areas from those that marked the majority of Zagreb and Croatian animated films. It is interesting that contemporary Croatian animation, if we want to talk about continuity, relies more on phenomena that arose a little outside the central discourse of the Zagreb School and films that did not deal with global issues or rely on newspaper cartoons and comics.

As we could see, already in Zdenko Gašparović's sentimental etude of unsurpassed charm, strength and beauty, *Satiemania*, Marušić's, in the context of his oeuvre, completely atypical work *Fish Eye* (*Riblje oko*, 1980) or Nedeljko Dragić's forays into the field of animated documentary *Diary* or *Pictures* from *Memory*, the search for new forms and different thematic areas from those that characterized the main current of Zagreb and Croatian animated film is quite noticeable. For the time being, it has gone rather unnoticed in the literature that the champion of the Zagreb School, Dušan Vukotić, in his lesser known films such as *Stain on His Conscience* (1968) or *Ars gratia artis* (1970), contributed to the emergence of different tendencies in the home-style of Zagreb film animated production. If we look back a little further, we will notice that authors from the so-called painting current such as Vladimir Kristl (*La Peau de chagrin*, 1960), the Marks/Jutriša tandem with their anxious Kafkaesque films, visionary works by Vatroslav Mimica, animated films of high artistic quality made by Pavao Štalter (*Mask of Red Death*, *House No. 42…*) as well as original creations by Dragutin Vunak (*Between the Lips and the Glass/Između usana i čaše*, 1968) or Boris Kolar (*Warf Warf*, 1964) did not really deal with global issues, but with individual destinies, often expressing dark feelings, cynicism and that characteristic bitterness that developed in the border areas between Central Europe and the Balkans. Those films are devoid of humorous and optimistic points and are full of unhappy motifs such as funerals, grey rains, muddy roads, black screeching birds that portend diseases and wars (Figures 6.1 and 6.2).

A particularly interesting author in this context was Zlatko Bourek. He was a top graphic artist and animator, who established a kind of grotesque expressionism in his visually superior works and also one of the few Zagreb profiles who successfully used the collage technique, which is halfway between cartoon and puppet-film, to convey and retain tactility on the screen, artistic wealth and a peculiar atmosphere of horror and nightmare (Figure 6.3).

A further return to the past would also lead us to the film *Heart in the Snow* (*Srce u snijegu*, 1959), an almost 10-minute-long attempt by Branko Ranitović to establish a production of a puppet-film intended primarily for a children's audience in the wake of the works of Jiri Trnka. It is interesting that Zlatko Grgić appeared as an animator in that film, who in the rest of his career would establish himself as, in the technical sense, probably the most competent cartoon animator who ever worked in the Zagreb studio.

FIGURE 6.1 *Mask of the Red Death* (1969) by Pavao Štalter.

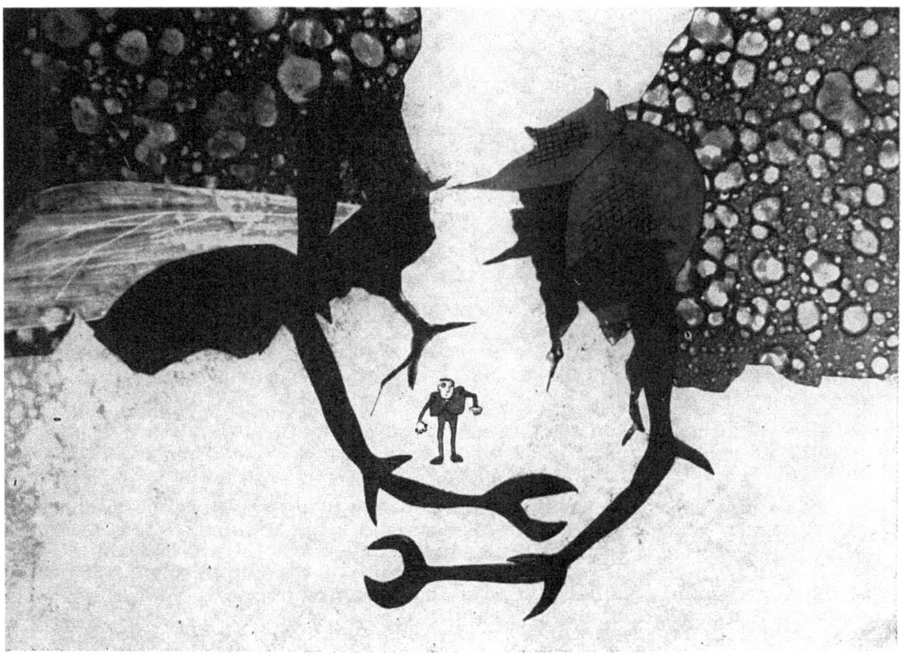

FIGURE 6.2 *The Fly* (1968) by Marks & Jutriša.

FIGURE 6.3 *The Cat* (1971) by Zlatko Bourek.

A good number of authors, especially after the big boom in Croatian modernist comics at the end of the 1970s, were inspired by this medium, which is as we could see in the previous chapter most evident in the works of Krešimir Zimonić who introduced modern comic aesthetics into the house style of Zagreb film, which was continued by other comic authors turned into animators (Magda Dulčić, Milan Trenc…). In addition, many authors have tried their hand at children's films, and I am referring not only to the cult series *Professor Balthazar* (main creator Zlatko Grgić) but also to the works made in this domain by Radivoj Gvozdanović, Darko Kreč or Milan Blažeković who, as we saw, managed to make three animated features aimed at children audience. Finally, let's notice the increasingly pronounced use of various animation techniques emerging after the 1990s as in the works of for example Daniel Šuljić (*The Cake*, *Kolač*, 1997), Nicole Hewitt (*Individu*, 1997) or Simon Bogojević Narath (*Leviathan*, 2006), which was accelerated by the change of technical paradigm – from cinematography to digital (Figures 6.4–6.8).

FIGURE 6.4 *Professor Balthazar* (1967–1977) by Zlatko Grgić et al.

STYLISTIC PLURALISM AND GENDER EQUALITY OF THE "DIGITAL GENERATION"

"The Digital Revolution is also an Animation Revolution" claims Feyersinger (2017) in his book on metalepsis in animation medium. Croatian animation could be taken as an illustrative example that confirms his suggestion. The radical change of the state context, the turbulent disintegration of the former state and the independence of Croatia, as well as new production paradigms, strongly influenced all aspects of animation production.

New Croatian animated films come to the audience in a radically changed time characterized by a significantly different sociological-political framework, a new "globalized" world without a "Cold War", but maybe more unsecure and unstable than before. And animation itself became something more important in new age. Animation is no longer a marginal phenomenon, but it has become the most important area in the process of total reshaping of not only moving images but also modern visual culture in general in all its paradigmatic areas. Filming (if it can even be called that today) is digital, which above all makes it cheaper and simpler and more accessible for young people who have embraced animation as their central means of expression. Although the ontological properties of animation remained essentially unchanged, in the period between the end of the 1980s and the middle of the 1990s of the last century, the production paradigm was changed so that instead of cinematographic animation we can exclusively talk about digital animation. Finally, the

Stonožica bosica (1977)

Veseli most (1977)

FIGURE 6.5 *Professor Balthazar* (1967–1977) by Zlatko Grgić et al.

distribution of films itself has completely changed; films are increasingly displayed on Internet sites or sent as e-mails. The entire history of animation is available on the Internet, so what seemed like a futuristic dream back in the 1980s, when you had to travel to festivals to see animated films, has become a reality.

Since the middle of the 1990s, viewers have already begun to encounter a wide range of animation forms and techniques, 3D CGI appears, various 2D surrogates for cel-animation, but more and more often we have both classic and digitally made

FIGURE 6.6 *Perpetuo* (1964) by Josko Marušić.

puppet-films. Movies are, of course, first and foremost the result of the energy and creativity of their authors, but it is certain that the education of animators in institutions founded in the 1990s as well as the rich tradition on which they are based play a significant role in their creation. The animation of the new century brought a new creative wave that ebbed and flowed during the last decade of the former century and during the first decades of the new one.

FIGURE 6.7 *Miramare* (2010) by Michaela Müller.

But the animation itself has become something else. It is the most important area in the process of total transformation of moving images. The pixel has replaced celluloid, which means that film production and distribution are undergoing major changes in all their paradigmatic areas. Filming is digital, which makes it cheaper and easier for young people to produce their first films. Post-production is also done digitally, which enables the use of advanced visual effects even in low-budget films and in small and poor countries. Editing is linear today and the film grows organically part by part by testing in

Kolač

FIGURE 6.8 *The Cake* (1997) by Daniel Šuljić.

animatics all possible angles and points of view, timing, plans, speed and rhythm. The film team can be geographically scattered literally all over the world, but the distance between collaborators is no longer a problem. On the contrary, working at a distance has become routine through so-called on-line communities, where digital communication enables daily conferences and conversations regardless of where any of the team members are located. Finally, the distribution of films itself is changing, home consumption of films has long surpassed that in cinemas, films are sent as electronic letters, electronic cinemas are becoming an everyday phenomenon and in all this, animated films are leaving the festivals and art cinemas ghetto and for the first time in film history, that form of moving images becomes an equal, if not even dominant, in comparison to live action.

The main feature of the new Croatian animation is the technological, genre, stylistic and thematic diversity of the films, which was noticeably strengthened by the arrival of the "digital generation", whose most excellent representatives would over time more and more successfully apply the possibilities of new technology for creating animated images. The viewer encounters a wide range of animation forms and techniques (CGI, various surrogates for cel-animation, classically made puppet-film etc.); some authors use a realistic simulation of three-dimensional space, while others are more inclined to a more classic approach with geometrically understood space and caricature stylization of the characters.

The thematic spectrum is visibly expanding. On one side one can see films with distinctly surrealistic textures or expressionistic internal constructions; on the other side there are works of documentary animation type "everyday realism", satirical views of the modern age and abstract games with rhythm, colour gradation and graphic-animation manipulation of movement and time. Some authors use a realistic simulation of three-dimensional space ("3D space"), while others are more inclined to a more classical approach with geometrically understood space and caricature stylization of characters.

Maybe the first noticeable change was the issue of gender equality since female animators like Ljubica Heidler or Magda Dulčić use to be a real rarity during the golden age of Zagreb School. During the 1990s and after, a large number of interesting female authors continued to appear, so it is definitely seeming like the idea of animation as a "man's job" is pronounced in the past tense in Croatia. It is interesting that for some reason female animators often appear in co-production collaborations between Croatia and other countries.

Let's mention some of them.

In her film *Airport* (2017), Michaela Müller demonstrates a superb sense of colour and form. The viewer experiences the film as fascinating exhibition of rhythmic animation in which light is cropped in multicoloured stripes that are set into motion. The airport serves as a metaphor for the modern world where people are portrayed as the material particles they are made of. This film stands out above all because of its strong visual-poetic qualities. Sensual paintings set into motion represent a young girl's inner fantasies.

Canada-based Eva Cvijanović's *Hedgehog's Home* (2017) is a puppet-film that charmed the audience at many film festivals around the world in 2016. It is based on a poem about a hedgehog who loves his modest but beautiful home by the great Yugoslav (Serbian, Bosnian and Herzegovina) children's author, Branko Ćopić. Just like the original piece of poetry, the film managed to convey a message of universal importance.

Estonian-born Chintis Lundgren has established herself as an original cartoonist and animator who has created a unique fantasy world in a series of short cartoons. Her funny characters, a strongly personal style recognizable by its minimalism where the drawing is stripped down to the essentials and a penchant for odd love triangles distinguish her works. One typical film is *Life with Herman H. Rott* (2017) where we watch a cartoon relationship comedy where everyday life and the complicated relationship between the sexes are in focus. Many of us will identify with the main character who becomes uncomfortable with the daily demands of life. A distinctive sense of humour based on the comic tradition from Lundgrens in both countries, Croatia and Estonia, results in healthy laughter.

Lucia Mrzljak who usually works together with Morten Tsinakov is another example of an author who combines Croatian and Estonian animation traditions with the difference that she moved from Croatia to Estonia. As a large part of Estonian animators, Mrzljak is strongly influenced by Priin Pärn's style and way of thinking. Her films are similar works within the absurd animation where she created a bizarre world like in *The Stork* (2020). Although stylized in a grotesque manner, her figures retain anatomically almost correct body proportions like in *Eeva* (2022), because she wants to emphasize her characters physical sexuality, especially in the scenes between the woman and countless suitors in which she skilfully plays with hidden sexual fantasies.

Besides her short cartoons like *Real Boy* (2021), the well-known comic book author Irena Jukić Pranjić prefers somewhat bizarre stories in which the visual language recalls problems connected to relations between the sexes. Jukić Pranjić particularly distinguished herself by animating comics in real space. Her goal was to create real, that is, "non-biological" movement, by using the technology from pre-film animations that were created by the process of merging the magic of the pre-industrial age and the technological outgrowths of the industrial revolution.

In her films like *Her dress for the final* (*Haljina za finale*, 2023), Martina Meštrović paints nuanced portraits of women experiencing the societal and ideological shift in modern society, while Ana-Marija Vidaković (*Tale From the Rooftop/Priča s krova*, 1997) formed an artistic sensibility based on the tradition of children's book illustration.

The daring project *Simulacra* (2014) by Ivana Bošnjak and Thomas Johnson is a competent use of 3D-digital technique that actualizes the French philosopher Jean Baudrillard's idea about images that today are separated from reality, so it is no longer possible to distinguish between the real and the unreal. Baudrillard's term meaning a copy without an original acquires a fine poetic meaning through a technically very competently performed story about the grown-up Tom Thumb, who in Plato's cave is looking for an answer to the question, am I really me or am I my own shadow?

Family Portrait by Lea Vidaković (2023) is a puppet-film that points out conflict between urban and rural. The film distinguishes itself both with respect to modelling the figures and the quality of the animation. *Family Portrait* is one of a series of stop-motion films, a technique that was almost completely neglected in the glorious era of the Zagreb school.

At first sporadically, and then more and more often, puppet-films such as *Soldat* (2006) by David Peroš-Bonnos appear as an animated satire about the great leader that is the subject to merciless lampoon. Digital and traditional animations are skilfully combined in that anti-militaristic allegory following the traditional conceptual discourse of the Zagreb school. Božidar Trkulja, who seems to have completely decided on the puppet-film, shows a preference for fantasy and folklore traditions. His *The Story from the Beginning of Time* (*Priča s početka vremena*, 2010), inspired by vivid Central African folklore, uses plasticine animation, while *The Last Challenge* (Posljednji izazov, 2017) was made with hard dolls. Bruno Razum mastered stop-motion to a new level in for instance *Can You See Them* (*Vidiš li ih ti?*, 2021) using setting, lighting and characters as a powerful storytelling tool. Particularly successful appear to be Zdenko Bašić *Gulliver* (2009) with expressionistic updated version of the famous fairy tale where he used digitally supported puppetry. In the most recent case, Ivana Bošnjak Volda and Thomas Johnson Volda managed to distinguish themselves internationally by very pedantically made stop-motion films such as *Remember How I Used to Ride a White Horse* (*Sjeti se kako sam jahala bijelog konja*, 2023), which is a psychological drama pondering state of mind of main character (Figures 6.9 and 6.10).

FIGURE 6.9 *Gulliver* (2009) by Zdenko Bašić.

FIGURE 6.10 The Real Boy (2021) by Irena Jukic-Pranjic.

Puppet-film aesthetics is also applied in the first Croatian digitally animated feature film, *Cricket and Antoinette* (*Cvrčak i mravica*, 2022), produced and directed by Dino Krpan and Luka Rukavina. This charming children's film which in the best possible way is reminiscent of *Antz* (Eric Darnell, Tim Johnson, 1998) achieved significant success with cinema audiences.

VUKOTIĆ'S EXCURSION INTO THE THREE-DIMENSIONAL

Even the former "king of cartoons" in Zagreb film, Dušan Vukotić, in his last film *Welcome to Earth* (*Dobrodošli na planet zemlju*, 1993), moved towards three-dimensionality in a formal expression. Something that has always characterized Vukotić and set him apart from others, an excellent knowledge of the history of animation and film, is today a prerequisite for anyone who wants to work in animation. After the completion of *The Game*, where he made a very skilfully directed combination of animated children's drawings and a feature film and thus for the first time significantly deviated from the two-dimensional canon of the "school", which brought him a new Oscar nomination and a handful of other awards, 38-year-old Vukotić finds himself in a paradoxical situation: he has reached the very top in the field of modernist cartoons, and from the top, clearly, he could only move in one direction – downwards. The choice was to continue doing the same and expose himself to the risk of stagnation and decline or to look for some other thematic and aesthetic possibilities of his own creative activity. In addition, according to the logic of things, animation as a form developed and what was at one moment the freshest idea will soon become just a historical fact that will retreat before new forms and expressions. I assume that this was the reason why Vukotić made the radical decision to focus more on work on feature films and pedagogy, instead of intensively dealing with cartoons (Figure 6.11).

FIGURE 6.11 Dušan Vukotić.

The continuation of Vukotić's career was seemingly search for a new aesthetic direction or film form in which it would be meaningful to invest new creative efforts. Each of his occasional returns to animation was therefore an attempt to join the central contemporary tendencies in the aesthetics of that form of expression. It was already evident from the mid-1960s that animators began to abandon the two-dimensional flatness of modernist cel-animation. In Canada, Poland, Czechoslovakia, Great Britain and elsewhere, authors were beginning to explore new artistic expressions and techniques in order to master spatial depth and plasticity. At least twice, Vukotić tried to join this trend, in the less successful cut-out film *Opera cordis* (1968) and the excellent *Ars gratia artis* (1970), which stands out for its tactile sensitivity and consistent montage rhythm. The same applies to his work outside of animation, where, for example, in *Visitors From The Arkana Galaxy* (*Gosti iz galaksije*, 1981), where the great Czech surrealist in the field of animation Jan Švankmajer was a collaborator, Vukotić tried to join the trend launched by Lucas and Spielberg with their fairy tale sci-fi films.

Welcome to Planet Earth should also be viewed in this context. Namely, as always, Vukotić unmistakably captured the spirit of the times and the central aesthetic features and techniques of current animation production, he applied some of them and anticipated others to a good extent. He articulated the critique of civilization in the form of a visually powerful and imaginative cinematic work by applying an aesthetic appropriate to the time. Today, it is quite clear that a tectonic change in the development of human civilization took place at the turn of the 1980s and 1990s. The relationship of political power, geography, economic and technological circumstances was radically changed, which logically all together affected the sphere of art, culture and spirituality in general.

If we look at films that achieved festival success at the time and were celebrated by critics, such as Švankmajer's *The Death of Stalinism in Bohemia* (1990), we will see that the hybridization of techniques and three-dimensional spatial simulation are the fundamental characteristics of the best animated films of that time.

Changes in technology, distribution, a different audience and cultural context conditioned a new approach in the articulation of ideas with adequate technical solutions. Admittedly, Vukotić has shown a tendency to hybridize before in, for example, *Stain on His Conscience* (1968) or *The Grasshopper* (*Skakavac*, 1975) as well as in some of his didactic-educational works, but never before in any of his films has such a radical conceptual conflict between different art-animation energies been applied. On the one hand, we can see a very risky process of animating a photographic image, which was successfully tested earlier, among others, by the Belgian Raoul Servais in the film *Harpia* (1978). The point of this method, otherwise quite similar to pixilation, is to create anatomically and physically impossible movements and positions of figures that are obviously living human beings.

Such figures are combined with the figure of a visitor from space, presented with the help of a completely different technique, the puppet-film (stop-motion). The figure of the alien is three-dimensional and stylized in such a way as to resemble a reanimated doll that expresses curiosity, play, naivety, innocence and, finally, confusion with what he finds on planet Earth. The artistic sensibility as well as the message of the entire film is therefore based on the friction between these two visual and animation concepts.

According to external generic indicators, the film *Welcome to Planet Earth* can easily be defined as a satire in the genre of science fiction that criticizes consumerism. Human beings are presented as aggressive intruders, greedy and selfish creatures prone to all kinds of violence, ready to compromise only if it is in their interest and to co-exist only in case they are weaker than the other. The film came at a time of a certain crisis in the science fiction genre, which, especially in the era of the so-called Cold War, produced great films, comics and significant literature in the works of authors such as Zamyatin, Orwell, Lem, Clark, Bradbury, the Strugacki brothers, Lessing or Dick. In the late 1980s and early 1990s, classic science fiction was becoming more or less meaningless in comparison to what reality had become. The future looked like a part of the present, not an extension of it. Namely, the visions of SF authors began to be realized in the worst possible way, from our everyday slavish dependence on machines, the complete subordination of medical and other sciences to prolonging the lives of unfathomable rich capitalists, to the fact that the real world in a political sense looks like the harshest dystopia. Love has been reduced to sex, reading has become clicking on the computer, pictures are not enjoyed in the gallery but in front of the screen, films are watched only "for skipping" and democracy is a kind of interactive game characterized by negative choice or avoiding of any choice.

Today's world, which was in the making in 1993, was fiercely criticized in Vukotić's easy-to-read metaphor about giant pigs as a symbol for the coming tide of insatiable greed. As it usually happens, reality will replicate art, so the so-called the Belgian "super bull", a monstrous creature created artificially to increase muscle mass and thus achieve greater profits, looked like it stepped out of Vukotić's film.

With his film, Vukotić symbolically marked a turning point in the development of Croatian animation. What came after that was the definitive end to the dominance of two-dimensional animation, animated cartoons and global metaphorical anecdotes.

GIPSY SONG: STORY TOLD IN WHISPERS

It is certainly difficult for any scholar to keep track of all trends, techniques, major achievements within a process taking place in the present or the recent past. Many authors distinguished themselves with their notable creations during the first three decades in which Croatia existed as an independent nation. The richness of narrative techniques, the poetic quality of stories, creativity in character design, the exploration of subjectivity, relevance and precision in portraying the historical moments of humanity, originality, seriousness and humour can be found in their films.

It is possible to single out, for example Vuk Jevremović for strong visual sensations in his films such as *11* (2022) or Marko Dješka for a minimalistic approach in *All Those Sensations in My Belly* (*Sve te senzacije u mom trbuhu*, 2020). Branko Farač appears to be a competent graphic artist with propensity towards visual research of human psyche as could be seen in his *Psychomorph* (2011). Goran Stojnić made his visually rich animations as *The Cat* (*Mačka*, 2011) under supervision of the legendary animation artist Jerzy Kucia and then continued his career mainly as a freelance animator contributing to films made by Popović and Mrzljak among others. Laura Martinović based her *10 Days of Lovid* (*Deset dana lovida*, 2022) on music rhythm. Some films by Hana Tintor are made as educative historical instructions in which her stories appear like the real world seen by an imaginative artist. Matija Pisačić is a competent draftsman stylistically very close to the Franco-Belgian comics school. His films such as *Murder in the Cathedral* (*Ubojstvo u katedrali*, 2017) are grounded in classic storytelling skills, thoughtful character development and clever dialogue. Natko Stipaničev made his films, among others *Arka* (2017) using 3D CGI in which he demonstrated a strong tendency to express himself through a surrealistic visual vocabulary (Figure 6.12).

FIGURE 6.12 *Leviathan* (2006) by Simon Bogojević Narath.

Nevertheless, some films can be singled out as central ones that came at the right moment to open new possibilities for the development of animation in the Croatian environment. Such a film of a particular significance because of the timing in which it was created and the way it paved the way for the films that followed is *Gipsy Song* (*Ciganjska*, 2003) by Marko Meštrović and Davor Međurečan. The duo created the film based on ethno-music and executed it in digital graphics of a harmonious expressionistic configuration.

Marko Meštrović and Davor Međurečan do not have any generational points of contact with the Zagreb School, and therefore, they can relate to this phenomenon quite unencumbered. Their author's work *Gipsy Song*, one of the most interesting animated films ever made in independent Croatia, came before the audience in a radically changed time characterized by a fundamentally different sociological-political framework, a new world that, instead of the balance of fear created by two opposing blocs, is now trying to globalize (Figure 6.13).

Gipsy Song is definitely an expression and part of that whole process, but at the same time it is also firmly rooted in the tradition of Croatian animation and art in general, which is the main reason that this work somehow functions as a synonym for the new wave of Croatian animation. This wave, made up of the works of authors such as Nicole Hewitt, Simon Bogojević Narath, Veljko Popović, Darko Bakliža and others, was created in a radically changed production (digitalization instead of film) and social (independent Croatia is no longer part of Yugoslavia) context.

There is a direct link between art and perception in an age. Of course, this is especially true for cinema in all its forms and expressions, including animation. Therefore, the authors' decision to construct *Gipsy Song* as a modern replica of German Expressionism, especially the central masterpiece of that stylistic direction *Metropolis* (1926) made by the tandem Thea von Harbou & Fritz Lang, is a fact that decisively determines the experience of their film.

Metropolis, a work of unsurpassed visual power and design that revolutionized the way twentieth-century man perceived the world, has never ceased to inspire artists around the world, and not just those of cinema. So, for example, we saw a remake of *Metropolis* under the same title in the medium of a Japanese anime film. This kind of existential pessimism can be read so clearly in Croatian writer Miroslav Krleža's

FIGURE 6.13 *Soldat* (2006) by David Peroš-Bonnos.

ballad *Gipsy Song*, written in 1936, which served as a poetic armature for the animation composition of the same name by Meštrović and Međurečan.

If the Zagreb cartoons during their golden age spread optimism in a gloomy and pessimistic world of Cold War, *Gipsy Song* is an extremely pessimistic work created in a time and a world networked with mass media that relentlessly and constantly bombard us with false and suffocating optimism.

Gipsy Song is a film with a carefully balanced rhythm and a harmonious expressionistic image configuration, and functional ethno-music naturally merged with the animation, which helps us to discover and recognize our own feelings while watching the film. It is a short film that, although made with computer technology, relies on the hand-drawing, the one that lingers in our memory for the longest time. *Gipsy Song* is constructed as a musical animation film, the structure and rhythm of which is a dance expressed above all by an interplay of black surfaces on a grey, rainy background, details such as black umbrellas and hats, dark glasses on the singer's face, the black "eye" of the guitar and the dark hole of the grave.

Despite its musical basis, or perhaps thanks to it, *Gipsy Song* is a muted, quiet film, whose story is told in whispers. It is a visual-musical narrative about old age and transience, about the futility of human life and music as the best way to go through life with a little less scar on the soul. At the same time, it is a collective portrait of the Balkans who drown their sorrows in brandy, which is sometimes not hot enough for them, so they want to spice it up with snake venom.

We find the participants of the film on the island of their mother tongue and memories (which are forms of oblivion, as Kundera would say) where they dance their death dance and only at the end, after the bottle containing the brandy and the venom is drunk, do we realize that it is about a group of outsiders who came to the bottom (or ghetto) of a megalopolis, to people caught in a gigantic concrete trap and suffering from depression as a result of industrialization, inhumane projects, demolished monuments, factories and chimneys spewing death for the surrounding nature. In a world that feels like a trap, it is impossible to desert from one's own life, to escape into another and different reality in no other way than by abandoning life.

HYBRIDIZATION AND COMMUNISM NOSTALGIA

Gipsy Song opened space for the hybridization of various techniques in Croatian animated films, which in many cases resulted in a certain aesthetic quality. Live action and animation, two equal and parallel tracks in the history of film, have long since been integrated on the silver screen. There are a number of examples of successful blends where photographic images portray a war refugee's loneliness, while animated images visualize invisible, ineffable and unrecordable, but just as real as visible reality. One artist animator who often combines live action and animation is Ana Hušman, who, for example, successfully applies the time lapse technique in her films *The Market* (*Plac*, 2006) and *Lunch* (*Rucak*, 2008). She was mentored by Nicole Hewitt and Ladislav Galeta, two experimental artists who used animation and film in their work that obviously inspired Hušmans ventures. Each in their own way, Bruno Razum, Darko Bakliža and Dino Krpan made several films characterized by stylistic experiments based on the technological possibilities of digital animation.

With his short films such as *Astronaut of Featherweight* (*Astronaut od perolaka*, 2017) and especially feature long *Accidental Luxuriance of the Translucent Watery Rebus* (Slučajna raskoš prozirnog vodenog rebusa, 2020), Dalibor Barić established himself as a consistent practitioner within the genre that Sitney calls "the graphic cinema" (2000). In his formal experiments made by using digital software, cut out, live-action and traditional animation, Barić continues where authors who used cinematographic techniques like Kenneth Anger, Stan Brakhage or Harry Smith left off.

How Steel Was Tempered (*Kako se kalio čelik*, 2018) stands out as a remarkably combination of animation and live action which particularly attracts attention with its subject matter and approach to it. The Croatian conceptual artist Igor Grubić created a film of social conscience that deals with last generation of communism. Yes, sooner or later, a film had to be made about the painful awakening of the generation born under communism and about their disorientation and disillusionment with the world of democracy and the free market into which the former socialist countries transformed in the early 1990s.

Grubić's film is essentially very simply structured. In many ways, it reminds of Dziga Vertov's classic *Man with a Movie Camera* (1928), where animation and editing are used to achieve a dialectical confrontation of detail and panorama, individual and collective. This genius artist and one of Stalin's many victims wrote as his credo: "Truth is always simple. What is not easy is to tell the truth".

Everything changed in the life of Grubić's main character. People are passive and accept injustice as a natural state. To get rich as the only ideology, hatred and nationalism becoming modern religions, and the most primitive and inflexible nationalists and fascists elected to power by most of the population have long ceased to be specific to the Balkans. Is this the free world and freedom that we aspired to when we were in socialism, asks Grubić in his animated film. Is this the freedom that those who were lying in communist prisons and gulags dreamed of? Differences between classes are being measured in light years. Each of them lives in a separate world where the ordinary people cannot even imagine what the world looks like for those who have no obligation to work and at the same time have unlimited means and power. The thin class of few billionaires is so far away that it is impossible to see it without a telescope, while what should have been the middle class has practically become a basement in a high-rise skyscraper, all floors of which are empty except for the luxurious penthouse at the top. In poor countries, such as the vast majority in the world, people today live in more terrible conditions than the biblical visions of hell itself. And they are still happy if they are only hungry, and no one bombards them.

Grubić uses an artistic sensibility taken from modern comics (the visual stylization in the film is similar, for example, to that used by Nick Drnaso or Craig Thompson in their comic books), a medium that far exceeds contemporary literature and feature films when it comes to quality and relevant storytelling. As a multimedia artist, he shows skill in using different means of expression, hybrid image, sound, animation, symbols and, in which he is particularly successful, montage equally on the macro and micro level of his film. In this respect, Grubić reminds in the best way of the master of animation montage, another Igor, Kovalyov, who creates his brilliant allegories based on meaningful nonsense or senseless connotation, mostly by editing.

In the opening of the film, we see an elderly man with a drooping head and a limp body, whose only company is a dog and a boy under a hood. The dog is most often a symbol of loneliness, which indicates that all close people are either distant or gone. Whether the boy is his descendant, an accidental companion or a figment that reminds the old man of the present's contempt for the past – each viewer can make their own judgement about that. The scene is combined with a skilfully executed suggestive montage of a train rumbling in front of the old man's eyes, taking him and the viewer back to the past. The old man passes through a dilapidated fence with a no-entry sign that ironically testifies to a world where there are no more rules. An economic transition to the photographic part of the film follows a documentary texture in the scenes of neglected machines, muddy puddles on the floor, rot, hardened tar and soot left by the coal long ago loaded into the blast furnace. A flock of pigeons crouched in front of long-broken windows confronted with a lonely old man. The old man's conflict with reality underscores the idea of a spirit that miraculously still lingers in the material world. Youth memories rush over him with dizzying force and symbolic figures act as identifying objects against the backdrop of the foreign world of capitalism.

Pictures from the past penetrate like bayonets into the old man's new reality. In the crescendo of the film from the bowels of the factory, an oath to Tito and songs from propaganda films about the working class are launched from an ancient 16-millimetre projector. In that place we easily recognize and identify with the human being symbolized by the drawn character of this film. Grubić's old man in the factory spent his youth futilely stoking the blast furnace, which hopelessly went out and exists today only on the projection of tattered celluloid films.

SIMON BOGOJEVIĆ NARATH: THE MOST DECISIVE STEP FORWARD INTO 3D CGI

Among the creators in modern Croatian animation, Veljko Popović and Simon Bogojević Narath emerged as two particularly interesting authors. Both have absolutely reached the quality of leading profiles from the famous Zagreb school with their work so far and are already recognized as such on the international level. So while Popović dealt with his conceptual projects in the form of a short film on the one hand with the problems of modern society and man, "homo consumericus" in *She Who Measures* (*Ona koja mjeri*, 2008) or with the revival of prominent Croatian painter Josip Vaništa's "puppet" characters in the brilliant and unspeakably charming composition *Cyclists* (*Biciklisti*, 2018), Bogojević is more interested in encroaching on space on a formal level in his artistic endeavours. At the same time, he shows an interest in some fundamental existential questions of human in general.

Already in his early works, Narath presented himself as an ambitious artist determined to work through visual media and digital technology. After several notable installations and experimental films, he managed to realize the first animated film *Plasticat* (2002) and one of the pioneering works of 3D CGI animation in Croatia. Even then, it was clear that he was an eclectic as confident as he was ambitious, who resolutely stepped into the world of modern visual storytelling. The film is a soft dystopia, which from today's perspective could be criticized for the cautiously modelled characters and stereotyped gestures, as well as the communication in general that is overrun with obvious symbolism. Finally, there is the inevitable naivety of an extremely young author. And yet, despite a certain conceptual and dramatic impurity, Bogojević already succeeds in the basic thing in that film: formulating his philosophical position and articulating it convincingly visually and animatedly. On the surface, *Plasticat* is a film about video games, but in the subtext, it deals with a very serious topic of our time, the relativization of the relationship between good and evil and violence as a means that justifies the goal, which is always money. Those who knew how to watch could already see that an artist who was determined to dig a deep furrow had entered the animation, film and art scene in general.

Four years after *Plasticat* comes *Leviathan* (2006), Bogojević's most mature film to date and a work that is certainly one of the most significant animated films created in Croatia in this century. The fact that it will become one of the most awarded films in modern Croatian animation, including winning the most important prize for many animators, the one awarded at the Annecy festival, will only support that statement. *Leviathan* first of all shows the astonishing progress the author made in terms of practically all aspects of artistic articulation in the four years between his two film projects. From today's perspective, it is clear that this was the result of the author's need for permanent regeneration of his own style and expression, which is why, among other things, he will move with ease and self-confidence not only from work to work but also from medium to medium, keeping his author's personality unchanged. The task that Narath has set before himself implies technically brilliantly executed innovation, which will be fulfilled to perfection in Leviathan (Figure 6.14).

The film opens with a flock of upset birds whose shadows swarm in a surrealistic ambience of quasi-historical architecture combined with modern posters and graffiti. The simulation of the view that moves through space and time leads us to the symbols of religious, economic, militaristic and ideological causes of human destruction,

Mačka

FIGURE 6.14 The Cat (2011) by Goran Stojnic.

presenting us the author's position on human hatred as a destructive energy in and around man. The fascinating mass scenes that follow are directly inspired by Hobbs and hence the film's title. Hobbs was a philosopher who essentially dealt with violence as a constant of human nature. According to him, the fundamental meaning of the state is contained in the social agreement that protects us from other people's violence and others from our own, but in exchange it takes away a large part of our freedom. Studying early capitalism, Hobbs saw society as a collection of human atoms struggling daily to survive in a world of scarce material resources. The truth about society, just like a clockwork, is therefore found in the relationship between its smallest parts. The macrocosm is mirrored in the microcosm. *Leviathan* is a film-mirror that reflects human society throughout history. And the history of people is presented through the orgies of physicality, the dominance of the stomach over the brain and the advantages of physical pleasures over spiritual achievements – the goal of man, this great work tells us, is primarily physical pleasure, not moral and intellectual progress. In his digital-animated interpretation of Hobbes's philosophy, the author does not miss to pay a clear tribute to the animation artists whose work continues to develop the heritage, the bursts of stylistic allusions to the works of Kucia, Švankmajer, Harryhausen and Norstein serve to create a flavour that even today after many years has lost nothing of its strength.

For someone who expected that Bogojević would continue to focus his creative efforts on orthodox 3D CGI, a pleasant surprise comes already in the next, equally successful film *Morana* (2008). Here, computer software is combined with visual morphology recognizable from Franco-Belgian comics, especially those works that Giraud signed as Moebius (*Arzach*, *L'Incal*, *Le Monde d'Edena…*) and Japanese anime films, above all those of Hayao Miyazaki, Mamoru Oshii, Katsuhiro Otomo and Satoshi Kon. The peculiarity of such a process is that the characters are drawn but have volume and move through space, the depth of which is convincingly simulated. In an idyllic area, which we will understand to be a pre-technological world inhabited by winged dogs, we find a man whose clothing functions as an indicator for the age from way back. The man is constantly running, climbing to the top of the cliff to perform some ritual. Swirling clouds, fog and a storm in the background make the animals flee in a stampede. The man calmly continues the ritual and when he lights his pipe the film takes us into a parallel space-time dimension: the world and time of the film's creation, the beginning of the twenty-first century with dystopian iconography as inaugurated by Otomo in his masterpiece *Akira* (1988).

When we return to the dimension of the Runner's world, we realize that he somehow manages to stop the overflow of negative energy from our world and returns home to his wife and family idyll, which is only possible in a world without hatred and technology that people use above all to rule one over others or destroyed each other.

A similar premise is the basis of Bogojević's next project *The Flower of Battle* (*Cvijet bitke*, 2011), a film that confirms him as the author of an already recognizable iconography and competence.

And suddenly, in the light of a veritable flood of new techniques, themes and creative curiosity of the new generation of animators, we become aware that that cute little man with a hat has long since remained in history.

Sources

Abbott, Edwin: *Flatland. A Romance of Many Dimensions.* Dover Thrift Editions. Dover, Chatham, 1992.

Adamson, Joe: *Tex Avery: King of Cartoons.* Popular Library, New York, 1975

Ajanovic, Midhat: *Karikatura i pokret.* Croatian Film Association, Zagreb, 2008.

Ajanovic, Midhat: *Den rörliga skämtteckningen.* Optimal Press, Göteborg, 2009.

Ajanovic, Midhat: *Life in a Cartoon.* Croatian Film Association, Zagreb, 2010.

Ajanovic, Midhat: *The Man & the Line.* Croatian Film Association, Zagreb, 2014.

Amidi, Amid: *Cartoon Modern. Style and Design in Fifties Animation.* Chronicle Books, San Francisco, 2006.

Arnold, Fritz. "Die bitteren Narren sind die guten Narren, Der Simplicissimus und das Kaiserreich". Goete-Institut, München, 1982.

Balázs, Béla. *Theory of the Film.* Dover Publications, New York, 1970.

Barrier, J. Michael: *Hollywood Cartoons. American Animation in Its Golden Age.* Oxford University Press, Oxford, New York, 1999.

Bashara, Dan: *Cartoon Vision. UPA Animation and Post War Aesthetics.* University of California Press, Oakland, 2019.

Beckman, Karen (ed.): *Animation Film Theory.* Duke University Press, Durham and London, 2014.

Bendazzzi, Giannalberto: *Cartoons. One Hundred Years of Cinema Animation.* John Libbey, London, 1994.

Chion, Michel: *Audio-Vision. Sound on Screen.* Columbia University Press, New York: 1990.

Cotte, Olivier: *Il était une fois le dessin animé.* Dreamland, Paris, 2001.

Crafton, Donald: *Shadow of a Mouse. Performance, Belief and World-Making in Animation.* University of California Press, 2013.

Dick, Philip K.: *Flow My Tears, the Policeman Said.* Orion Publishing Co., London, 2001.

Dobson, Nichola et al: *The Animation Studies Reader.* Bloomsbury Academic, London, 2019.

Dow, Christopher: "Private Snafu's Hidden War, Historical Survey and Analytical Perspective". In Bright Lights Film Journal, nr 42, Oakland, 2003.

Eidsvik, Charles. "Mock realism: The comedy of futility in Eastern Europe," in Andrew S. Horton (ed.), *Comedy/Cinema/Theory.* University of California Press, Berkeley; Los Angeles; London, 1991, 91–105.

Feyersinger, Erwin: *Metalepsis in Animation. Paradoxical Transgressions of Ontological Levels.* Universitätsverlag Winter GmbH, Heidelberg, 2017.

Fiske, Lars och Steffen Kverneland: *Olaf G.* Optimal Press, Göteborg, 2007.

Furniss, Maureen: *Art in Motion. Animation Aesthetic.* John Libbey, London, 1998.

Gombrich, Ernst Hans: *The Essential Gombrich. Selected Writing on Art and Culture.* Edited by Richard Woodfield. Phaidon Press, London, 1996.

Halas, John: *Masters of Animation.* Salem House Publishing, London, 1987.

Harvey, Robert C.: *Children of the Yellow Kid. The Evolution of the American Comic Strip.* Frye Art Museum, Seattle, 1998.

Hašek, Jaroslav: *Den tappre soldaten Švejks äventyr.* Klassikerförlaget, Stockholm, 1998.

Hermann, A. H.: *A History of The Czeshs.* Penguin Books Ltd., London, 1975.

Hillier, Bevis: *Cartoon and Caricatures.* Studio Vista Limited, London, 1970.

Holloway, Ronald: *Z is for Zagreb. A Guide to the Films of One of the World's Major Cartoon Studios.* The Tantivy Press, New York, 1972.

Horn, Maurice (ed.) *The World Encyclopedia of Comics*. Chelsea House Publishing, New York, 1976.
Hubley, John & Zack Schwartz: *Animation learns a new language*, A conference paper. Hollywood Quarterly 1.4, Oakland, 1946.
Hudson Hich, Darren: *Introducing Aesthetics and the Philosophy of Art*. Bloomsbury, London, 2017.
Jurander, Claes: *När man ritar hästar*. Gidlunds förlag, Stockholm, 2010.
Klein, Norman M.: *Seven Minutes. The Life and Death of the American Animated Cartoon*. Verso, New York, 1993.
Klein, Norman M.: *The Vatican to Vegas. A History of Special Effects*. The New Press, New York, London, 2004.
Kundera, Milan: *Skämtet*. Rabén & Sjögren, Stockholm, 1987.
Kunzle, David: *The Early Comic Strip – Narrative Strips and Picture Stories in the European Broadsheet from c. 1450 to 1825*. University of California Press, Berkley and Los Angeles, 1973.
Kunzle, David: *The History of the Comic Strip - The Nineteenth Century*. University of California Press, Berkley and Los Angeles, 1990.
Leslie, Esther: *Hollywood Flatlands. Animation, Critical Theory and the Avant-Garde*. Verso, New York, 2002.
Lönroth, Lars. *Östeuropeisk animerad film*. Liber Läromedel, Lund, 1979.
Magnusson, Helena. *Berättande bilder. Svenska tecknade serier för barn*. Makadam Förlag, Göteborg & Stockholm, 2005.
Maillet, Raymond, 1982. "Besjeda jednog sinefila kojemu je mnogo stalo do filma "kvadrat po kvadrat" Filmska kultura, 137, Zagreb, 1982.
Majcen, Marinić, Mihaela: *Prema novoj animaciji. Povijest novijeg animiranog filma u Hrvatskoj*. Meandermedija, Zagreb, 2015.
Maltin, Leonard: *Of Mice and Magic. A History of American Cartoons*. New American Library, New York 1987 (1980).
McCloud, Scott: *Serier, den osynliga konsten*. Epix Förlags AB, Stockholm, 1995.
Mimica, Vatroslav: "Razmišljanja o filmskoj umjetnosti", Filmska kultura, 37, Zagreb, 1963.
Munitić, Ranko: *Uvod u estetiku kinematografske animacije*. Filmoteka 16, Zagreb, 1982.
Munitić, Ranko & Sudović, Zlatko (ed.): *Zagrebački krug crtanog filma*. Knjiga prva. Ex Libris. Zagreb, 1978.
Munitić, Ranko & Sudović, Zlatko (ed.): *Zagrebački krug crtanog filma*. Knjiga druga, Ex Libris. Zagreb, 1978.
Munitić, Ranko & Sudović, Zlatko (ed.): *Zagrebački krug crtanog filma*. Knjiga treća, Ex Libris. Zagreb, 1978.
Munitić, Ranko & Sudović, Zlatko (ed.): *Zagrebački krug crtanog filma*. Knjiga Četvrta. Ex Libris, Zagreb, 1986.
Nowell-Smith, Geoffrey: *Oxford History of World Cinema*. Oxford University Press, London, 1996.
Pikov, Ülo: *Animasophy. Theoretical Writings on the Animated Film*, Estonian Academy of Arts, Department of Animation, Tallin, 2010.
Pintoff, Ernest: *Animation 101*. Michael Wiese Productions, California L.A., 1988
Reidelbach, Maria: *Completely Mad. A History of the Comic Book and Magazine*, Little, Brown & Company, USA, 1991
Rohdin, Mats: Vildsvinet i filmens trädgård. *Metaforbegreppet inom filmteorin*. Aura. Stockholm, 2003.
Rössel, James: *25 amerikanska skämttecknare*. Folk i Bild, Stockholm, 1955.
Roth-Lindberg, Örjan: *Skuggan av ett leende. Om filmisk ironi och den ironiska berättelsen*. Fischer & Co, Stockholm, 1995.

Shull, Michael S. & David E. Wilt: *Doing Their Bit. Wartime American Animated Short Films, 1939-1945*, McFarland, London, Jefferson, North Carolina, 1987.
Sitney, P. Adams. *Modernist Montage: The Obscurity of Vision in Cinema and Literature.* Columbia University Press, New York, 1990.
Sitney, P. Adams. *Visionary Film. The American Avant-garde 1943 – 2000.* Oxford University Press, Oxford, 2000.
Skirbekk, Gunnar & Nils Gilje: *Filosofins historia.* Daidalos. Göteborg, 1993.
Sorlin, Pierre. *European cinemas, European societies 1939 – 1990.* Routledge, London, 1991.
Stephenson, Ralph: *Animation in the Cinema.* International Film Guide, New York, 1967.
Sutil, Nicolás Salazar: *Motion and representation.* The Language of Human Movement. Massachusetts Institute of Technology. Cambridge, Massachusetts, London, 2015.
Thomas, Bob: *Disney's Art of Animation.* Hyperion, New York, 1991.
Torre, Dan: *Animation – Process, Cognition and Actuality.* Bloomsbury, London, 2017
Turkovic, Hrvoje: *Život izmišljotina.* Ogledi o animiranom filmu, HFS. Zagreb, 2012.
Wellek, Rene: *Essay on Czech Literature.* Mouton Co., The Hague, 1963.
Wells, Paul: *Understanding Animation.* Routledge, New York, 1998.
Wells, Paul: *Animation and America.* Edinburgh University Press, Edinburgh, 2002.
Wells, Paul: *Animation, Genre and Authorship.* Wallflower Press, London, 2002.

Index

Note: *Italic* page numbers refer to *figures*.

M

N

O

Y

Z

FSC
www.fsc.org
MIX
Papier | Fördert
gute Waldnutzung
FSC® C083411

Kolibri 360 GmbH
Ferdinand-Jühlke-Straße 7
99095 Erfurt, Deutschland
produktsicherheit@kolibri360.de